The Ultimate Scrapbooking Book

The Ultimate Scrapbooking Book

Rebecca Carter
Lael C. Furgeson
Stephanie F. Taylor
Vanessa-Ann
Sandi Genovese

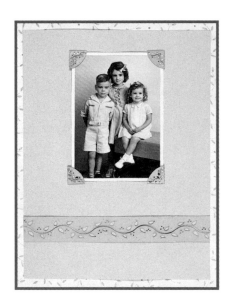

A MAIN STREET BOOK

Library of Congress Cataloging-in-Publication Data Available

10 9 8 7 6 5 4 3 2

Published in 2001 by Sterling Publishing Company, Inc.
387 Park Avenue South, New York, N.Y. 10016
Material in this collection was adapted from
Scrapbooking for the First Time ©1999 by Rebecca Carter
*Making Scrapbooks: Complete Guide to Preserving Your Treasured
Memories* © 1998 by Vanessa-Ann
515 Scrapbooking Ideas © 2000 by Vanessa-Ann
Family Scrapbooking: Fun Projects To Do Together © 2000 by Lael C.
Furgeson & Stephanie F. Taylor
*Creative Scrapbooking: Over 300 Cutouts, Patterns & Ideas to Embellish
& Enhance Your Treasured Memories* © 1999 by Sandi Genovese
© 2001 by Sterling Publishing Co., Inc.
Distributed in Canada by Sterling Publishing
C/o Canadian Manda Group, One Atlantic Avenue, Suite 105, Toronto,
Ontario, M6K 3E7, Canada
Distributed in Great Britain and Europe by Cassell PLC, Wellington
House, 125 Strand, London WC2R OBB, United Kingdom
Distributed in Australia by Capricorn Link (Australia) Pty Ltd.
P.O. Box 704, Windsor, NSW 2756 Australia

Printed in China
All rights reserved

Sterling ISBN 0-8069-5831-6

Table of Contents

Scrapbooking for the First Time

Introduction

"Scrapbooking" is a hobby that not only provides a creative outlet for the scrapbook designer, but also promotes a strong sense of self-esteem and belonging for those whose lives and accomplishments are creatively chronicled and compiled into an album or collection of albums.

Great scrapbooks start with great photos. Although professional photos are wonderful additions to a scrapbook, using a professional photographer for all photos is not practical, or necessary. Your own snapshots are going to capture the most memorable moments in life.

The best times and conditions, as far as lighting is concerned, for taking photographs outside are before 10 am and after 4 pm and on a slightly overcast day. The subject should be positioned so the sunlight is hitting them from the side instead of facing directly into the sun.

Add variety to photos by changing the angles at which photos are taken. Try looking through the camera viewfinder at the subject from low, high, and normal camera angles to see which will look best. Children's photos are often better if the photographer kneels down to the child's level before taking the shot. Many older people find photos taken from a slightly higher angle more appealing.

Get closer to the subject when you are taking the photograph. The one comment I hear most often is, "Your pictures are so close-up! In my photos the people are always so far away." At first, it is a little awkward to get so close, but the results are great. The only exception to using this technique is when you are using a flash—especially indoors—as the subject can appear washed out or over-exposed.

Try enlarging your photos. If you have a photo where the image is very small and you would like it to appear larger, either enlarge it on a color copy machine or have the photo printed larger from the negative. Then simply crop the photo so the subject is the main focus.

Good photos come from good photo processing labs. Avoid the temptation to save money by going with a lower-quality lab. Incorrect developing can mean the difference between a photo that lasts and a photo that quickly fades.

Use both black-and-white and colored photos in your scrapbooks. While black-and-white photos last longer, the value of colored photos cannot be denied. Many scrapbook designers recommend taking colored photos for the most part and taking a set of black-and-white photos every six months to one year to preserve family history, in the event that color photos deteriorate.

Keep duplicates of favorite photos and negatives somewhere besides in the home. In the event of a fire, flood, or other natural disaster, at least some photos will survive. Duplicates can be kept with family, friends, or in a bank safe deposit box.

Many photos suggest a theme or represent a special event. For example, a photo of a child blowing out candles on a birthday cake can be used to build a page with a birthday theme. Decide what emotion or mood is reflected by the theme and use it as a guide when choosing paper patterns and accents.

Add color to scrapbook pages by using colored paper products, pens, markers, and more. You may choose to use colors that traditionally represent the theme of the scrapbook page or colors that are complementary to the colors found in the photos. Choose colors that reinforce and enhance the page's theme, not detract from it.

Use a few of the many available scrapbook supplies to accentuate the photos, theme, and colors.

As acid damages photos, it is important to use acid-free supplies when creating scrapbook pages. Scrapbook suppliers and most standard craft stores are great sources for papers, stickers, die-cuts, pens, and other acid-free products.

When you have pages that face each other, try to use complementary or coordinating colors and themes. Your scrapbook will appear neat and organized, not cluttered and hard to follow.

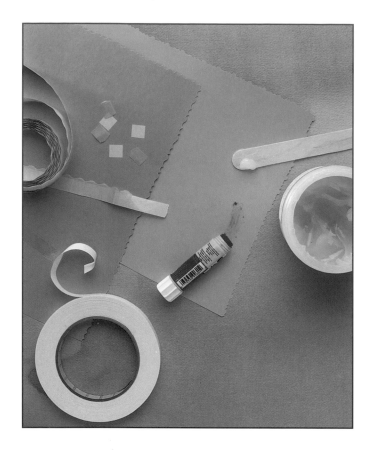

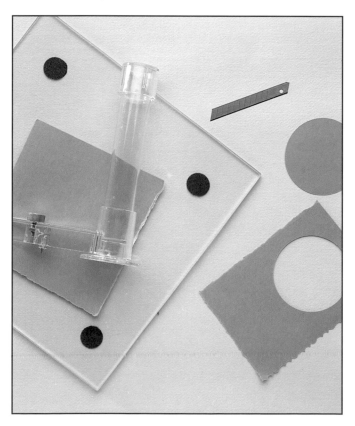

Chapter 1: *Basic Tools and Supplies*

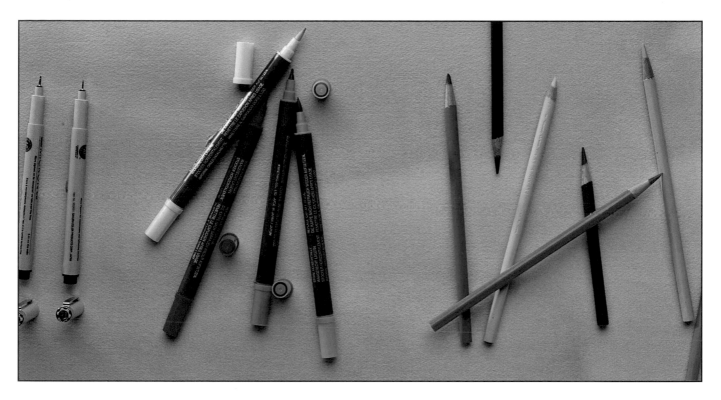

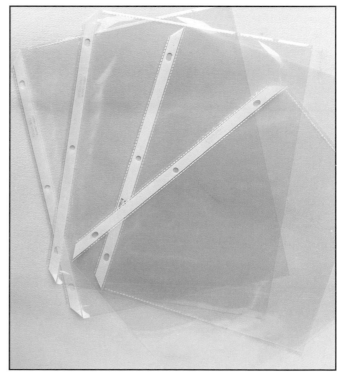

What do I need to get started?

Getting Started

Scrapbooking can be an overwhelming project if it is not broken down into categories. When I first began scrapbooking a few years ago, I bought everything in sight just because it was there, "Oh, that's cute," and "I must need that." From every store I went into, I came out with bags of "stuff" with no plan in mind. The kids and I sat down with boxes of photos and bags of stuff and in no time at all we had a big mess and only one page done. It was not fun.

Being organized has got to be the first priority on the list before beginning.

Organize Your Space

Arrange a place or even designate a "spot" where your supplies and photos are going to be stored. If at all possible, set up a table that can be left up with all of the supplies at hand. This will save time in having to gather the supplies and photos each time you would like to work on a page.

Organize Your Memories

Wash hands thoroughly before handling photos. Natural oils from skin can be harmful to photos, so even clean hands must be washed frequently while working on scrapbooks. When possible, try to handle photos by the edges or wear lightweight gloves.

When you receive the photos back from developing, discard any photos that are out of focus—a blank wall or the back of someone's head. Take a moment to identify the who, what, where, when, how, and why of each photo. Then, later, when you are ready to create the scrapbook page, the memories and thoughts will be fresh in your mind and it will make journaling easier. Write the information on the back or top edges of the photo, using a photo safe labeling pencil.

Many varieties of labeling pencils can be used to safely write on both front or back of a photo and will wipe off with a tissue. Do not use a ballpoint, felt tip, or water-based pen to label photos. These pens may create indentation lines on the photo's face and their inks may eventually bleed through, becoming visible on the face of the photo.

Next, sort these and any other photos and memorabilia that you may already have sitting in that drawer or shoe box. Obtain a box for each member of your family. I suggest a larger box to hold memorabilia, drawings, and special school papers; and another box specifically for photos. These boxes should be acid-free. There are many styles available and they are just the right size to protect the photos. Label the boxes either by the year or by the event.

Employ the knowledge of friends and family members to help identify dates, people, places, and events pictured (a family reunion or gathering is a good place to find such help).

This will take a bit of time, but once they are organized, the photos and momentos will be easily found and the craft of scrapbooking will be a positive experience instead of a headache.

Organize Your Supplies

Here is a list of basic supplies you will need to get started:

Adhesives (acid-free)
Card stock (acid-free)
Photo album
Photo corners
Photo safe pencil
Scissors
Sheet protectors (acid-free) (optional)
Templates
Transparent ruler

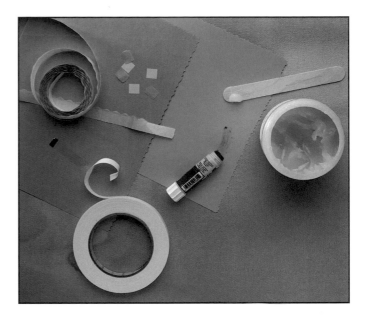

Adhesives: There are several different types of adhesives for mounting photos, ground paper, die-cuts, etc. When choosing any adhesive, make certain it is acid-free and photo-safe.

The adhesive a scrapbooker chooses is a personal preference. Some of the different products available are:

Glue stick—This is a basic glue that you may already have at home. It is clean and easy to use. It works well for mounting die-cuts and punch-outs.

Mounting tape—This adhesive is best to use for mounting a photo onto a prefinished photo matte.

Photo sticker squares—Although these double-sided tape squares were developed for adhering a photo, they can be used to adhere just about anything. These are quick and easy.

Wet bond—This is a liquid glue that is available with a jumbo tip for larger coverage or a pencil tip for smaller projects.

Card Stock: Acid-free colored card stock is one of my favorite items to use on a page because it adds color and dimension without detracting from the photos. It is inexpensive and, by adding the effect of a few different decorative-edged scissors, a thousand layouts can be created. Card stock comes in hundreds of colors, textures, and weights. Be certain to familiarize yourself with the product available.

Card stock is the most widely used paper for scrapbooking and comes in lightweight, medium weight, and heavy weight (sometimes referred to as cover weight). Decide which weight works best for your purposes. Here are a few characteristics to consider:

Lightweight card stock—Choose this weight when you want to use decorative-edged scissors and craft punches, as it leaves a very clean edge. Lightweight card stock is not the best for the ground or background sheet, as it tends to be flimsy once photos are mounted onto it.

Medium-weight card stock—This weight is the most widely used as it is acts well as a ground paper and also is easy to cut with decorative-edged scissors and craft punches.

Heavy-weight card stock—I like to use this weight whenever possible for the ground or background paper, making the page very sturdy. Avoid using this weight when using decorative-edged scissors or punches. The thickness of the paper wears the blades and results in unclean cuts.

Photo Album: Albums and binders are available in all sizes, colors, styles, and formats. The main difference between scrapbooks is in the binding. Album bindings should allow pages to lie flat. Choose from three-ring binders, expandable binders, and bound scrapbooks

Take some time to decide the size of album you want to use. The 12" x 12" format allows more space to arrange the photos, whereas there may be a larger assortment of stationery and decorative papers available in the 8½" x 11" format.

One approach may be to have at least one album for each family member and another to represent the entire family. Choose a scrapbook album that allows for the greatest amount of flexibility and creativity.

Photo Corners: Photo corners have been used for many years to secure photos on a page without adhering the photo itself. Today, photo corners are available in a variety of styles and colors from transparent to gold and silver.

Decorative photo corners—These photo corners are laser-cut and come flat in a sheet. They need to be folded and assembled and require the use of an adhesive, but they are well worth the time.

Mounting corners—These photo corners are available in a wide range of colors. They are made of heavy paper and must be moistened to adhere onto the page.

Transparent photo corners—These photo corners are self-adhesive. They are designed to hold a photo without detracting from the photo.

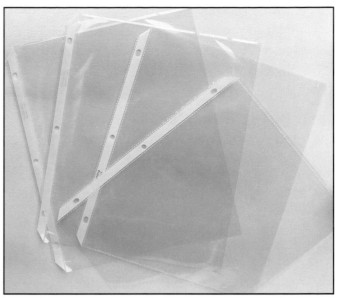

Photo Safe Labeling Pencil: A photo labeling pencil should be used for recording information about the photo and for tracing a stencil or template to a photo.

Scissors: It is important to have a good sharp pair of scissors to ensure clean lines. I prefer to use the type that has a spring in the handle which makes it so your hand does not get tired when cutting for a long time. The spring makes it very easy when cutting around shapes—especially ovals and circles. I use a large pair for general cutting and a small pair for small intricate cuts.

Sheet Protectors: Sheet protectors envelope the scrapbook pages and keep photos on facing pages from rubbing together. They are available in both 12" x 12" and 8½" x 11" formats—for both the three-ring binder and the expandable binder pages. Sheet protectors come in different weights and finishes from nonglare to high-gloss. Choose one that you are comfortable working with and stay consistent from book to book.

Top-loading sheet protectors—These are available in both 12" x 12" and 8½" x 11" formats.

Templates: Templates are used to crop photos and papers into shapes, such as hearts, circles, stars, balloons, etc., to eliminate unnecessary background or to match a theme.

Templates are available in a wide range of shapes and sizes. Transparent templates are useful for exact placement of the design. Cookie cutters also work well as templates

Position templates over item to be trimmed, trace shape, and cut out. Use a photo safe labeling pencil when tracing to a photo as any remnant tracing will wipe off with a tissue.

Transparent Ruler: I use a transparent ruler on almost every page I create. Getting straight lines and making certain the photo is adhered straight are very important on a scrapbook page, and this ruler makes it easy to achieve both.

Beyond the Basic Supplies

As interest grows, so will a collection of fun-to-have supplies. The following is a listing of the many available supplies that I would recommend for quick and easy ways to complete your pages.

Circle Cutter: This tool adjusts to the desired diameter of the circle. It makes a perfectly clean circular cut. The circle cutter is great when a template does not have the exact size of circle you may need.

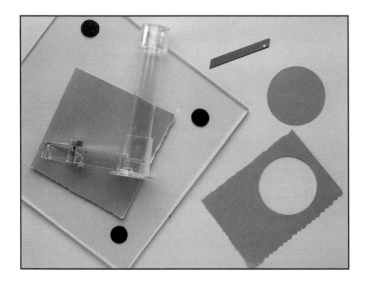

Clip-art: Lined art images are available in booklets to copy and cut to accent scrapbook pages. Clip-art is also available in the form of computer software and can be printed to paper and cut out for quick and easy page decorations.

Color Wheel: This tool is a visual representation of the spectrum of colors in the shape of a wheel. When choosing colors, select a primary color and use the wheel to choose complementary colors.

Corner Rounders: These are similar in appearance to craft punches. They trim square corners off photos and papers, leaving curved corners.

Corner Templates: These are used to trim corners on photos and papers into shapes. Position clear acrylic templates over item to be trimmed, trace shape, and cut. Use a photo labeling pencil when tracing to a photo as any

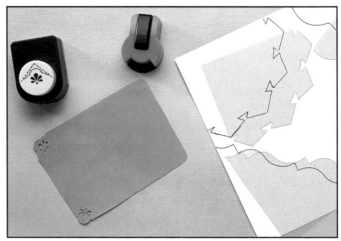

remnant tracing will wipe off with a tissue.

Craft Knife: A knife with a replaceable blade makes cutting straight edges and tight corners clean and easy.

Craft Punches: These are available in several sizes and motifs, from hearts to dinosaurs, stars to palm trees, and more. These are used to punch colored paper or card stock for small shapes to enhance a page.

Crimper: A crimper corrugates papers and cards, adding dimension and texture to a page.

Decorative-edged Scissors: Use these fun scissors to cut paper with distinctive edges. There are several different edges to choose from to accent any theme.

Avoid cutting photos with decorative-edged scissors. These scissors are primarily for cutting and trimming card stock.

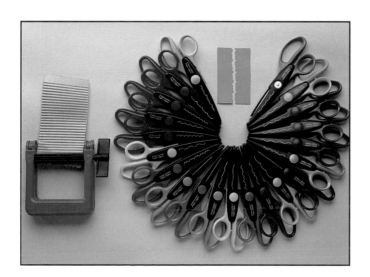

Die-cuts: Die-cuts are available in several colors and sizes. They are cut from varied weights of paper and are a quick way to add thematic shapes and colors to a page. Die-cuts can be purchased individually or in theme packets. Many paper stores have a die-cut machine that patrons can use to cut their own papers, to get both the shape and color they desire.

Embossing Stencils: These brass plates are available in several designs that can be gently pressed into scrapbook papers, creating a raised effect.

Lettering Booklets: Learn creative techniques of writing and decorating the alphabet. These booklets demonstrate how to complete styles, such as dot, outline, and block lettering. Refer to photo on page 16.

Light Box: Available in varied sizes, these boxes have an acrylic top and a light enclosed within. Use them to transfer clip-art or lettering designs directly to the ground paper or paper label. Place the design, right side up, on a light box and the ground paper or paper label on top, right side up. Trace the design to the paper. Note: This technique can be duplicated by holding the design and ground paper or paper label up to a sunlit window. Refer to photo on page 16.

Novelty-edged Rulers: These rulers are used to create a continuous pattern along one or more edges of a paper. Patterns include wavy, zigzag, scallop, and more. Position clear acrylic rulers on paper, trace pattern, and cut.

Paper: Add dimension and color to a scrapbook with paper. Card stock (mentioned on page 11) is a heavier weight paper often used as a ground paper or for creating die-cuts. Decorative or novelty papers and stationery are often used for page backgrounds and to create patterns and borders.

Paper Cutter: A good compact paper cutter is a nice addition to your tools. It will cut the 12" x 12" paper, extend out to 15" for measuring left- or right-handed, and has an inexpensive replaceable blade. I often use this to cut ground paper and trim photos.

Pens, Pencils & Markers: Use these for labeling, highlighting, and journaling. Make certain pens and markers are fade-proof, waterproof, and use pigment ink. Pens and markers are available in all colors and with several different tips, such as .01 tip for creating fine lines, and tiny accents; .05 tip for standard clean lines; and a 45° angle for calligraphic effect for titles and special emphasis. Colored pencils that are water-resistant and light-fast can also be used to decorate scrapbook pages.

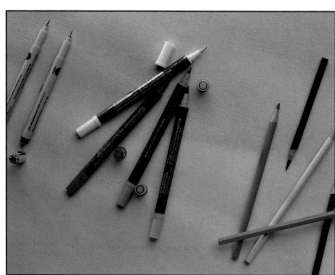

pH Testing Pen: This amazing pen instantly tests acid content of paper.

Premade Photo Mattes: These are available in several colors. Embossed and of card stock thickness, these can be used to matte studio portrait photos.

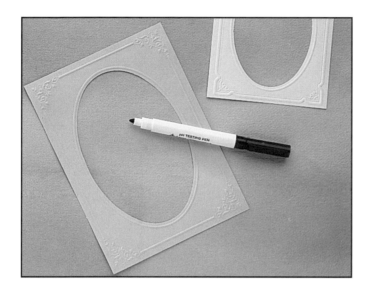

Red Eye Pen: This pen fixes red eyes on photos. It contains a dye that filters out the color red, allowing natural eye features to show through.

Rubber Stamps, Pigment Ink Pads, Embossing Powder & Heat Tool: There are numerous individual rubber stamps, rubber stamp kits, and pigment ink pads available to use to enhance a scrapbook page. After stamping, color in the designs with pigment ink brush markers and/or apply colored embossing powder and heat-set with a heat tool.

Stickers: Stickers are available in all sorts of themes, sizes, and colors. They add instant artistic impact, or color, or humor.

Organize Your Storage

Once you have collected a few basic supplies, store them in a safe place. Shoe boxes with lids work great for storing adhesives, craft punches, and scissors.

Tools such as these can also be stored in clear, plastic, stackable drawers. Portable canvas bags with multiple pockets also prove useful for storing and carrying needed supplies.

Keep items such as stickers, die cut shapes, punch shapes, papers, and scraps either in zipper-type baggies with holes punched along one side of the bags, or in clear 2" x 2" slide size, 3½" x 2" sports card size, 4" x 6" photo size, or 8½" x 11" top-loading protector sheets. Organize them by occasion and color and store them together in a 3-ring binder.

I believe it is important to keep your supplies handy and in a safe place, so the time you spend scrapbooking is time spent creating instead of searching for the lost scissors or glue sticks.

Creating Scrapbook Pages

Once you have gathered and organized your supplies, you are ready to begin creating pages. Here are a few tips for a smooth start.

Sharing Costs

Sharing the expense can really ease the cost of scrapbooking supplies. If a group of friends gets together on the cost of some supplies, such as the decorative-edged scissors and craft punches, you will all have a larger variety of products to create with. Also, there is such a large number of styles of scissors—where do you start? Before you make a large purchase, start with the basics and share the others.

Color-copying Photos

One important tool you may want to consider is a laser or color copier. Copy the photo that seems to be missing its negative or an older photo of parents or grandparents. The laser copier is so advanced that you can make a copy of an old black-and-white photo and mount it onto a page. Black-and-whites are so important to have in photo albums. I have made many laser copies of old photos, framed the copies, and shared them as Christmas presents. What a treat!

Finding a Starting Point

Start where you feel the most comfortable. This may be designing a page for last month's birthday or last year's Christmas celebration. The idea is to just start. Once your first few pages are complete, the rest will become very easy.

Layout

For each page, choose two to four photos. Be selective when choosing and mounting photos. They should be well-focused, interesting, and varied.

The layout of the pages seems to frighten people the most. In 90% of designs, the triangle rule is the easiest to follow. On pages that have more than one photo, place them in a triangle pattern. Refer to examples below.

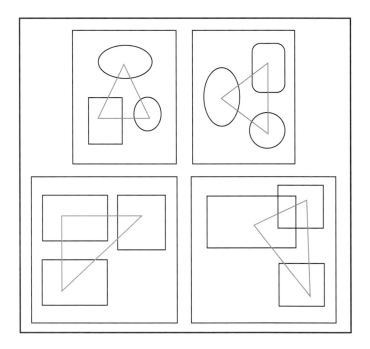

The placement of stickers, die-cuts, and memorabilia can also follow this same rule. After practicing this rule on a few pages you will find it easier to do. The pages are more pleasing to the eye because they are balanced.

Finding Balance

Do not feel like every inch of the paper needs to be filled up with stickers or lettering. A very simple rule to follow is, "Less is sometimes better." Remember that the photo is supposed to be the main focus, not the sticker or the printed ground paper. Leave some empty areas, or negative space, and you will find that these are much more appealing pages to look at.

There are some pages that lend themselves to a lot of stuff. Refer to "Life as a Teen" on page 86. This page is purposely filled to capacity because of the intent. However, you should keep these pages few and far between.

Scrapbooking Terms

Sometimes it seems as if scrapbookers speak their own language. The following listing of common terms will help you feel comfortable when you visit the local scrapbook store.

Adhere: Adhering is the actual process of mounting the item or photo, using mounting strips, glue, or photo corners.

Background Paper: Background paper is the paper used as a border onto which the ground paper is adhered or mounted.

Crop: This term is often used to refer to a gathering of friends on a set date at a set time and place to work together on individual scrapbooks and share supplies and ideas for pages. Scrapbookers often plan monthly get-togethers that last for several hours and include potluck-style refreshments. The crop can be held in a scrapbooker's home or in a larger facility, such as a church building. Sometimes a crop is the main event in a getaway weekend with family or friends.

Cropping Photos: Many scrapbook designers will choose to crop, or cut, photos to remove unwanted background, emphasizing the foreground or people, and to create fun shapes. Snapshots, which are often incorrectly framed at the time of photographing the subject, are candidates for cropping. This technique will not affect the stability of a photo. Cropping is completely safe, but it is irreversible. Consider cropping color copies of irreplaceable one-of-a-kind photos.

Cropping studio photos is not recommended, since professional photos are typically framed well, with little unnecessary background. Studio portraits can be framed with decorative paper cutouts or premade photo mattes. NEVER crop an instant photo. Make color copies of instant photos. The color copies can then be cropped as desired and added to pages.

Ground Paper: Ground paper is that onto which the photos are adhered or mounted.

Journaling: Journaling is documenting photos by either hand-writing or lettering names, dates, and events—again, the who, what, where, when, how, and why—on the ground paper. Write personal feelings and humorous captions about the event. Include family stories, poems, and songs that correspond with the photo. For a child's scrapbook, write down first words, favorite phrases, and any grammatical errors and manners of speech to capture the child's development over time.

When adding a journal entry that is quite lengthy, type it or use a computer to avoid making mistakes that would cause you to have to start again.

Lettering: Lettering is the technique of creatively writing and decorating words, phrases, and titles. This technique makes the text an element of page design, drawing attention to the words. There are many different styles to choose from. Write the words in the lettering style on the page in pencil first, then go over pencil with a pen or marker.

Memorabilia: The purpose of creating a scrapbook is to provide a place to keep "scraps!" Tangible reminders of people, places, and events can include any of the following memorabilia.

Announcements
Awards
Birth certificates, hospital bracelets, sonogram
   copies, etc.
Brochures
Certificates
Children's drawings
Greeting cards
Handprints
Letters
Locks of hair
Maps
Marriage licenses
Menus
Newspaper clippings
Obituaries
Post cards
Programs
Report cards
Ribbons
Ticket stubs
Wedding invitations

Make certain to use page protectors to keep these momentos in place.

Pocket Pages: To hold memorabilia separate from a photo page, create a pocket page by gluing two ground papers together along bottom and both sides. Remember to cut a curve into the top edge of the top page for easy access to the contents of the pocket page.

Creating an Archival-quality Scrapbook

Many scrapbookers want their scrapbooks to be archival, or able to stand the test of time. The primary enemy to this goal is acid.

An object that has a pH less than 7.0 is said to have acid, an unstable chemical substance that will weaken paper and photos, leading to yellowing and brittleness. Items kept in a scrapbook or used to decorate the pages should be acid-free or have a pH of 7.0 or more.

When shopping for paper for pages, choose acid-free, lignin-free papers which have had acid removed from the manufacturing process or have been treated to neutralize acids.

Buffered paper, which is not only acid-free, but is also acid-absorbent. Buffered paper has added calcium carbonate that will absorb acid that may come into contact with the paper. Many designers will use buffered paper at the front and back of a scrapbook to protect pages from gasses or acids given off by the binder.

Fusible Appliqué

To appliqué fabric to scrapbook pages, use double-sided fusible web. Enlarge pattern from book as necessary. Trace pattern onto translucent tracing paper. Turn tracing paper over so pattern is visible in reverse. Place fusible web facing reverse side of pattern, paper side up. Trace pattern on paper side of fusible web.

Follow manufacturer's instructions to fuse the web to the motif fabrics.

Cut out pattern following pattern line.

Peel off the paper backing and fuse the fabric motifs to paper or background fabric.

Archiving

Archival Quality

When a scrapbook supplier says their products are archival quality, just what does that mean? It does not mean the products will last forever. There is no way to guarantee a scrapbook will last forever, unless a scrapbook designer intends on chiseling memories in stone. However, archival quality supplies, techniques, and preservation methods are intended to make scrapbooks last for several generations.

There are few binding industry standards when it comes to archival quality products. The term itself is not uniformly used. There is no set number of years a product must last before it can be considered archival quality. Just a label that says archival quality or photo safe is not enough to ensure a product is completely safe. Manufacturers can, and in some cases do, slap the label on any product they sell. Since the term has yet to be uniformly defined, false advertising claims are not an issue.

Archival Terms

acid: an object that has a pH less than 7.0; an unstable chemical substance that will weaken paper, board, and fabric leading to yellowing and brittleness.

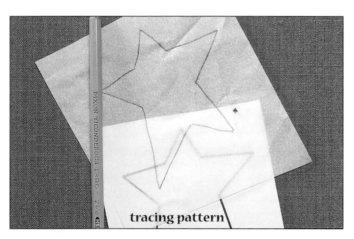

tracing pattern

fusing web to fabric

applying first color of paint to paper

applying second color of paint to paper

acid free: An object that has a pH of 7.0 or more is said to be free of acid.

acid migration: Even when a product starts out as acid free, there is no guarantee it will stay that way. Acid can move into the product from other high acid objects in close contact, from environmental pollutants, or even from contact with oils in human hands. Acid from high acid products will always migrate to acid free products.

buffering: Calcium carbonate, a colorless or white alkaline chemical is added to buffered products to absorb migrating acids. Buffering adds extra protection, but is still no guarantee against acid. Even buffered products will eventually become acidic if kept in close contact with high acid products for extended periods of time.

chemical stability: Products are said to be chemically stable when their elements are neutral. Chemically stable products do not easily decompose or deteriorate. These products are said to resist changes brought on by contact with natural elements and outside chemicals.

Paper Terms

acid free paper: products have either had acid removed from the manufacturing process or have been treated to neutralized acids.

lignin free paper: Lignin, the acidic portion of wood pulp, has been removed from the paper making process.

buffered paper: This paper is not only acid free, it is acid absorbent. Buffered paper has added calcium carbonate that will absorb acid that may come into contact with the paper. Many designers will use buffered paper at the front and back of a scrapbook to protect pages from gasses or acids given off by the binder.

acid & lignin free paper: Papers that are both acid free and lignin free are of the highest quality. Products that are only acid free still have lignin in them. Acids in the lignin can build up over time eventually creating problems. These problems may not arise for 20 to 30 years, if at all.

cotton or linen paper: Papers made from wood or wood products can damage photographs if not properly treated. Papers made from cotton or linen are safer, since they do not contain the same acids common in wood products.

permanent paper: A product given this name meets a standard set by a government and paper industry committee. To meet this standard, the product must have a pH level of 7.5 or more, must be free of chemical impurities, must be resistant to tears and folding, and must contain a buffer of calcium carbonate or some other approved alkaline buffer. Permanent paper should also contain cotton or rag fibers.

Plastic Terms

For maximum protection, archival quality album pages can be enclosed in protective plastic sleeves to prevent damage from dust and handling. Off gassing is the big threat to watch for in plastics. Plastics that are not pH neutral and chemically sound can emit gasses that over time will eat away at the emulsion on photographs, causing colors to fade. Aside from reading labels, the best way to tell a plastic is unsafe is by smelling it. If the plastic has a strong detectable smell, it is probably unsafe for storing photographs.

Several safe plastics are readily available. The following are a few widely used plastics considered safe for direct contact with photographs.

mylar: is the clearest and most expensive way to cover photographs and documents. Mylar is ridged and has a tendency to scratch easily. It is the first choice of professional archivists. This plastic may be purchased in set sheet sizes, in rolls, or in envelopes. Double sided film tape holds the mylar in place around the photograph or document, encasing contents against the elements. Unlike laminating, mylar casing is removable with no damage to the contents.

polypropylene: Like mylar, polypropylene is a clear, translucent plastic. Unlike mylar it is flexible, and scratch resistant. It is also a more economical option. Polypropylene is available most commonly in sheet protectors.

polyethylene: This plastic is very similar to **polypropylene.** The difference is that polyethylene has a frosted appearance and is less likely to be affected by static than polypropylene. Polyethylene is also available in sheet protectors.

Most paper is acidic by nature. If at all possible, keep acidic papers out of scrapbooks. Many craft stores or scrapbook outlets now carry acid free, lignin free paper. Archival quality paper may be slightly more expensive, but the expense is worthwhile. Scrapbooks made with low quality highly acidic papers will fade and tear over time. Low quality paper may even irreversibly damage the very photographs a scrapbook is intended to protect.

Don't use crepe paper or construction paper in a scrap book. These papers will fade and tear quickly, and their colors may bleed onto photographs.

Remember, never place photographs in a "magnetic page" self adhesive photo album. Self stick albums are covered in polyvinyl chloride (PVC), a plastic that releases hydrochloric acid. Acids will actually eat away at pictures, causing them to become yellow and brittle. To make matters worse, the adhesives in these albums will absorb into photographs over time, making them difficult, if not impossible, to remove. Several companies have tried to reintroduce magnetic page albums using archival quality papers, plastics, and adhesives. Whether or not these products are completely safe is still undetermined.

Items kept in a scrapbook or used to decorate the pages should also be acid free. Scrapbook suppliers sell acid free stickers, cards, photo corners, and pens to compliment acid free background paper and photographs. Permanent pigment pens are the best, since their colors last longer and are less likely to run or smear over time. Read the label on any pen, or call the manufacturer's customer service line if the label does not indicate the pen is acid free.

A number of materials have been found to be unsafe in direct contact with photographs. Some of these include wood or wood based products, lacquer, or enamels.

Although long term testing hasn't been completed, most scrapbook designers agree that fabric, laces, and ribbons also may be used to embellish scrapbooks. Cotton polyester fabric and notions are recommended and should be washed before use to remove any acids, sizing chemicals, or excess dyes. While the fabric itself may break down over extensive amounts of time, it should not harm photographs. If potential long term fabric problems are still a concern, consider placing buffered paper cutouts between photographs and fabric. Some scrapbook designers have found that brightly colored, poorly made ribbons can occasionally fade or bleed onto photographs. To avoid this, consider placing ribbon around, but not directly on a photograph; or use color copies or duplicates of irreplaceable photographs in questionable designs.

High acid background and embellishing materials are not the only danger to photographs; adhesives used for scrapbooks can also be a source of potential damage. Again, do not use regular trans-parent tape, high acid rubber cement, super glue, or high acid craft glue in a scrapbook. There are several new acid free adhesives out on the market, some specially designed for scrapbooks. Others, like acid free glue sticks, have been around for some time. Carefully read product labels to make certain adhesives are acid free before using them. If there is a question, call the product customer service line. While they may reveal acid content, many manufacturers will not openly reveal that their product is unsafe.

Truly archival quality scrapbooks should be reversible. This means that photographs placed in the scrapbook can be taken out again with no resulting damage. To make this possible, a scrapbook designer would need to use either a removable adhesive, or photo corners to secure photographs.

removing photographs from self adhesive albums

It may not be too late to save photographs stored in old magnetic page albums. Photographs still in these damaging albums should be removed immediately. If photographs don't come up easily, they may have already begun bonding with the adhesive. Try using a thin cake spatula to pry up old photo-graphs. If they still stick, use a warm blow dryer to melt the gum between the picture and the page. Running waxed dental floss between the photograph and the adhesive page can also help to remove photographs. If, even after effort, photographs still won't come free, get color copies of them to add to an archival quality scrapbook.

saving non-archival quality memorabilia

Some scrapbook designers may want to include high acid papers in their scrapbooks such as news-paper clippings, children's artwork, school report cards, or event tickets. All of these paper mementos can be a source of high acid

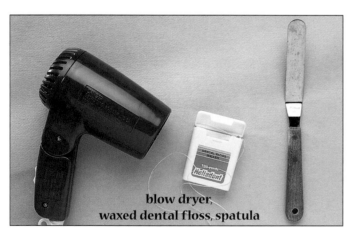

blow dryer, waxed dental floss, spatula

content. Newspaper, one of the highest in acid content, is made with a low grade paper which will become yellow and brittle within only a few years. Photographs and papers that come into contact with high acid paper may absorb some of the acids. Newspaper inks are unstable, high in acid, and may bleed onto surrounding photographs or papers.

There are a number of safe ways to include these high acid memories in albums. High acid items can be photocopied onto acid free paper.

Original documents may be placed in clear mylar envelopes where they can be viewed without acid escaping. Documents can also be sprayed with a neutralizer. The spray coats the paper and neutralizes acid levels. Display the sprayed document on buffered paper. The buffered paper will absorb acid as the levels rise over time. Buffered paper should be changed every few years to keep it's absorbency effective.

finding acid-free scrapbook supplies

Scrapbook suppliers are a great source for papers, stickers, pens, and other acid-free products. Standard craft stores are starting to carry the items too. If a product is not labeled acid free, a pH testing pen may be used to test for acid content. These pH pens can also be used to check for acid content in documents, certificates, or other paper mementos a scrapbook designer may consider including in page design.

creating albums just for fun

Often, scrapbook designers may decide to create short term scrapbooks just for the fun of it. These albums are intended to be used now, without the extra care needed to make photographs last for future generations. There is nothing wrong with breaking all the rules and putting together a quick, fun album. When creating this type of scrapbook, consider using color copies of irreplaceable photo-graphs or duplicates of photographs instead of running the risk of sacrificing one-of-a-kind priceless pictures. Duplicates or color copies of photographs may also be used when the acid content of fun designs may cause long term damage to photographs. So go ahead and use wood, bright fabrics or ribbons, water based pens, newspaper clippings, and high acid papers. Just think twice before using photographs that can not be replaced.

alternatives to traditional scrapbooks

Scrapbooks are not the only safe way to store memories. While a standard shoe box is not safe, an archival photography storage box can be a great place to tuck away mementos.

Photographs and clippings can also be arranged in a simple collage and displayed on a wall. A collage of items from a vacation can include more than just photographs. Local currency, event tickets, maps, post cards, stamps, local magazine or newspaper clippings, travel brochures, and more can be included to preserve memories of time away from home. If the collage is only intended for short term display, extensive archival precautions may not be necessary. If the collage is intended to hang for several years, consider testing papers and other mementos for acid content before including them, or using color copies or duplicates of irreplaceable photographs.

alternatives to plastic page protectors

Photographs should not be allowed to rub up against each other in a scrapbook. Plastic page protectors are only one way to keep photographs on adjacent pages from touching. Many of the designs in this book are interactive, providing scrapbook browsers an opportunity to open pop-out features, or slide out designs. These features would be inaccessible trapped in a plastic covered page. Fortunately, there are other options for page protection. Many scrapbooks have built in tissue paper dividers used to separate pages from each other. If a scrapbook does not have dividers and plastic page protectors are not an alternative, consider placing photographs on every other page to keep designs from rubbing against each other.

storing negatives

Many people consider the printed picture the most important part of the photography experience to preserve. Negatives, though frequently ignored, are just as important as the photographs themselves. With preserved negatives, unlimited new photo-graphs can be obtained at a minimal price. If only the photograph is saved, reproduction or restoration prices are more expensive.

Negatives should be organized and stored with just as much thought and care as prints. Negatives are not always safely stored in the envelopes sent from the photo lab. Negatives

should not be stored touching each other, since rubbing can damage negatives. The best way to store negatives is in archival quality plastic sleeves. These clear divided sheets allow negatives to be organized and viewed while protecting them from the elements. The sleeves can then be organized into 3-ring binders. Negative storage sleeves can be purchased from a photography supply store.

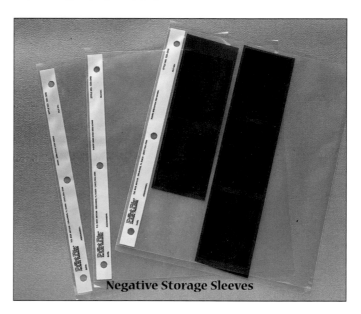
Negative Storage Sleeves

Photographs can be reproduced from well-preserved black and white negatives almost indefinitely. Color negatives, no matter how carefully stored have a shorter life. The color dyes in negatives will begin to shift over time. Within 15 or 20 years, the color negative will no longer produce a first rate image. While colors may not be true, an image will still be present. Professional photo labs can correct some of the color problems in old negatives.

safe scrapbook storage

Most people unknowingly store their scrapbooks in the worst possible places. Attics and basements are never the place to store photographs. Photographs don't stand up well under extremes of heat, cold, or humidity. Commercial storage sheds are also an unwise place to store photographs. Even though some storage units are climate controlled, potential water damage or theft can not be completely ruled out.

The best place to keep scrapbooks is in the part of the house the family lives in. Since heat and cold are controlled for human comfort in living areas, scrapbooks will stay within safe limits. Another option, is to keep archival scrapbooks, photographs or negatives in a bank safe deposit box. Most bank boxes are kept secure and many are even climate controlled to keep humidity and temperature levels constant.

It is always a good idea to keep duplicates of favorite photographs somewhere besides home. In the event of a fire, flood, or other natural disaster, at least some photographs will survive. Duplicates can be kept with family, friends, or in a bank deposit box.

Light can also be damaging to scrapbooks. Just as direct sunlight will eventually fade carpet and furniture, it will fade scrapbooks and pictures. Although scrapbooks can be safely displayed on a coffee table or bookcase, they are safest in archival quality storage boxes. Boxes keep out light and dust.

If scrapbooks are displayed in the open, make certain they are kept out of direct sunlight.

storing photographs on CD-ROM

The safest and most compact way to store photo-graphs is on CD-ROM's. Photographs scanned in a high resolution format into a computer and stored on a computer compact disc will last throughout the years without fading, tearing, or deteriorating. Best of all, home storage space is saved since just one small compact disc will hold hundreds of photographs. In addition, short sound or video clips can be added to CD-ROM's to compliment photographs.

While CD-ROM manufacturers frequently claim this medium lasts forever, many industry analysts disagree. A number of studies conclude the lifetime of a compact disc is only about 75 to 100 years.

To store photographs on CD-ROM at home, a computer, color scanner, and compact disc writer or burner are necessary. While many homes have computers, few families own scanners or burners. Lower resolution photographs can also be scanned and stored on a removable storage disk. The re-movable disks are less expensive, but the life of the stored photographs may not be as

Removable Storage Disks   **CD-ROM**

long as for those stored on CD-ROM.

If purchasing expensive computer hardware is not an option, photographs can be taken to computer graphic imaging centers for scanning and storage. Look in the yellow pages for a local graphics center that offers the scanning service.

Some graphics centers will allow customers to lay out their photographs in a page layout similar to a standard scrapbook, allowing space for further embellishment and text. Many centers even provide indexing utilities to assist customers in organizing and finding photographs on the compact discs.

Most photographic developing services provide less elaborate scanning and compact disc duplication services. Just about anywhere photographs are dropped off for developing, CD-ROM scanning and duplication service is available. Customers can have almost anything transferred onto compact disc: unprocessed film, negatives, slides, or color or black & white photographs. Prices vary by store, but usually run around $1 per scan, which, in this case, includes the price of the compact disk. Services can usually store at least one hundred high resolution scans on a compact disk. Some, with more advanced systems, may be able to store more.

Although many scanning services provide mail order services, most say customers should never mail irreplaceable photographs. Send color copies of one-of-a-kind photographs in for placement on compact disc.

family history

researching family history

Scrapbooks are more than a way of preserving the present for the future, they are a way of discovering the past. As scrapbook designers prepare pages to preserve memories of their current family, they may also want to consider researching their family origins.

start at home

The best place to start a search for origins is at home. Look around the house for items of genealogical value. These include:

Birth certificates
Family bibles
High school or college diplomas
Marriage announcements or invitations
Marriage certificates
Military discharge papers
Needlework samplers
Obituaries
Old initialed flatware
Old passports
Old quilts (often signed by their maker)
Photographs

Look through the items for clues from the past to find the answers to the commonly asked questions, who, what, where, when, how, and why.

Again, when home resources run out, try checking with extended family members. Contact older living relatives. They may have more items of genealogical value, or may remember family stories that can be of help in the search for past generations.

assembling clues from the past

A pedigree chart is the best way to compile genealogical information. The chart resembles the branches of a tree and has room for names and the dates and places of birth, marriage, and death of each individual in a family.

The first name on the list should be the person who the research is done for. Branching out from that person is their mother and father. Branching out from both mother and father are

grandparents and then great-grandparents on each side.

With each progressive generation back, ancestors multiply. Many researchers choose to go back four or five generations. Many Americans choose to research back far enough to identify their family's first immigrants.

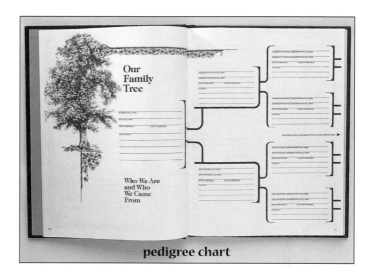

pedigree chart

Do not make the mistake many researchers make in only researching the surname line. A person is just as closely related to ancestors who bare different surnames as to those who bare the same last name. Leaving a mother's, grandmother's, or great-grandmother's line unexplored, leaves the research process unfinished.

To begin, try putting together a four- or five-generation pedigree chart. Fill in the chart as much as possible. Make certain to use complete names when known. Dates and places for birth, death, and marriage can be estimated if they are not known.

filling in the gaps

After all known information about a family has been recorded in the pedigree, the real detective work can begin. Look for gaps and holes in the assembled information to find out where to begin the search.

To fill in the gaps, go from the known to the unknown. Knowing the name of a grandfather, can lead to the names of his father and mother. His parents' names may be found on his birth certificate or marriage certificate. Once his

birth & marriage certificates

parents' names are found, their parents can be found in the same way. By digging through public records, the search can begin to turn up the names, dates, and places necessary to complete the family pedigree.

where to find records
—local records

Birth certificates, death certificates, and marriage certificates are typically kept in town or county courthouses. If accessing them in person is impossible, requests can also be made by mail. Many requests can not be met since town or county records departments do not always have the time or the employees to spare looking up information. It is always a good idea to include an offer for payment for research services and a self-addressed stamped envelope with any request. Many courthouses have set prices for records searches. A quick phone call, to obtain specific procedures, is a good idea. Include in any request for a records search the complete name of the individual and important dates that may identify the record.

Other official records kept on a county level can be of help to the researcher. Probate records provide a wealth of information. The most important variety is the last will and testament. Wills typically list the names of children and spouses. In some cases wills may be the only time the first name of a wife will be mentioned.

—state records

Many states keep duplicate birth, death, or marriage records at the state level. Each state has an address researchers can write to to ask for records searches. The Department of Health and Human Services produces a booklet called, "Where to Write for Vital Records–Births, Deaths, Marriages, and Divorces". An up-to-date copy of the booklet can be obtained by sending a self addressed envelope and $2.25 to:

Superintendent of Documents
Government Printing Office
Washington, D.C. 20402-9325

The information is also available free of charge on the internet at the following address: http://www.cdc.gov/nchsww/nchshome.htm

If the state does not have the records requested, they will usually forward the request to the local office that does. Most states have specific fees for document searches. Fees are listed in the Department of Health's booklet.

—federal records

Federal records of use to the researcher include: census records, military pension records, passenger arrival lists, and naturalization records. Census records can be obtained for a fee by writing to the following address:

U.S. Department of Commerce
Bureau of the Census
Pittsburgh, Kansas 66762

Military pension records and passenger arrival lists are kept in the National Archives. Although a personal visit to the archives is encouraged by many professional genealogists, records can be requested by mail by writing:

National Archives and Records Service
NNC
Washington, D.C. 20408

When requesting information, provide as much information as possible. Including full names, dates, and, places.

—other sources

Government documents are not the only source of information for researching family history. A researcher can also turn to newspaper archives, internet web sites, records of private organizations and societies, school records, church records, and even cemetery grave markers.

Most newspapers print birth, marriage, and death announcements. If a researcher has good idea of when an event occurred, they may be able to find the announcement of it in local newspaper archives. Marriage announcements and obituaries contain valuable genealogical information. Together, the two announcements usually contain birth, marriage, and death dates; names of parents and children; places of residence; occupation; schools attended; and organization membership information. Although many newspapers have been microfilmed and indexed, many have not. Phone calls to the papers covering the locality where an ancestor married or died can tell a researcher whether or not the obituaries and marriage announcements have been archived.

The world wide web via the internet is a vast and valuable resource when searching for family members. With a computer, a modem, and an internet service provider, information that would have taken an extended amount of time to receive by more traditional means can now be acquired in minutes. Once logged on to the internet, access a search engine and use keywords (special words or phrases that go instantly from one location, or site, to another over the web) that relate to this topic such as "geneology," "family origin," or "birth and death record." If a home computer setup as described above is not an option, look to the local library. Many libraries now have up-to-date computers that are designated for patrons' use in performing internet research.

Records of private organizations, clubs, and societies may turn up some clues worth looking for. Much of the information stored by organizations may be as simple as the member's name and date of joining, but occasionally records also include names of the member's parents, wife, or children. Some membership records include detailed information on a member's age, educational background, occupation, religion, and occasionally even a photograph.

College and university records can also be a source of information. Rosters, rolls, yearbooks, and enrollment records kept by many colleges and universities may include information about a student's residence and may include the names of parents.

Churches kept records of births, marriages, and deaths before the government ever began documenting vital statistics. To obtain information from existing churches, first contact the ecclesiastical leader of the local church. Even if church leaders don't have the records, they may know where records are stored. For churches no longer in existence, contact the local historical society, to find out where the old records are kept.

Many churches offer family history services to the public. The Church of Jesus Christ of Latter Day Saints (the Mormons) has one of the largest family history services in the world. Since they consider genealogy a moral imperative, the LDS church has sent microfilm crews throughout the world to duplicate documents. The family history library, located near the church's headquarters in Salt Lake City, Utah, contains millions of microfilmed documents. These documents are available to the public and copies can be requested through any local LDS church branch throughout the world. Many researchers have found an afternoon spent in the family history library can save years of research.

Local historical societies can be a source of genealogical help and advice. Check with a local society, or call or write to the society near the ancestor being searched for.

Cemetery gravemarkers can be a help to the researcher. In the past when people more frequently stayed in the same place for generations, entire families were often buried together. Many early graves were even dug on a family's own land. A pilgrimage to a family grave site can sometimes help turn up potential clues. Complete names are often recorded on gravemarkers when they were never written down on other documents. A woman who was listed only as Mrs. John Smith in documents will sometimes have her given name and maiden name on a marker.

laws associated with records

The Right to Privacy Act of 1974, makes some recent records inaccessible. Frequently, even though the records are not available to the public, they will be made open to genealogical researchers who are themselves listed in the records.

Many states have their own laws governing the release of records. Some will only release records to the public which were created 75 to 100 years ago. Since most information about the last 75 to 100 years can be found in home sources, record holds do not bar many genealogists from learning about their ancestors.

Laws sealing adoption records are much harder to research past. In old birth records, information about the biological parents of a child or the child's legitimacy was openly recorded in public documents. Modern adoption records are typically sealed by courts, unable to be opened without a court order rescinding the sealing.

displaying family histories

Once a family pedigree chart has been completed, it makes a perfect addition to a family scrapbook. Even a partially complete chart is of value to future generations.

photography

improving photographs

Great scrapbooks start with great photographs. Although professional photographs are wonderful additions to a scrapbook, using a professional photographer for all photographs is not practical, or necessary. With a few tips, even inexperienced photo-graphers can improve the quality of their snapshots.

camera viewfinders

The viewfinder on a camera is not a window through the lens. Often lens obstructions will not be visible though the viewfinder. It is up to the photo-grapher to make certain lens obstructions are removed. Before taking a photograph, make certain the lens cap is removed, the camera strap is clear, and no fingers cover the lens. Periodically, check to see if the lens needs cleaning. A dirty lens will only show in the photographs, not the viewfinder.

correct image cropping

What is seen in the viewfinder is not always what shows up in a photograph. Black or faint yellow lines in a viewfinder show where the image is cropped. Even though the area around the lined off rectangle is visible, it will not get

camera viewfinder

into the picture. Avoid mistakes, such as cropping off people's heads, by keeping the desired image within the lines.

camera angles

Variety can be added to photographs by changing the angles at which photographs are

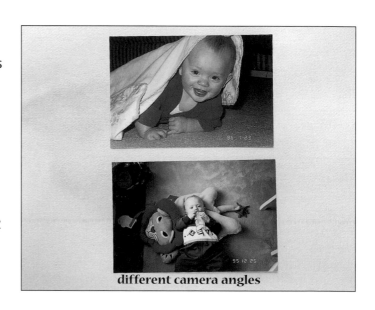

different camera angles

taken. Try looking through the camera viewfinder at the subject from low, high, and normal camera angles to see which will look best. Children's photographs are often better if the photographer kneels down to the child's level before taking the shot. Many older people find photographs taken from a slightly higher angle more appealing.

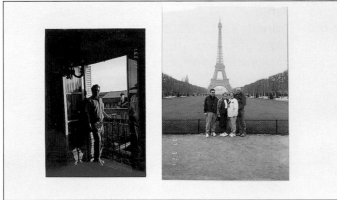

shadows & under cloud cover

outdoor photographs

Direct sunlight is too strong for taking photographs. Direct sunlight can cause harsh shadows on a squinting subject's face. In the past, film was not sensitive enough to take photographs without sun in the subject's face. Today's film is sensitive enough to work without the harsh lighting.

The best lighting for outdoor photographs comes at sunrise and sunset. When taking photographs during other times of day, try taking the shots in the shade or under cloud cover. Light harshness can also be cut down when the photographer faces the sun, using the subject to create shade for the photograph. When using this method, the sun acts as a backlight on the subject. If at all possible, try to avoid taking photographs at noon. At noon, the sun comes straight down on subjects creating dark shadows on their faces.

causes of red eye

The flash from the camera travels into the subject's eyes and reflects at almost a straight angle back to the camera lens. This reflects the blood vessels in the eye, making the eye appear red.

preventing red eye

Red eye is most common in cameras where the lens is too close to the flash. When selecting a camera, try to choose a model with the lens as far away from the flash as possible. The wider the angle of reflection, the less likely red eye will occur. Some cameras also have a red eye reduction feature. The red eye reducing cameras emit a small flash before the main photo flash. The two flashes meet, counteracting the red eye reflection. Some photographers have found that placing a light behind the photographer may also help to cut down on the problem.

correcting red eye

Fixing red eyes on photographs is possible using special red eye pens. The pens contain a dye that filters out the color red, allowing natural eye features to show through. Pen dye should be applied only to the red area on the eye. If applied to the white of the eye, the pen dye will cause the white to appear blue.

film tips

A film's sensitivity to light is rated by its speed. The higher the film speed, the more sensitive it is to light. A lower film speed needs more light. A higher film speed needs less light. While a multi-purpose film speed might meet most photography needs, a photographer may want to purchase additional rolls of film for special lighting situations. Film should be used promptly and developed quickly. Use negative film for prints and slide film for slides. Don't allow film to be exposed to x-rays. Ask to have film hand checked at airports and don't ever put film in luggage where x-ray inspections are strongest. Don't expose film to heat. Never leave exposed or unexposed film in a hot car or in direct sunlight.

photo labs

Good photographs come from good photo labs. Avoid the temptation to save money by going with a lower quality lab. Incorrect developing can mean the difference between a photograph that lasts and a photograph that quickly fades.

black & white vs. color

Black & white photographs last a great deal longer than color photographs. As the years pass, the dyes that create the color in photographs shift, causing images to fade and blur. Often fading occurs so gradually, it is almost unnoticeable. When there is no perfect original to compare a faded photograph with, color fading can be virtually undetectable. Color photography can still have a place in an archival quality album. Black & white photographs should be taken periodically to add to a family photographic record, but they do not need to replace color photography. Many scrapbook designers recommend taking a set of black & white photographs every six months to one year to preserve family history, in the event color photographs deteriorate.

photographic restoration

Photographic restoration has come a long way in the last few years. It is now possible to effectively restore damaged photographs at an affordable price. In the past, damaged photographs could only be restored by hand using pencils, dyes, chalks, and oils. Work was typically done directly on the damaged photo. The process was time consuming and expensive. Traditional methods can still be used today, but a good photographic artist will charge $25 to $40 an hour on average.

The most popular new method for restoration is digital. The damaged photograph is scanned into a computer where the digital copy can be manipulated by a photographic artist. Using this method, restoration experts can mend torn photos, add backgrounds, remove staining, enhance images, correct colors, and fix water damage discoloration. Artists can even make cosmetic changes to photographs, like removing teen's braces or blemishes.

While the digital restoration process is still time consuming, it is much more efficient compared to traditional methods. Plus, a computer artist can always undo a change that doesn't work. A traditional artist has to start over if there is a mistake. Often when work is done on the photograph itself, mistakes can cause further damage to the photograph. Once a photograph has been restored, copies can be made from it.

Digital restoration prices can vary based on the complexity of the work being done. Typically prices begin at around $25 and can reach up into hundreds of dollars depending on the complexity of work requested.

Digital restoration does not repair the damaged photograph itself. It creates a new undamaged print that looks just like the old photograph. To restore or preserve the damaged photograph itself, a photographic conservator is needed. Conservators clean the original portrait, mend it, and, in some cases, can even intensify the original image. If possible, get a second opinion before turning a photograph over to a conservator for work. Many of the cleaning processes used in photographic conservation can cause more damage than good. Never give a cherished photograph to an inexperienced conservator. More damage to photographs can be caused by good intentions than by neglect.

before & after photographic restoration

designed by Rhonda Rainey

Our Family History

Hugh & Lorraine   married June 4, 1930
Charles & Geraldine   married Mar. 23, 1955
Charles Jr. & Laurie   married July 29, 1978
Michael & Julie   married June 27, 1980
Melanie & Kenneth   married Sept. 8, 1990
Leslie & Sebron   married Oct. 18, 1995
Patricia

Herman
Duffy
Boots

designed by Rhonda Rainey

May 19th 1998

← my cake!

Spencer

Braden

Jake

We had my party in our front yard. It was sooo windy!! I had a dinosaur cake and got a lot of dinosaur toys! It was so much fun!

Abby

← the can was empty!

then there are those who like to watch!

Barb

The camp site

Sophie

Sophie was finding all sorts of treasures!!

What a fun Halloween! We had purchased those teeth from a friend of ours and Ty, Rachel & Dad had a ball! The scary thing was... Rick fit into the character a little too well. Rachel & her friend, Jennifer laughed the whole time she was getting dressed, adding crooked pigtails, lipstick & tissue from her long-johns. Ty was a true hillbilly. He & his friend Christopher were gone for hours & came home with bags of candy. ♥ Sophie & Chantry were just your cute, normal halloween kids. They traveled the neighborhood with Dad but once home, Sophie squealed each time the door bell rang, running with candy in hand to fill the bags. We all are excited for next year... oh, what will we be? Come see!!

Chapter 2: *Techniques*

1996

Spring Lake

Trout Farm

Breanna ♥ 2 yrs.
Hannah ♥ 10 mo.

Sophie

7 mo. old

How do I mount a photo onto ground paper?

Start out simple when beginning to scrapbook. The main idea and focus is to get the photos into an album to protect them, instead of being piled into a box "somewhere" in the basement. Some of us prefer this simple style where the photos are nicely displayed on a page without a lot of decoration.

Antiquity

Here's How:
1. Arrange the photos on the ground paper as desired.

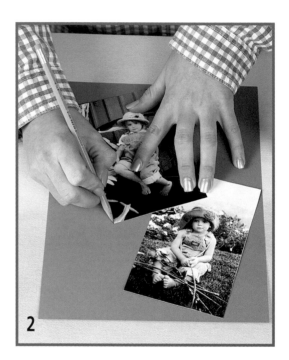

2. Using the pencil, lightly mark around the corners of the photos.

3. Remove the photos from the ground paper.

4. Beginning with the photos that are closest to the ground paper (if your photos overlap), apply adhesive to the back of each photo. Adhere them onto the ground paper, as marked, one at a time.

Troubleshooting:

Look for adhesives that are acid-free or that are labeled photo safe, meaning that the manufacturer has taken extra steps to ensure that the adhesive is free of materials that might damage the photo.

Avoid adhesives that emit odors or fumes. This is often a sign that the adhesive contains elements which can damage the photo.

Design Tip:

Experiment with different types of adhesives to find those that will make scrapbbooking easy and fun for you. There is such a wide variety to choose from—permanent or temporary, pen or stick, tape or tabs.

**What You Need
to Get Started:**

2 photos per
  page
Adhesive
Card stock:
  brown for
  ground
  paper; ivory
Scissors

How do I create
paper frames?

Placing a paper frame behind a photo gives it a finished look. Hold your photo next to several different colors of card stock to determine which color will best complement the image. Choose a contrasting ground paper so the paper frame stands out against the background.

Jake & the Twins

Here's How:

1. Apply adhesive to the back of each photo. Adhere them onto ivory card stock, allowing enough space around the entire photo for a paper "frame."

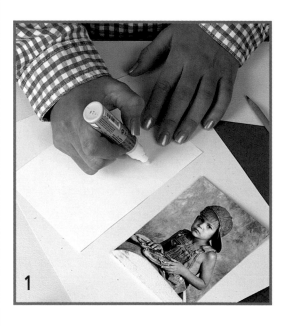

2. Using scissors, cut the card stock ⅜" larger than the large photos all around and ¼" larger than the smaller photos all around.

3. Refer to Technique 1 on page 36. Arrange and adhere the photos onto the ground paper.

3
technique

What You Need to Get Started:

1 photo per page
Adhesive
Card stock:
  olive green
  speckled for
  ground paper
Decorative
  border: light
  brown with
  vine design
Decorative paper:
  vine print for
  background
  paper
Decorative photo
  corners: light
  brown with
  vine design
Paper cutter
Pencil
Scissors
Transparent ruler

How do I mount ground paper onto background paper and use photo corners?

Photo corners are mostly for photos that you may not want permanently mounted in the photo album. Photos can be easily removed and used for other purposes. Some photo corners are self-adhesive while others may require the use of an adhesive to adhere them to the scrapbook page.

40

Mom, Uncle Roland & Aunt Marion

Here's How:

1. Using the pencil, transparent ruler, and paper cutter, measure, mark, and cut ¾" off of the bottom and one side of the ground paper.

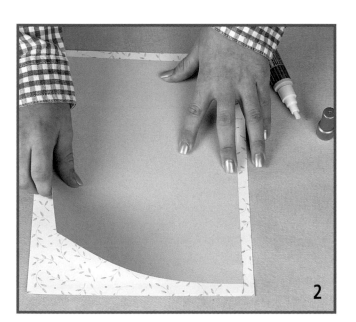

2. Apply adhesive to the back of the ground paper. Adhere it onto the center of the background paper, creating a ⅜" border.

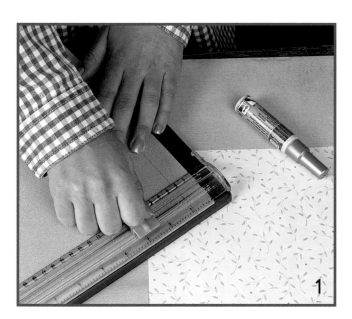

3. Arrange the photo on the ground paper as desired. Apply adhesive to the back of the decorative photo corner. Hold the photo in place with one hand and carefully slide a corner over the photo, adhering it onto the ground paper. Repeat for the opposite corner and then the two remaining corners.

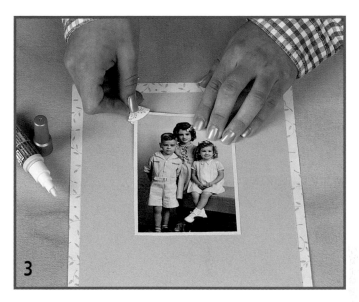

4. Using the scissors, trim the decorative border to fit the width of the ground paper. Apply adhesive to the back of the decorative border. Adhere it onto the ground paper.

Design Tips:

Depending on the type of photo corners you choose, there are a couple of different ways of adhering the corners onto the ground paper. Refer to Photos Corners on page 12 for options.

If the decorative photo corners are being used as decorative elements, apply photo sticker squares to the backs of the corners and adhere them onto the sides of the photo instead of at the corners.

What You Need to Get Started:

2 photos per
page
Adhesive
Decorative paper:
rose print for
ground paper
Marker: 0.5 mm
black liner
Paper labels
Premade photo
mattes to fit
photos
Tape

How do I use premade photo mattes on a printed ground paper?

Premade photo mattes are prefect for framing professional studio photos. They are cut to a standard size, which makes centering the photos very easy. Most mattes have embossed designs that add texture but do not take away from the image in the photo. Because the mattes are a solid color, they balance out a printed background that may otherwise be too heavy or overpowering.

Sophia

Here's How:

1. Place premade photo mattes face down on the work surface. Center each photo face down on the matte.

3. Using the marker, add journaling to the paper labels.

4. Refer to Technique 1 on page 36. Arrange and adhere the matted photos and paper labels onto the ground paper.

2. Place tape on the sides of the photo matte and adhere the photo.

Design Tips:

It is easier to tape the photo behind the frame, and then adhere the frame onto the background. It is much more difficult if you try to adhere the photo and then the frame. Avoid mistakes by centering the photo correctly before adhering it onto either the matte or the ground paper.

3 photos per page
Adhesive
Card stock: light blue; light green; ivory for ground paper; light kraft for background paper; lavender; pink
Decorative-edged scissors: cloud; scallop
Decorative photo corners: light brown with vine design
Markers: 0.5 mm black liner; 1.2 mm black liner
Paper cutter
Paper label
Pencil
Scissors
Transparent ruler

How do I use decorative-edged scissors?

Decorative-edged scissors are a wonderful way to dress up any paper frame or paper border. Most of these scissors will cut two different designs depending on how you hold them in your hand. Choose the edge that will best complement the photo or theme. Never use the decorative-edged scissors on the photo, as it detracts from the photo.

Easter Bunnies

Here's How:

1. Using the pencil, transparent ruler, and paper cutter, measure, mark, and cut ½" off the top and one side of the ground paper.

2. Position the cloud decorative-edged scissors in your hand so the desired edge will cut. Trim all sides of the ground paper, matching up the edge design with each cut of the scissors.

3. Apply adhesive to the back of the ground paper. Adhere it onto the center of the background paper.

4. Refer to Technique 3 on page 40. Arrange and adhere the photos and the decorative photo corners onto the light blue, lavender, and pink card stock, allowing enough space around the photo for creating a paper "frame."

5. Refer to Technique 2 on page 38. Using decorative-edged scissors, cut the card stock ¼" larger than the photo all around.

6. Apply adhesive to the back of the paper label. Adhere it onto the light green card stock. Using decorative-edged scissors, cut card stock ⅛" larger than the paper label all around.

7. Using the markers, add journaling to the paper label.

8. Refer to Technique 1 on page 36. Arrange and adhere each framed photo and the paper label onto the ground paper.

Easter
1994

2 photos per
   page
Adhesive
Card stock: olive
   green speckled;
   sage green
   speckled; ivory;
   tan parchment
   for background
   paper; tan
   speckled for
   ground paper
Decorative-edged
   scissors: stamp
Markers: 0.5 mm
   black liner;
   1.2 mm black
   liner
Paper cutter
Pencil: soft lead
Scissors
Templates: oval;
   rectangle
Transparent ruler

How do I use a template to crop photos?

Cropping becomes necessary when there is a lot of wasted space around the image on which you are focusing. Crop out the undesirable portions to make the most of your photo.

My Dad's Old Hat

Here's How:

1. Using the pencil, transparent ruler, and paper cutter, measure, mark, and cut ½" off the top and one side of the ground paper.

2. Using the decorative-edged scissors, trim all sides of the ground paper.

3. Apply adhesive to the back of the ground paper. Adhere it onto the center of the background paper, creating a ⅜" border.

4. To crop each photo, place the template over the photo to the best position. Using the pencil, trace the shape onto the photo.

5. Using scissors, cut around the pencil line on each photo. For a smooth cutting line, follow these steps:

• If you are right-handed, hold the photo in your left hand then, with your right hand, open the scissors all the way. Place the photo to the inside "v" of the scissors.

• Make the cut, using all but ¾" from the tip of the blade before opening the scissors again.

• Use long smooth cuts instead of short choppy ones and turn or guide the photo with your left hand not with the scissors.

• Do not cut all the way to the tip of the scissors in the middle of a shape as the paper tends to split.

6. Refer to Technique 2 on page 38. Adhere corresponding photos onto the coordinating card stock. Cut the card stock ⅜" larger than the photo all around.

7. Using the decorative-edged scissors, cut a 6¼" x 1¼" piece of ivory card stock. Adhere the ivory card stock onto the sage green card stock. Using scissors, cut the sage green card stock ½" larger than the ivory card stock all around.

8. Using the 0.5 mm marker, add journaling to the ivory card stock.

9. Apply adhesive to the back of the sage green card stock. Adhere it onto the ground paper, centered from side to side and ¼" from the bottom.

10. Refer to Technique 1 on page 36. Arrange and adhere the photos onto the ground paper.

11. Using the 1.2 mm marker, add journaling to the ground paper near the photos.

Design Tips:

The children were the focal point in the upper photo, but the excessive background was detracting. Cropping the image brought the focus back to the children and actually made them appear larger.

In the bottom photo, cropping in tight on the child, and using an oval shape to accentuate the hat, gave me the "close up" effect that I was looking for.

Practice first before tracing a template and cutting original photos. If this is your first time cropping a photo or cutting

around corners and ovals, I suggest making color copies of some photos and using them to practice cropping and cutting.

Ovals are the hardest shape to cut. You want smooth cuts—not jagged edges or straight cuts where the line begins to curve. It is better to have a pile of practice sheets instead of a pile of photos that are cropped and cut not to your liking.

Use different sizes and shapes of cropping templates to add interest to the page.

What You Need to Get Started:

1 photo per page
Adhesive
Card stock: navy
   blue for ground
   paper; cream;
   dark green;
   white
Corner rounder
   punch
Craft punch:
   snowflake
Markers: 0.5 mm
   blue liner;
   1.2 mm blue
   liner
Pencil
Scissors
Transparent ruler

How do I use corner punches and craft punches?

The corner rounder is perfect for rounding the corners of the photo instead of using scissors. The tool is easy to use and all of the corners will match. One simple way to enhance a page is by punching a motif from corners and edges. Use the punched out images for added design around the page.

Best Buddies

Here's How:
1. Using the corner rounder punch, insert the corner of the photo into the punch and round each corner.

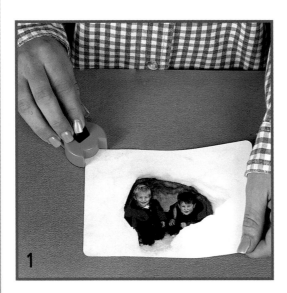

2. Refer to Technique 2 on page 28. Adhere photo onto the dark green card stock. Cut the card stock ⅜" larger than the photo all around.

3. Using the snowflake punch, punch each corner of the of dark green card

stock. Note: When you are punching out motifs in the corners, it is hard to see the placement. Turn the punch upside down, slide the card stock in, and punch. The punch is harder to hold this way, but you can see the placement of the motif easier.

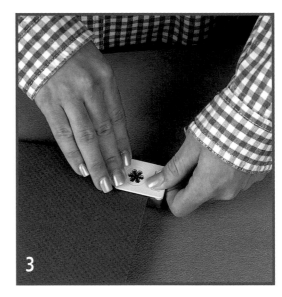

4. Apply adhesive to the back of the dark green card stock. Adhere it onto the cream card stock. Cut the cream card stock ¼" larger than the dark green card stock all around.

5. Apply adhesive to the back of the cream card stock. Adhere it onto the ground paper.

6. Refer to Technique 2 on page 38 to create a paper label. Using scissors, cut a 3¾" x 1¼" piece of white card stock. Apply adhesive to the back of the white card stock. Adhere it onto the dark green card stock. Cut the dark green card stock ⅛" larger than the white card stock all around. Adhere the dark green card stock onto the cream card stock. Cut the cream card stock ¼" larger than the dark green card stock all around. Using the corner rounder, round the corners of the cream card stock.

7. Using markers, add journaling to the paper label.

8. Apply adhesive to the back of the paper label. Adhere it onto the ground paper.

9. Using the snowflake punch, punch approximately 25 snowflakes from the white card stock.

10. Apply adhesive to the backs of the snowflakes. Randomly adhere them onto the ground paper and photo frame.

Troubleshooting:
The more intricate the craft punch, the more the blades will stick after punching. To release the button, press the dot of the design on the underside where the paper comes up, using a ballpoint pen.

Punch through waxed paper several times to lubricate the blades.

When the cuts from the punch are not very clean, punch through very fine sand paper several times to sharpen the blades.

Design Tip:
Overlap the punch designs onto the photo border. This will add some dimension.

What You Need to Get Started:

2 photos per
   page
Adhesive
Card stock:
   white; yellow
   floral for
   ground paper;
   yellow quilted
   for ground
   paper; yellow
   striped for
   background
   paper
Decorative-edged
   scissors: cloud;
   scallop
Handwritten
   words or
   computerized
   lettering
Marker: 1.2 mm
   green liner
Paper: blue plaid
Paper label:
   coordinating
Pencil
Scissors
Templates: circle;
   oval; rectangle;
   scallop-edged
Transparent ruler

How do I use templates to embellish pages?

Most of the new templates have a decorative-edged border. This is a larger design not found on decorative-edged scissors. I like to use these templates to divide up larger areas of paper—like the 12" x 12" papers. The templates take a little more time to use, but add a bit more variety to the pages.

Sophie

Note: If this is your first time working with stencils, begin with a very simple edge and work up to more difficult lines. Refer to photo on page 35 for facing page layout.

Here's How:
1. Using the transparent ruler, pencil, and paper cutter, measure, mark, and cut 1" off one side of the ground paper. (If you are using 8½" x 11" paper, measure from the 8½" width.)

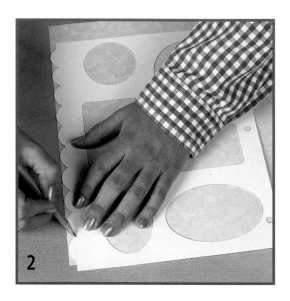

2. Place the scallop-edged template along the cut edge. Trace the design. Some of the decorative-edged templates may not be long enough to accommodate the 12" x 12" scrapbook pages. After tracing the design along the edge of your paper, slide the template up and continue the pattern.

3. Using scissors, carefully cut along traced line. Cut slowly to get nice smooth lines.

4. Cut a 1½" strip of white card stock that is the length of your page. Place the scallop-edged template along one

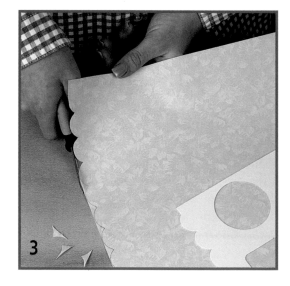

long edge and trace the design. Carefully cut along traced line.

5. Cut a 3" strip of background paper that is the length of your page.

6. Apply adhesive to the back of the ground paper along the scalloped edge only. Position the scalloped white card stock strip under the ground paper so about ⅛" of white is extending beyond the ground paper. Adhere them together.

7. Apply adhesive to the back of the white card stock strip along the scalloped edge only. Position the 3" strip of background paper under the ground paper and white card stock so the total width is equal to the total width of your page. Adhere them together.

8. Refer to Technique 6 on page 46. Using templates, a pencil, and scissors, crop selected photos as desired. Refer to Technique 7 on page 48. Round each corner of desired photos.

9. Refer to Technique 2 on page 38. Adhere photos onto the white card stock. Cut the card stock ¼" larger than the large photos and ⅛" larger than the smaller photos all around.

10. Using the cloud decorative-edged scissors, trim the edges of the journal entry paper. Adhere the journal entry paper onto the blue plaid paper. Using scissors, cut the blue plaid paper ½" larger than the journal entry paper all around.

11. Using the 1.2 mm liner marker, add journaling to the paper labels.

12. Refer to Technique 1 on page 36. Arrange and adhere the photos, journal entry, and paper labels onto the ground paper.

April 1998

Mom and Dad let Rachel and Tyrel decide on the Spring-break vacation. They decided on the Casa Blanca in Mesquite Nevada.

They HAD to buy me all new stuff from my levi hat to my flower sunglasses. I was all set to go.

It was the perfect weekend and we all had a great time especially in the pool which had a waterslide and a beautiful waterfall surrounded by flower gardens and palm trees. I loved to watch the kids come down the slide and splash water at me at the bottom.

I kept the hat on most of the time but the flower sunglasses were better just to chew on. That grass was a bit "prickly" and would rather sit on dad's lap and play with the camera.

9
technique

What You Need to Get Started:

3 photos per page
Adhesive
Card stock: blue;
  dark sage green;
  sage green; tan
  for ground paper;
  yellow
Die-cuts: cloud;
  flame; logs;
  mountains;
  tent
Markers: 0.5 mm
  black liner;
  1.2 mm black
  liner
Opaque pens: blue;
  white
Pencil
Scissors
Templates: circle;
  oval; rectangle;
  square
Transparent ruler

How do I use die-cuts on a page?

This is an easy and inexpensive way to add design and color to a page. Die-cuts are ready-made and available in all colors, shapes, and sizes.

South Fork Canyon

Note: Refer to photo on page 24 for facing page layout.

Here's How:

1. Refer to Technique 6 on page 46. Crop selected photos as desired.

2. Refer to Technique 2 on page 38. Adhere selected photos onto assorted colors of card stock. Cut the colored card stock ¼" larger than the large photos and ⅛" larger than the smaller photos all around.

3. Refer to Technique 1 on page 36. Arrange and adhere the photos and die-cuts onto the ground paper.

4. Using the markers and opaque pens, add journaling to the die-cuts and ground paper.

Design Tip:

Do not be afraid to overlap the die-cuts with each other and also with the photos. Try using them as a background. Layering die-cuts and photos adds dimension to the pages.

How do I silhouette photos?

Silhouetting is perfect if you have a lot of photos of the same event. It is also great if there is a large group of people to show on the same layout.

I Am Five Today

Note: Make plenty of color copies for silhouettes so original photos are not ruined. Refer to photo on facing page layout.

Here's How:
1. Using the transparent ruler, pencil, and cloud decorative-edged scissors, measure, mark, and cut ½" from the top and one side of the ground paper.

2. Apply adhesive to the back of the ground paper. Adhere it onto the of background paper, lining up the two uncut edges and leaving a colored border on the right and top edges. If you have a facing page, repeat with a second piece of ground paper and background paper, leaving a colored border on the left and top edges.

3. Refer to Technique 6 on page 46. Crop photos to be used at the top of the page as desired.

4. Refer to Technique 2 on page 38. Adhere one of the cropped photos onto green card stock. Cut the card stock ¼" larger than the photo all around.

5. Using a craft knife or scissors, carefully cut around the photographic or copied images to be used for silhouetting.

6. Arrange the blunt-edged silhouetted photos on the ground paper, lining them up along the bottom of the page, and placing them in varying heights, slightly overlapping them if necessary.

7. Arrange the cropped photos on the pages as desired.

8. Place remaining silhouetted photos on the pages as desired.

9. Using the die-cuts as "fillers," carefully slide them into place under and around silhouetted photos.

10. Apply adhesive to the back of each photo and die-cut. Adhere them onto the ground paper one at a time.

What You Need to Get Started:

8–10 photos per page
Adhesive
Card stock: green; red; white for ground paper;
Craft knife and cutting mat
Decorative-edged scissors: cloud
Die-cuts: birthday cake; star
Markers: 0.5 mm black liner; 1.2 mm black liner
Pencil
Scissors
Templates: oval; rectangle; square
Transparent ruler

11. Using the markers, add journaling to the die-cuts, and ground paper.

areas, use a craft knife, as scissors may bend or tear the photo.

Design Tips:

Not all photos are right for this technique. If you have plenty of photos to use, give it a try. Use this technique sparingly throughout your album.

Choose just a few photos that depict the main event. This will give nice variety to the layout.

Photos with a blunt edge should be used toward the bottom of the page. Photos that can be cut all the way around can stand on their own.

To get into those hard-to-cut

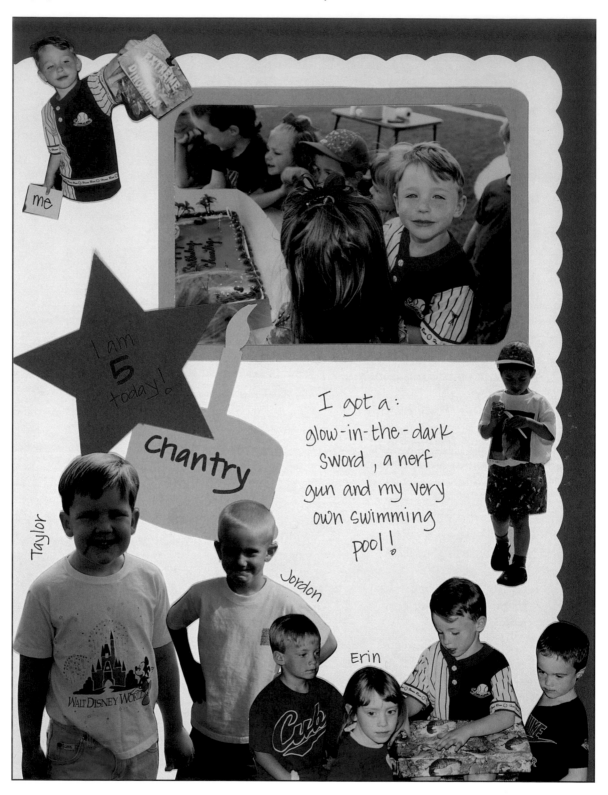

How do I use stickers to embellish a page?

What You Need to Get Started:

3 photos per
  page
Adhesive
Card stock: dark
  blue; burgundy;
  ginger speckled
  for ground
  paper; dark
  green
Corner rounder
Decorative-edged
  scissors:
  scallop; stamp;
  zigzag
Pencil
Scissors
Stickers: animals;
  letters
Transparent ruler

Jazz up any scrapbook page with inexpensive self-adhesive stickers. The variety is endless and the technique is quick and easy. These are also great for children to use when they are designing their own pages.

Hogle Zoo

Here's How:

1. Refer to Technique 7 on page 48. Round each corner of each photo.

2. Refer to Technique 2 on page 38. Adhere photos onto card stock. Cut the card stock ⅜" larger than the large photos all around and ¼" larger than the smaller photos all around.

3. Refer to Technique 1 on page 36. Arrange and adhere the photos onto the ground paper.

4. Carefully place stickers as desired to accent the page layout.

5. Add lettering to the page by carefully placing the letter stickers.

Troubleshooting:

When using stickers to add design to a page, try to keep the background very simple. Stickers tend to get "lost" on a heavily printed background; the page becomes very "busy," and the viewer's focus on the photos, the most important element, is diminished.

Remember, stickers are used to add to the story and perhaps a bit of color, not to become the reason you did the page in the first place. Be selective and use just a few stickers per page.

Design Tips:

Take your time placing the stickers. Some sticker brands allow you to remove the stickers and rearrange them before the adhesive becomes permanent, usually before 10–20 minutes.

If you are not certain where to place the sticker, do not peel it from the backing. Cut around the sticker, leaving the backing on, and lay it on the page to see how it looks. When you are satisfied, remove the backing and press the sticker onto the page. One time application is best with stickers, as removing and rearranging them causes the edges of the sticker to turn and sometimes bend.

Hogle Zoo

Spring

1997

How do I use decorative papers that have borders?

Combine a piece of decorative paper that has a border with a photo or two, a small die-cut, and perhaps a few stickers, and you have an almost instant scrapbook page.

School Days

Here's How:

1. Using the transparent ruler, pencil, and scissors, measure, mark, and trim the class photo to fit within the border on the decorative paper.

2. Refer to Technique 6 on page 46. Crop the portrait photo as desired.

3. Refer to Technique 2 on page 38. Adhere the photo onto card stock. Cut the card stock ¼" larger than the photo all around.

4. Refer to Technique 1 on page 36. Arrange and adhere the photos and die-cuts onto the decorative paper.

Troubleshooting:

Avoid layering photos with a heavily printed paper as it becomes very busy and takes emphasis away from the border and more importantly, the photos. Use colored card stock to place behind photos. If your border is really busy, be selective about choosing die-cuts or stickers. Sometimes less is better.

What You Need to Get Started:

1 class photo
1 portrait photo
Adhesive
Card stock: dark red
Decorative paper with border
Die-cuts: assorted
Pencil
Scissors
Template: oval
Transparent ruler

What You Need to Get Started:

3 photos per
   page
Acid-free paint
Adhesive
Adhesive dots:
   repositionable
   for stencils
Card stock: blue;
   brown; ivory
   for ground
   paper
Disposable
   palette
Makeup sponges
Paper towel
Pencil
Scissors
Stencil for
   memory page
Stickers: letters

How do I use stencils to decorate a page?

Many stencils that were designed for decorative painting techniques easily cross over into the craft of scrapbooking. With just a bit of acid-free paint and a makeup sponge, you can add subtle colored images directly onto the ground paper.

Spring Lake

Note: I moved the stencil to place motifs in different areas.

Here's How:

1. Begin to create the border by centering the stencil along the bottom edge of the ground paper. Secure the stencil to the paper, using the re-positionable stencil dots.

2. Pour a small amount of paint onto disposable palette. Dip makeup sponge into paint. Dab sponge on paper towel, removing excess paint.

3. Apply paint from the edge of the stencil onto the ground paper, lightly dabbing to avoid bending the stencil. The paint will be darker around the fish and lighter as it reaches the edge of the paper. Allow the paint to dry.

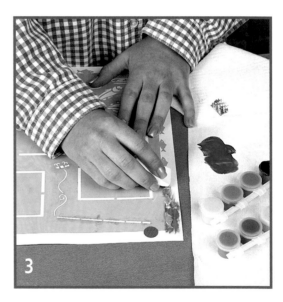

4. Repeat Steps 1–3 for the top edge of the ground paper.

5. Clean the stencil and flip it over. Repeat Steps 1–3 for both sides of the ground paper.

6. Stencil-paint the frames, fish, fishing pole, water, and cattails onto the

ground paper, lightly dabbing to avoid bending the stencil, from the outside toward the center of the motif.

7. Refer to Technique 6 on page 46. Crop selected photos as desired4

8. Refer to Technique 1 on page 36. Arrange and adhere the photos onto the ground paper within the painted frames.

Troubleshooting:

Begin stenciling slowly. This is a technique which requires patience. Use a small amount of paint to avoid the paint seeping under the stencil.

3 photos per page
Adhesive
Card stock: light blue speckled for ground paper; red; tan speckled; teal; white; yellow
Craft knife and cutting mat
Decorative-edged scissors: cloud; scallop; zigzag
Die-cuts: cloud; sun (2); umbrella
Lettering books
Light box
Markers: 0.5 mm black liner; 1.2 mm black liner; 0.5 mm baby blue liner; 1.2 mm baby blue liner; 1.2 mm red liner
Pencil
Self-adhesive die-cuts: glasses; pail; shovel; starfish (2)
Scissors
Templates: circle; oval; rectangle

How do I use creative lettering on a page?

A variety of lettering adds personality to any layout. Do not be afraid to experiment with different heights, widths, and colors of lettering on the same page. This technique is fun and very addicting.

Playa del Canto

Here's How:

1. Rip a piece of tan speckled card stock to create the "sand" and position it over the bottom portion of the ground paper.

2. Apply adhesive to the back of the torn paper. Adhere it onto the ground paper. Using scissors, trim tan speckled card stock flush with the ground paper.

3. Refer to Technique 6 on page 46. Crop selected photos as desired.

4. Refer to Technique 2 on page 38. Adhere photos onto card stock. Cut the card stock ¼" to ⅛" larger than each photo all around.

5. Using scissors, cut two pieces of white card stock for paper labels.

6. Place the selected lettering, right side up, on a light box with the white card stock on top, right side up. Using the pencil, lightly trace the lettering onto the card stock.

7. Using the markers, ink the lettering. Erase any pencil lines once the lettering is inked.

8. Adhere the lettered card stock onto colored card stock. Cut the colored card stock ¼" larger than each piece of lettered card stock all around.

the craft knife to make a small slit in the tan card stock and slide the edge of the die-cut into the slit.

9. Refer to Technique 1 on page 36. Arrange and adhere the photos, paper labels, and die-cuts onto the ground paper.

10. Using the markers, add journaling to the ground paper and die-cuts.

Trouble-shooting:
Ink the lettering before adhering the white card stock onto the colored card stock. If a mistake is made, the colored card stock is not wasted.

Design Tip:
To make certain the die-cuts appear as if they are down in the "sand," use

61

Mexico '97

digging for sand dollars

We buried Jake

How can I use rubber stamping to decorate a page?

Creating borders and backgrounds is simple with stamping. The most appealing aspect of working with rubber stamps is that the images can be used over and over without having to purchase the product every time.

What You Need to Get Started:

2 photos per
  page
Adhesive
Card stock: blue
  for ground
  paper; brown;
  tan
Colored pencils
Marker: 2.0 mm
  black
  calligraphy
Pencil
Permanent ink
  pad: black
Scissors
Stamp: sunflower
Transparent ruler

Jr. Performance

Here's How:
1. Refer to Technique 2 on page 38. Adhere photos onto tan card stock. Cut the card stock ⅛" larger than each photo all around.

2. Apply adhesive to the back of each piece of tan card stock. Adhere each piece onto brown card stock. Cut the brown card stock ⅛" larger than each piece of tan card stock all around.

3. Using transparent ruler, pencil, and scissors, measure, mark, and cut a 2¾" x 10½" strip of tan card stock.

4. Ink the sunflower stamp, using the black ink pad.

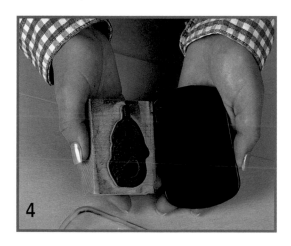

5. Print the image, by placing the stamp, rubber die side down, onto the card stock strip. Without rocking or twisting the stamp, give it a little pressure.

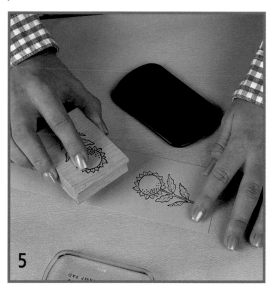

6. Lift the stamp straight up and off the card stock strip. Allow the ink to dry. Refer to photo on page 64.

7. Randomly print the image over the entire strip of card stock by repeating Steps 4–6.

6–7

11. Refer to Technique 1 on page 36. Arrange and adhere the photos onto the ground paper.

12. Using scissors, cut out the single stamped image, leaving ⅛" of card stock all around.

13. Apply adhesive to the back of the single stamped image. Adhere it onto the right side of the ground paper, overlapping the photo if desired.

8. Print a single image onto a scrap piece of tan card stock. Allow the ink to dry.

9. Using the colored pencils, color the sunflowers as desired.

9

10. Apply adhesive to the back of the stamped card stock strip. Center and adhere it onto the left side of the ground paper.

Jr. Performance Group '97–'98

How can I create 12" x 12" pages using 8½" x 11" stationery?

This is one of the funnest techniques to use. The variety of 8½" x 11" stationery is endless and converting these papers to 12" x 12" is so simple. Create your own borders, corner designs, and individual images from one piece of paper.

Big Hugs

Note: I cut up stationery and placed motifs at the corners of the pages.

Here's How:
1. Using the transparent ruler, pencil, and paper cutter, measure, mark, and cut ¾" off the top and 1¾" off one side of light peach ground paper.

2. Apply adhesive to the back of the ground paper. Adhere it onto the light kraft background paper, ⅜" from the left side.

3. Apply adhesive to the back of the stationery. Adhere it onto the ground paper, ⅛" from the left side.

4. Refer to Technique 11 on page 55. Carefully place stickers at different angles down the right side of the background paper.

5. Refer to Technique 2 on page 38. Adhere the photo onto the sage green card stock. Cut the card stock ⅜" larger than the photo all around. Adhere the sage green card stock onto the ivory speckled card stock. Cut the ivory speckled card stock ⅛" larger than the sage green all around. Adhere the

ivory speckled card stock onto the rose card stock. Cut the rose card stock ⅛" larger than the ivory speckled card all around.

6. Apply adhesive to the back of the rose card stock. Adhere it onto the stationery, 1" from the top and centered from side to side.

7. Cut the light yellow card stock to 3½" x 1" to create a paper label. Cut the olive green speckled card stock to 5" x 1¼".

8. Apply adhesive to the back of the yellow card stock. Adhere it onto the center of the olive green speckled card stock.

9. Refer to Technique 7 on page 48. Punch a heart from each side of olive green card stock on the paper label.

10. Using the markers, add journaling to the paper label.

11. Apply adhesive to the back of the paper label. Adhere it onto the stationery ¼" below the photo and centered from side to side on the stationery.

What You Need to Get Started:

1 photo per page
Adhesive
Card stock: olive green speckled; sage green; ivory speckled; light kraft for background paper; light peach for ground paper; rose; light yellow
Craft punch: heart
Decorative-edged scissors: deckle
Markers: 0.5 mm lavender liner; 1.2 mm lavender liner
Paper cutter
Pencil
Scissors
Stationery: Classic Pooh
Stickers: Classic Pooh
Transparent ruler

BIG HUGS
Breanna and Hannah '98

How do I use rub-ons to decorate a page?

What You Need to Get Started:

2 photos per page
Adhesive
Card stock: blue for ground paper; tan speckled for background paper
Corner rounder
Markers: 0.5 mm black liner; 1.2 mm black liner
Paper cutter
Pencil
Rub-ons
Scissors
Transparent ruler

Rub-ons are like using an oversized sticker—without the silhouette look that comes with a sticker. Rub-ons are great for layering and can be used on almost any surface.

A Little Worn Out

Here's How:

1. Using the transparent ruler, pencil, and paper cutter, measure, mark, and cut ¾" from the top and one side of the ground paper.

2. Refer to Technique 7 on page 48. Round each corner of the ground paper.

3. Apply adhesive to the back of the ground paper. Adhere it onto the center of the background paper.

4. Cut out the selected rub-ons, leaving the paper backing attached to the rub-on.

5. Arrange the rub-ons and photos on the ground paper as desired.

6. Rub the design onto the ground paper and background paper.

7. Carefully remove the paper backing by lifting from one corner. Watch for the small black lines to make certain they have adhered onto the paper.

8. Apply adhesive to the back of each photo. Adhere them onto the ground paper one at a time.

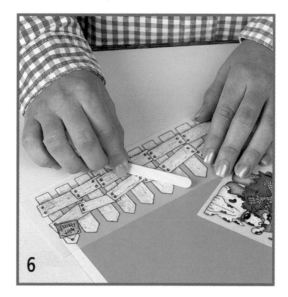

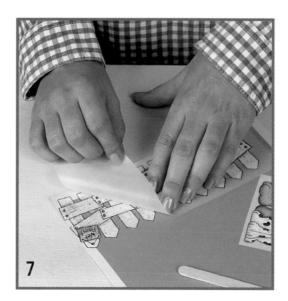

9. Using the markers, add journaling to the ground paper.

Trouble-shooting:

If you are uncertain where you are going to place the rub-on, cut around the motif, leaving the backing on, and lay it on the page to see how it looks.

When you are satisfied, remove the backing and press the rub-on onto the page.

One time application is best, as the back of the rub-on is very sticky and cannot be peeled up to be moved or it will tear apart.

Design Tip:

Do not be afraid to layer the designs—this is a great way to achieve dimension.

How do I create puzzle pages?

**What You Need
to Get Started:**

7 photos per
   page
Adhesive
Card stock: navy
   blue for ground
   paper; kraft for
   background
   paper; light
   kraft
Stencil: oval
   puzzle
Decorative-edged
   scissors: cloud
Marker: gold
   paint
Scissors

Puzzle templates take all the guesswork out of cropping. This technique is easily accomplished and uses several pictures on one page. A puzzle page is a fun addition to any photo album.

Bathtime

Here's How:
1. Using the transparent ruler, pencil, and decorative-edged scissors, measure, mark, and cut 1½" off two sides of the ground paper.

2. Using scissors, cut two 1½" x 12" strips from the light kraft card stock. Using the decorative-edged scissors, trim one long edge from each strip.

3. Apply adhesive to the back of the ground paper along the scalloped edges. Position the scalloped light kraft card stock strips under the ground paper so about ¼" of light kraft is extending beyond the ground paper and adhere them together.

4. Apply adhesive to the back of the ground paper with the scalloped light kraft strips. Adhere it onto the center of the background paper.

5. Refer to Technique 6 on page 46. Crop selected photos as desired.

6. Using the template as a guide, arrange the photos on the page with even spacing.

7. Apply adhesive to the back of each photo. Adhere them onto the ground paper one at a time.

8. Using the marker, add journaling to the ground paper.

Troubleshooting:
Use a small piece of removable tape to hold photos in place while adhering each photo permanently. It is important to space each photo evenly to achieve the puzzle effect.

Design Tip:
Decide upon a theme and keep to that theme. Use large subjects for each opening to simplify the look of it.

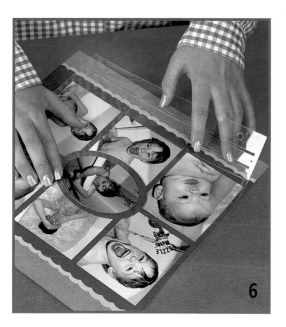
6

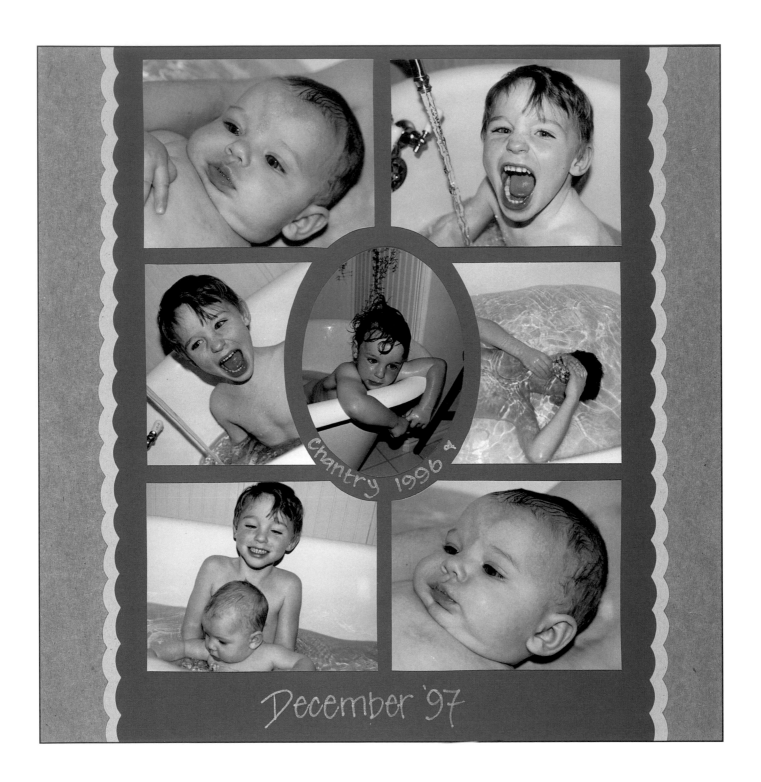

Chantry 1996 4

December '97

How do I use clip-art from pattern books?

This technique allows you to choose clip-art from books without using a computer. The images can be reduced or enlarged to fit the area you want to fill and may or may not be colored.

Halloween '98

Here's How:

1. Using the transparent ruler, pencil, and paper cutter, measure, mark, and cut ⁵⁄₁₆" from the top and one side of the ground paper.

2. Refer to Technique 7 on page 48. Round each corner of the ground paper.

3. Punch a star in each corner of the ground paper.

4. Apply adhesive to the back of the ground paper. Adhere it onto the center of the background paper.

5. Refer to Technique 6 on page 46. Crop selected photos as desired.

6. Refer to Technique 2 on page 38. Adhere photos onto card stock. Cut the card stock ¼" to ⅛" larger than each photo all around or large enough to accommodate punching either on each corner or along one edge.

7. Punch stars from each corner of the selected card stock.

8. Select clip-art images from the pattern book. Using a photocopy machine, copy the images onto white card stock or watercolor paper, reducing or enlarging as desired.

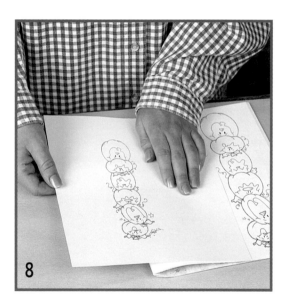

8

9. Dilute acrylic paints with water to the consistency of a wash for a watercolor effect. Using the paintbrush, color the images as desired, beginning with a light wash and apply darker washes to create the shading. Allow paint to dry. Refer to photo on page 72.

What You Need to Get Started:

4 photos per
   page
Acrylic paints and
   paintbrushes
Adhesive
Card stock: black
   for ground
   paper; blue;
   olive green;
   orange; rusty
   red; white;
   yellow for
   background
   paper
Corner rounder
Craft punch: star
Decorative-edged
   scissors:
   scallop;
   stamp; zigzag
Lettering books
Markers: 0.5 mm
   black liner;
   1.2 mm black
   liner; 1.2 mm
   wheat liner
Paper cutter
Pattern book
Pencil
Scissors
Templates: circle;
   oval; rectangle
Transparent ruler
Watercolor
   paper:
   lightweight

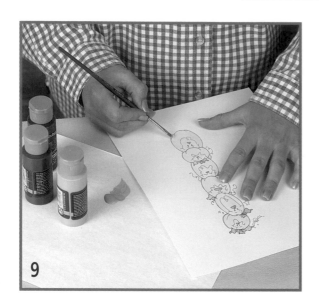

Troubleshooting:

Choose designs that are easy to color. Make certain the designs do not overpower the page or compete with the photos.

Lay out your page and make certain the size of the clip-art works before adding color.

Color the image first before cutting it out. You can use colored pencils, markers, acrylic paints and paintbrushes, or watercolor paints and paintbrushes to color patterns. Seal these with an acrylic sealer.

Use scissors with a sharp point to cut around the colored image.

10. Using scissors, cut out images.

11. Refer to Technique 14 on page 60. Cut a piece of white card stock for paper label. Pencil and ink in the lettering.

12. Adhere the lettered card stock onto colored card stock. Cut the colored card stock ¼" larger than each piece of lettered card stock all around.

13. Refer to Technique 1 on page 36. Arrange and adhere the photos, clip-art images, punched stars, and paper label onto the ground paper.

How do I use computer clip-art?

In this technological age of computers, software made up of clip-art images is readily available and provides a quick and easy way to decorate a scrapbook page. Most clip-art programs contain both black line art and colored images.

What You Need to Get Started:

2 photos per
   page
Adhesive
Cardstock: sage
   green; orange;
   red for back-
   ground paper
Computer clip-art
Decorative-edged
   scissors: zigzag
Paper: white
Paper cutter
Pencil
Scissors
Transparent ruler

Turkey Day

Here's How:

1. Refer to Technique 6 on page 46. Crop selected photos as desired.

2. Refer to Technique 2 on page 38. Adhere photos to card stock. Cut the card stock ¼" to ⅛" larger than the photos all around.

3. For reference, arrange the photos on a piece of white paper as desired.

4. Select clip-art images from the booklet provided with the computer clip-art. Arrange the images on a page in your document, positioning them to correspond with the layout of your photos, leaving ½" of white along the top and one side of the page.

5. Choose a coordinating font. Add journaling on your page by typing the information on the page within the document.

6. Print the page with the clip-art images and lettering. Using paper cutter, trim ½" from the top and one side of the printed page.

7. Apply adhesive to the back of the printed page. Adhere it onto the center of the red card stock.

8. Apply adhesive to the back of each photo. Adhere them onto the printed page one at a time.

Design Tip:

After choosing your photos for the page, measure the openings where the clip-art images will be placed. Size your image correctly before printing to save time that might otherwise be spent reducing or enlarging on a copy

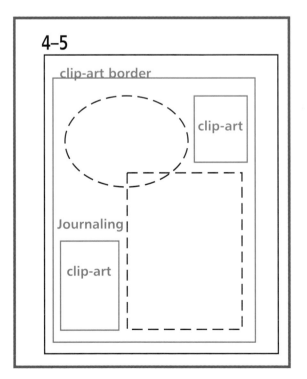

Turkey Day
November
1998

How do I make a pocket page to hold memorabilia?

What You Need to Get Started:

1 photo per page
Adhesive
Cardstock: sage green; orange; red for ground paper
Computer clip-art
Jute: 2-ply (1½ yards)
Memorabilia
Paper: white
Paper punch
Pencil
Scissors
Transparent ruler

The purpose of creating a scrapbook is to provide a place for keeping "scraps." Pocket pages are a wonderful way to keep special momentos close to the photos of the same event.

Rain Dance

Here's How:

1. Using transparent ruler, pencil, and scissors, measure, mark, and cut orange card stock to 5½" x 8½" for the pocket.

2. Punch holes along the top 8½" edge of the pocket, ⅜" apart.

3. Align the bottom edge of the pocket with the bottom edge of the ground paper. Using the paper punch, punch holes through both pieces of paper, ¾" apart all around.

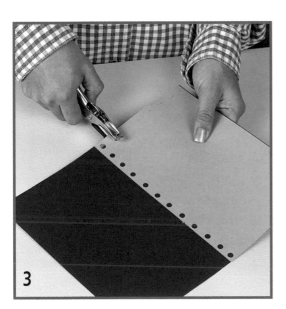

4. Tape one end of the jute to avoid fraying. Beginning at the top center hole of the pocket and leaving a 6" tail, weave the jute through the holes. Weave through both pieces of paper around the edges and finish weaving through the holes on the top of the pocket. Tie a bow where ends meet.

5. Using transparent ruler, pencil, and scissors, measure, mark, and cut a 4½" x 7½" piece of sage green card stock.

6. Refer to Technique 10 on page 53. Carefully cut around the photographic or copied image to be used for silhouetting.

7. Refer to Technique 20 on page 73. Prepare print, and cut out clip-art images and journaling.

8. Position the blunt edge of the silhouetted photo along the bottom of the sage green card stock. Arrange the clip-art images and journaling on the card stock as desired.

9. Apply adhesive to the back of each image. Adhere them onto the card stock one at a time.

10. Apply adhesive to the back of the sage green card stock. Adhere it onto the center of the pocket.

11. Place memorabilia into the pocket.

Troubleshooting:

Be aware that memorabilia-filled pocket pages may cause indentations on pages that are place next to them in a binder. Place these and pages with one-of-a-kind photos far apart.

Design Tip:

There are kits available that you can use to create your own pocket pages in no time. The kits are themed and contain stickers, die-cut shapes, colored paper, patterned paper, adhesive strips, and step-by-step directions.

How do I use embossing templates to emboss paper?

What You Need to Get Started:

1 large photo
Adhesive
Card stock: dark green; light green; dark lavender; light lavender; dark pink; light pink; pre-embossed white for ground paper
Embossing templates: flower; leaf
Scissors
Stylus
Tape

Embossing is the nearly forgotten art of gently pressing a shape or motif into the paper's surface. While embossing is not a complex technique, it adds a wonderful texture and dimension to any page.

Little Angel

Here's How:

1. Refer to Technique 1 on page 36. Apply adhesive to the back of the photo. Adhere it at an angle onto the embossed ground paper.

2. Place the flower template on the front of the dark lavender card stock and lightly tape the stencil to the card stock.

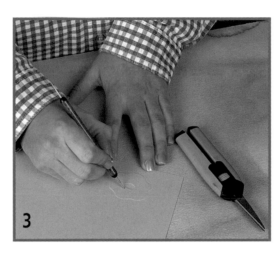

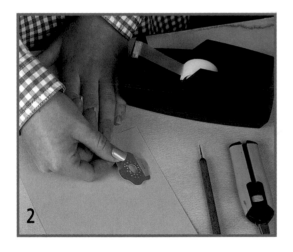

3. Turn the stencil over so the card stock is on top. Using the stylus, gently press the paper through the grooves of the template, creating a raised design. Repeat for a second flower.

4. Using the scissors, carefully cut out the embossed flowers and leaves.

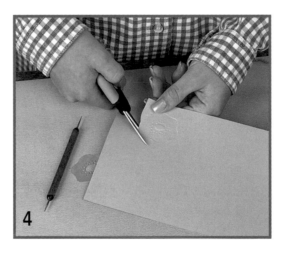

5. Repeat Steps 2–3 to emboss two

flowers onto light lavender card stock, two flowers onto dark pink card stock, and two flowers onto light pink card stock. Using the leaf template, emboss seven leaves onto dark green card stock and five leaves onto light green card stock.

6. Arrange and adhere the embossed flowers and leaves around each corner of the photo and onto the ground paper.

Troubleshooting:

Avoid scrubbing the stylus across larger areas of the design as this may leave grooves in the paper.

Because work is being done from the backside, the embossed design will be a reverse image of what is seen on the stencil front.

How do I use natural papers on a page?

Natural papers made with bits of flowers and leaves seem to lend new life to the photos. Most natural papers are hand-made and have a wonderful texture that stands out against the flatness of "run-of-the-mill" papers.

The Wedding

Here's How:

1. Using the transparent ruler, pencil, and paper cutter, measure, mark, and cut 1½" off the top and one side of the ground paper.

2. Refer to Technique 7 on page 48. Round each corner of the ground paper.

3. Apply adhesive to the back of the ground paper. Adhere it onto the center of the printed background paper.

4. Refer to Technique 2 on page 38. Adhere the photo onto the ivory card stock. Cut the card stock ¼" larger than the photo all around.

5. Refer to Technique 3 on page 40. Adhere the photo corners with the photo onto the olive green card stock. Cut the olive green card stock ⅜" larger than the ivory card stock all around.

6. Adhere the olive green card stock onto the natural paper. Cut the natural paper ⅜" larger than the olive green card stock all around.

7. Round each corner of the natural paper.

8. Adhere the natural paper onto the pink speckled card stock. Cut the pink speckled card stock ½" larger than the natural paper all around.

9. Punch each corner of the pink speckled card stock.

10. Apply adhesive to the back of the pink speckled card stock. Adhere it onto the ground paper, ½" from the top and centered from side to side.

11. Cut a piece of ivory card stock for a paper label. Punch each corner.

12. Adhere the ivory card stock onto the olive green card stock. Cut the olive green card stock ⅛" larger than the ivory card stock all around.

13. Using the marker, add journaling to the paper label.

14. Apply adhesive to the back of the olive green card stock. Adhere it onto the ground paper, ⅛" from the photo and centered from side to side.

What You Need to Get Started:

1 photo per page
Adhesive
Card stock: olive green; ivory; ivory for ground paper; pink speckled
Corner punch: fan
Corner rounder
Decorative paper: roses print for background paper
Decorative photo corners: black with leaf design
Decorative-edged scissors: deckle
Marker: 0.5 mm black liner
Natural paper
Paper cutter
Pencil
Stickers: green bow; pressed flowers; rose
Transparent ruler

15. Refer to Technique 11 on page 55. Carefully place the stickers on the ground paper and paper label as desired.

Troubleshooting:

Make certain you know where the natural stickers are going to be placed. These cannot be removed once they are placed onto the surface. They are extremely delicate, but well worth the extra care.

Design Tip:

If you want to give a photo an old-time look, create a small white border, using deckle decorative-edged scissors and some ivory card stock. This effect finishes a color copy made from an original.

How do I color-tint black-and-white photos?

24
technique

What You Need to Get Started:

2 photos per page
Adhesive
Card stock: blue speckled; brown speckled ; olive green speckled; olive green speckled for background paper; sage green speckled; ivory; light kraft speckled for ground paper; lavender; plum; yellow
Decorative border: light brown with vine design
Decorative corner punch: fan
Decorative photo corners: light brown with vine design
Decorative-edged scissors: deckle
Marker: 0.5 mm black liner
Natural paper
Paper cutter
Pencil
Pressed flowers
Scissors
Self-adhesive laminate
Spot pens: photo tinting set
Templates: circle; oval; rectangle; square
Transparent ruler

Color-tinting black-and-white photos now is so easy, and spot pens have made it that much easier. This technique is almost like filling in the color in a coloring book.

Sunday Afternoon

Note: Carefully read all manufacturer's instructions for the photo tinting pen set.

Here's How:

1. To avoid scratching photos, soften pen tips by rubbing them vigorously on a discarded photo for 20 seconds.

2. Using a sponge, moisten the area to be colored with water and solution provided in the photo tinting set. Make two or three swipes with the sponge from top to bottom or from side to side so the photo is slightly tacky, but not wet.

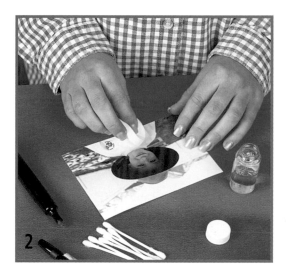

3. Lightly touch the pen tip to the black-and-white photo. Fill in the area, using circular motions and gradually building color.

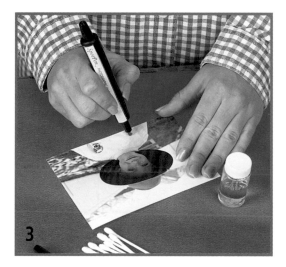

Note: If streaking occurs, either the photo has become too dry and needs to be moistened again or you are using too dark a color on a light area.

4. Using a cotton swab, blot excess dye from the photo.

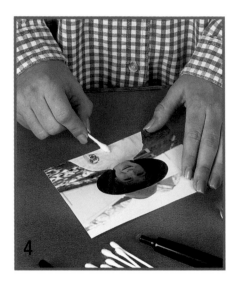

5. Using the transparent ruler, pencil, and paper cutter, measure, mark, and cut 1" off the top and one side of the ground paper.

6. Refer to Technique 7 on page 48. Punch each corner of the ground paper.

7. Apply adhesive to the back of the ground paper. Adhere it onto the center of the background paper.

8. Refer to Technique 6 on page 46. Crop selected photos as desired.

9. For each photo, refer to Technique 2 on page 38. Adhere photos onto coordin-

ating pieces of card stock and natural paper. Cut the card stock and natural paper ⅝", ⅜", and ¼" larger than the photo all around.

10. Refer to Technique 3 on page 40. For selected photos, adhere photos with photo corners onto the center of the smallest piece of natural paper or card stock.

11. For remaining photos, adhere the photo onto the center of the smallest piece of natural paper or card stock. Repeat the process for the remaining pieces of natural paper or card stock for the desired number of paper layers.

12. Measure, mark, and cut ivory card stock to 2⅜" x 2" for a paper label. Trim off corners.

13. Adhere the ivory card stock onto the lavender card stock. Cut the lavender card stock ⅜" larger than the ivory card stock all around. Punch each corner of the lavender card stock.

14. Using the marker, add journaling to the paper label.

15. Measure, mark, and cut four 1¾" squares, one 2" circle, one 2⅝" oval, and one 2½" x 5" rectangle from ivory card stock.

16. Adhere each piece of ivory card stock onto a coordinating piece of card stock. Cut coordinating pieces of card stock ⅛" larger than each piece of ivory card stock all around.

17. Position pressed flowers on the ivory card stock as desired. Apply adhesive to the back of each flower. Adhere them onto the card stock. Following manufacturer's instructions, apply self-adhesive laminate over the card stock to enclose the pressed flowers.

18. Apply adhesive to the back of the decorative border. Adhere it onto the ground paper ⅞" from the left or bottom edge.

19. Refer to Technique 1 on page 36. Arrange and adhere photos, paper label, and pressed flower cards onto the ground sheet as desired.

Troubleshooting:

Save all the photos you may have otherwise discarded so you can practice the tinting technique on them. This is not only for selecting color placement but also for experimenting with the moisture needed on the photo to avoid streaking. It is better to practice on a few disposable photos than on a photo that may be difficult to replace.

Design Tip:
Sometimes less color is better. Some photos may need only one or two colors to be the most dramatic.

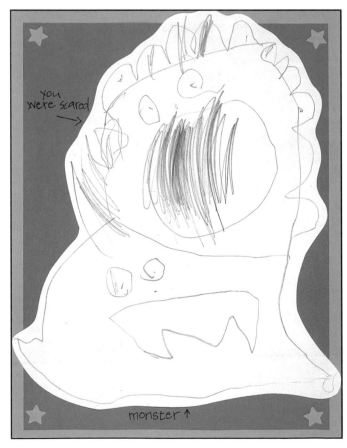

Chapter 3: *Projects Beyond the Basics*

What You Need to Get Started:

3 photos per page
Adhesive
Card stock: lime green; hot pink; teal; white for ground paper; bright yellow
Decorative-edged scissors: cloud; scallop; zigzag
Die-cuts: assorted
Lettering book
Markers: 1.2 mm black liner; 1.2 mm green liner
Paper label
Pencil
Scissors
Stickers
Templates: circle; rectangle; square

How do I create a "teen" page?

These types of pages are great because "anything goes." The more the better. This technique fits the personality of the theme and is exciting to look at.

Life as a Teen

Note: Refer to photo on page 84 for facing page layout.

Here's How:

1. Using the transparent ruler, pencil, and zigzag decorative-edged scissors, measure, mark, and cut ¾" from the top and one side of the ground paper.

2. Apply adhesive to the back of ground paper. Adhere it onto background paper, lining up the two uncut edges and leaving a colored border on the left and top edges. If you have a facing page, repeat with another piece of ground paper and background paper, leaving a colored border on the right and top edges.

3. Refer to Technique 6 on page 46. Crop selected photos as desired.

4. Refer to Technique 2 on page 38. Adhere photos onto card stock. Cut the card stock ¼" to ⅛" larger than each photo all around.

5. Refer to Technique 14 on page 60. Pencil and ink in the lettering on the paper label.

6. Refer to Technique 1 on page 36. Arrange and adhere photos, paper label, and die-cuts onto the ground paper.

7. Refer to Technique 11 on page 55. Carefully place the stickers on the ground paper as desired.

How can I display dimensional items on a page?

Incorporate purchased memorabilia pockets into your page design to display items that have real or sentimental value. These durable pockets keep small items safe and sound.

Kids in Our Neighborhood

Note: Before creating the scrapbook page, gather some autumn leaves and place them between two layers of paper toweling. Stack heavy books on top of the toweling. Allow the leaves to dry for approximately two weeks. Take the leaves to a professional copy shop and have them color copied.

If leaves are out of season, they can be purchased already pressed. They are expensive so take good care of them and they can be used over and over.

Refer to photo on page 85 for facing page layout.

Here's How:
1. Using the transparent ruler, pencil, and paper cutter, measure, mark, and cut ½" off the top and one side of the ground paper.

2. Using the paper punch, punch holes ½" apart all around the edges of the ground paper.

3. Tape one end of the jute to avoid fraying. Beginning at the top right hole of the ground paper, weave the jute through the holes all around.

4. Apply adhesive to the back of the ground paper. Adhere it onto the center of the background paper.

5. Position the natural paper at an angle on the ground paper. Using the scissors, trim the corners of the natural paper flush with the inside edge of the punched holes.

6. Refer to Technique 6 on page 46. Crop selected photos as desired.

7. Refer to Technique 2 on page 38. Adhere photos onto card stock. Cut the card stock ¼" to ⅛" larger than each photo all around. If desired, adhere this piece of card stock onto a second piece of card stock. Cut the second piece of card stock ¼" to ⅛" larger than the first piece of card stock all around.

8. To create photo labels and layered paper for memorabilia pockets, cut two pieces of ivory card stock. Adhere each piece of ivory card stock onto a coordinating piece of card stock. Cut the coordinating piece of card stock ¼" larger than the ivory card stock all around.

9. Remove the paper backing from the adhesive on the back of the memorabilia pocket. Adhere the pocket onto

What You Need to Get Started:

5 photos per page
Adhesive
Card stock: navy blue; navy blue for background paper; brown; ivory; light kraft for ground paper; dark tan; light tan
Color copies of green leaves
Decorative-edged scissors: deckle; zigzag
Jute: 2-ply (1½ yards per page)
Markers: 0.5 mm black liner; 5.0 mm brown calligraphy
Memorabilia
Memorabilia pockets: self-adhesive
Natural paper
Paper cutter
Paper punch
Scissors
Tape
Templates: circle; oval; rectangle; square

the center of the ivory card stock on the selected layered piece.

10. Refer to Technique 14 on page 60. Using the markers, add lettering and journaling to the paper labels.

11. Using scissors, cut out the color copied leaves, making edges wavy for a realistic look.

12. Refer to Technique 1 on page 36. Arrange and adhere the photos, memorabilia pockets, photo labels, and leaves onto the ground paper.

13. Fill the pockets with memorabilia.

How can I display my child's artwork on a scrapbook page?

Photos are not the only things that are displayed in a scrapbook. It is a great place to put artwork. It tells such a wonderful story about a child, and they are so proud to see it displayed in book form.

A Monster Under Your Blanket

Here's How:
1. Using the transparent ruler, pencil, and paper cutter, measure, mark, and cut ¾" off the top and one side of the ground paper.

2. Refer to Technique 7 on page 48. Punch a star in each corner of the ground paper.

3. Apply adhesive to the back of the ground paper and adhere it to the center of the background paper.

4. Refer to Technique 6 on page 46. Crop selected photos as desired.

5. Refer to Technique 2 on page 38. Adhere photos onto card stock. Cut the card stock ¼" to ⅛" larger than each photo all around.

6. Using the marker, add journaling to the paper label.

7. Refer to Technique 1 on page 36. Arrange and adhere the child's artwork, paper label, and photos onto the ground paper.

8. Using the marker, add any additional children's drawings and journaling to the ground paper.

Design Tip:
Instead of using stickers to decorate the pages, have your child draw some borders or small items to decorate the pages. It will make it much more personable.

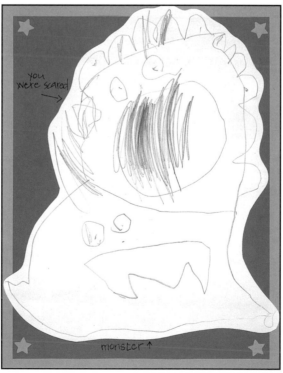

What You Need to Get Started:

2 photos per page
Adhesive
Card stock: green; green for ground paper; orange for background paper; red for ground paper; yellow; yellow for background paper
Child's artwork
Craft punch: star
Decorative-edged scissors: scallop; zigzag
Paper cutter
Paper label
Pencil
Marker: 0.5 mm black liner
Scissors
Templates: circle; rectangle

"Mom this is when a monster was under your blanket"

Chantry age 4

March 24, 1998

ghost monster

ghost team monster.

How should I use bright colors?

Summer time usually means bright and fun colors. Keep the ground paper simple and the photos will pop off the page.

Tessa & Rylee

Here's How:
1. Using the cloud decorative-edged scissors, trim the ground paper ¼" all around.

2. Apply adhesive to the back of the ground paper. Adhere it onto the center of the background paper.

3. Refer to Technique 6 on page 46. Crop selected photos as desired.

4. Refer to Technique 2 on page 38. Adhere photos onto card stock. Cut the card stock ¼" to ⅛" larger than each photo all around.

5. Refer to Technique 1 on page 36. Arrange and adhere the

photos and die-cuts onto the ground paper.

6. Using the markers, add journaling to cloud die-cut.

3 photos per page
Adhesive
Card stock: neon green; neon pink; teal for ground paper; white for background paper; bright yellow
Decorative-edged scissors: cloud; scallop; zigzag
Die-cuts: cloud; flower; palm tree; star; sun; swirl
Markers: 0.5 mm black liner; 1.2 mm black liner
Pencil
Templates: oval; rectangle
Scissors

What You Need to Get Started:

4 photos per
  page
Adhesive
Card stock: olive
  green speckled;
  plum; tan
  speckled
Color copies of
  leaves
Colored pencils
Marker: 0.5 mm
  black liner
Pencil
Scissors
Scrapbook kit
Tape

How do I use a full kit to design several pages?

This is a simple way of assembling many pages at once without having to buy many components. Depending on the company that compiled it, a kit contains a variety of materials from the background paper and framed corners to separate frames and labels, to decorative pieces.

Fall Colors

Note: Refer also to photos on pages 84 and 85 for coordinating page layouts.

Here's How:
1. Divide the kit into separate pages. Carefully punch out the die-cut borders and images.

2. Coordinate the premade photo mattes with the photos. Using scissors, trim selected photos as necessary.

3. Refer to Technique 4 on page 42. Place premade photo mattes face down on the work surface. Center each photo face down on the matte. Place tape on the sides of each photo matte and adhere each photo.

4. Using the colored pencils, lightly color the embossed areas to tint the images.

5. Refer to Project 2 on page 87. Using scissors, cut out the color copied leaves.

6. Refer to Technique 1 on page 36.

Arrange and adhere the matted photos and leaves onto ground paper.

7. Using the marker, add journaling to the pages.

Design Tips:
I loved using this embossed kit. It came with eight pages—two completely ready and four that I could create myself, using the frames and corners that were provided.

I chose the fall packet because I have many pictures from past years' Christmas card photos. I have a pile of photographer's proofs that fit many of the smaller frames. Proofs are a great way to fill several pages because not everyone looks good in every photo. Cropping out someone who may have had their eyes closed or who was looking in another direction places the focus on the person who looks great. This makes the most of your photos.

You do not have to stay with the exact kit unless it fits everything you like. Do not be afraid to replace the ground sheet with a piece of colored card stock.

When using colored pencils to tint the embossed images, do not use a sharp point. Sharp points create lines that are not very attractive. Dull the pencil point by first coloring several strokes on a piece of scratch paper, creating a flat edge. A dull point makes a nice even color on the embossed image. You are high-lighting the embossed image and therefore should color only the top surface of the image and avoid coloring down into the engraved areas or around the sides. Do not press hard or you may dent the embossed image. Several light applications will achieve a darker color.

Watercolors or water-based, blendable pens will also work for tinting the embossed images.

Some kits only come in 8½" x 11". If you need some-thing to fit a 12" x 12" album format, you can off-set the 8½" x 11" framed sheet to one side of the 12" x 12" ground sheet.

Adhere a piece of card stock to the back of any embossed frame complete with photos that is the size of a page. The cardstock will protect the back side of the photos.

6
project

What You Need to Get Started:

5 photos per page
Adhesive
Card stock: blue; green; kraft for ground paper; red; white; yellow
Craft knife and cutting mat
Decorative-edged scissors: scallop; stamp; zigzag
Markers: 0.5 mm black liner; 1.2 mm black liner
Scissors
Stationery: patterned 8½" x 11"
Templates: circle; oval; rectangle
Transparent ruler

How can I use stationery cut-outs to decorate a page?

Stationery is so versatile. Cut out individual images from one sheet of stationery to decorate one scrapbook page. You can use a full sheet of stationery on facing scrapbook page to complement the first with journaling or additional photos.

Boys & Bugs

Here's How:

1. Using the craft knife or scissors, carefully cut out the images from the patterned stationery.

2. Refer to Technique 6 on page 46. Crop selected photos as desired.

3. Refer to Technique 2 on page 38. Adhere photos to card stock. Cut the card stock ¼" to ⅛" larger than each photo all around.

4. Arrange the cut-out images on the page to create a border. Arrange the photos on the page as desired. Fill in any large gaps with cut-out images.

5. Adhere the cut-out images and photos onto the ground paper one at a time.

6. Using the markers, add journaling to the ground paper.

How do I create theme pages?

Because there are so many products available, a theme page is easy to assemble. Add a few momentos and some stickers and the page quickly comes together.

Mickey & Friends

Here's How:

1. Using the transparent ruler, pencil, and paper cutter, measure, mark, and cut 1" off the top and 2" off one side of the ground paper.

2. Apply adhesive to the back of the ground paper. Adhere it onto the background paper, ½" from the left side and centered top to bottom.

3. Refer to Technique 6 on page 46. Crop the selected photos as desired.

4. Refer to Technique 2 on page 38. Adhere the photos onto the blue, green, and red card stock. Cut the card stock ¼" larger than each photo all around.

5. Refer to Technique 1 on page 36. Arrange and adhere the memorabilia, photos, and punch-outs onto the ground paper

6. Using the markers, add journaling to the ground paper.

7. Refer to Technique 11 on page 55. Carefully place the stickers on the ground paper as desired.

What You Need to Get Started:

3 photos per page
Adhesive
Card stock: blue; green; red; yellow plaid for ground paper
Decorative paper: theme print for background paper
Marker: 0.5 mm black liner
Memorabilia
Paper cutter
Punch-outs: theme motifs
Scissors
Stickers: numbers
Templates: circle; oval; rectangle
Transparent ruler

What You Need to Get Started:

2 photos per page
Adhesive
Card stock:
 blue; light
 blue; green;
 light green;
 ivory; ivory for
 ground paper;
 light kraft;
 light kraft for
 background
 paper; pink;
 rose; white;
 light yellow
Decorative-
 edged scissors:
 deckle
Marker: 0.5 mm
 brown liner
Paper cutter
Pencil
Scissors
Stationery with
 multiple motifs

How can I get the most out of my stationery?

Assemble two or more layouts from one page of stationery by cutting out each image, creating any size of surface area. You will stretch your supplies and your money.

Peter Ty

Here's How:

1. Using the transparent ruler, pencil, and paper cutter, measure, mark, and cut 1½" off the top and one side of the ground paper.

2. Apply adhesive to the back of the ground paper. Adhere it onto the center of the background paper.

3. Using scissors, cut out motifs from the stationery, leaving a ⅛" silhouette all around each image.

4. Apply adhesive to the back of each silhouetted image. Adhere them onto light shades of coordinating card stock and cut each piece of card stock ⅛" larger than the image on four sides.

5. Apply adhesive to the back of each piece of card stock. Adhere them onto darker shades of coordinating card stock, allowing enough space around each for creating a paper "frame."

Using scissors, cut each piece of card stock ⅛" larger than the first all around.

6. Refer to Technique 2 on page 38. Adhere each photo onto ivory card stock. Cut card stock ⅛" larger than the combined photos all around.

7. Apply adhesive to the back of each photo. Adhere them side by side, ¼" apart, onto light blue card stock, allowing enough space all around for creating a paper "frame." Using scissors, cut card stock ¼" larger than the photos all around.

8. Measure, mark, and cut a 5" x 1⅛" piece of ivory card stock to create a paper label. Adhere the ivory card stock onto brown card stock. Cut the brown card stock ⅛" larger than the ivory card stock all around.

9. Using the brown marker, add journaling to the ivory card stock.

10. Apply adhesive to the back of two remaining silhouetted images. Adhere them onto the paper label.

11. Arrange and adhere the images, photos, and the paper label onto the ground paper.

What You Need to Get Started:

3 photos per page
Adhesive
Card stock: ivory
Craft knife and cutting mat
Decorative paper: print with frames
Marker: 0.5 mm black liner
Scissors
Tape

How do I use paper with printed frames?

The page design is already created for you. Simply insert your favorite photos. This process makes completing several pages in one sitting quick and worry-free.

Tori Anne

Here's How:

1. Using the craft knife and cutting mat, cut out openings within printed frames on the decorative paper.

2. Refer to Technique 4 on page 42. Treat this piece of paper as a premade photo matte. Place paper face down on the work surface. Center each photo face down on the openings. Tape the sides of each photo to the back of the paper.

3. Apply adhesive to the back of the paper complete

with photos. Adhere it to a piece of card stock that is the same size as the decorative paper. The cardstock will protect the back side of the photos.

4. Using the marker, add journaling to the page.

How do I use different patterned papers together?

Layering different patterned papers is a great way to make one photo on a page stand out. Do not be afraid to use several papers on one page.

August 1994

Here's How:

1. Using the pencil, transparent ruler, and paper cutter, measure, mark, and cut 2" off the top and one side of the ground paper.

2. Apply adhesive to the back of the ground paper. Adhere it onto the center of the background paper.

3. Refer to Technique 6 on page 46. Crop the photo as desired.

4. Refer to Technique 2 on page 38. Adhere the photo onto the light blue speckled card stock. Cut the light blue card stock ¼" larger than the photo all around.

5. Adhere the light blue speckled card stock onto the dark blue card stock. Cut the dark blue card stock ¼" larger than the light blue speckled card stock all around.

6. Adhere the dark blue card stock onto the ground paper, ⅜" from the top and centered from side to side.

7. To make a paper label, cut a 3½" x 1" piece of tan striped paper. Adhere the tan striped paper onto dark blue card stock. Cut the dark blue card stock ⅛" larger than the tan striped paper all around.

8. Adhere the dark blue card stock onto light blue speckled card stock. Cut the light blue speckled card stock ⅛" larger than the dark blue card stock all around.

9. Using the marker, add journaling to the paper label.

10. Adhere the light blue speckled card stock onto the ground paper, ¼" from the photo and centered from side to side.

2–4 photos per page
Adhesive
Card stock:
  lavender;
  peach; pink;
  yellow
Keepsake kit:
  text; borders
  and back-
  grounds
Markers: 0.5 mm
  black liner;
  0.5 mm
  lavender liner;
  1.2 mm
  lavender liner
Memorabilia
Pencil
Scissors
Transparent ruler

Are there premade pages I can use?

Premade keepsake kits are a great way to record events that share a common theme and are accompanied by a lot of photos, such as a wedding or birth of a baby.

Keepsake Kits

Note: The kits are made up of two parts. The first includes a variety of borders with text for recording information, such as the mother's thoughts during pregnancy, the birth statistics, the family tree, the birth certificate, the baby's prints, and a year of journaling month to month events. The second kit includes frames, borders, backgrounds, and stickers.

Kits are available in both the 12" x 12" and 8½" x 11" formats.

Here's How:

1. Refer to Technique 6 on page 46. Crop selected photos as desired.

2. Refer to Technique 2 on page 38. Adhere photos onto card stock. Cut the card stock ¼" to ⅛" larger than each photo all around.

3. Refer to Technique 1 on page 36. Arrange and adhere photos and memorabilia onto the ground paper.

4. Refer to Technique 11 on page 55. Carefully place the stickers on the ground paper as desired.

5. Using markers, add journaling to the page.

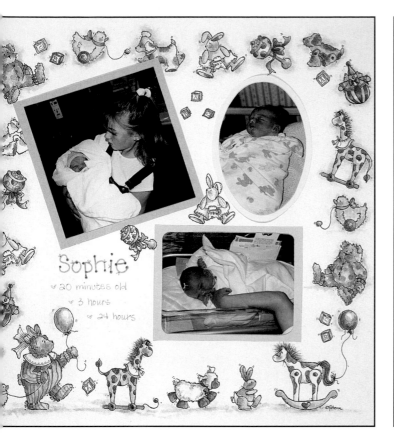

Sophie
- 20 minutes old
- 3 hours
- 24 hours

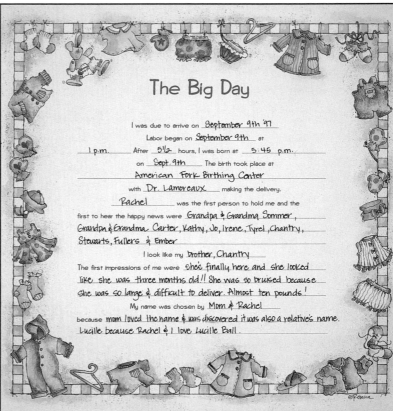

The Big Day

I was due to arrive on *September 9th '97*

Labor began on *September 9th* at

1 p.m. After *5½* hours, I was born at *5:45 p.m.*

on *Sept. 9th* The birth took place at

American Fork Birthing Center

with *Dr. Lamoreaux* making the delivery.

Rachel was the first person to hold me and the

first to hear the happy news were *Grandpa & Grandma Sommer,*

Grandpa & Grandma Carter, Kathy, Jo, Irene, Tyrel, Chantry,

Stewarts, Fullers & Ember

I look like my *brother, Chantry*

The first impressions of me were *she's finally here and she looked*

like she was three months old!! She was so bruised because

she was so large & difficult to deliver. Almost ten pounds!

My name was chosen by *Mom & Rachel*

because *mom loved the name & was discovered it was also a relative's name.*

Lucille because Rachel & I love Lucille Ball.

*A Little Girl
to Fill Your Home
with Love*

Memorable Moments

My first		I first	
bath	2 wks	rolled tummy to back	6 mo.
tooth	3/25/98	slept through the night	13 mo.
smile	10/6/97	held a bottle	1 yr.
coos	11/2/97	held a toy	12/1/97
face recognition	1 mo.	sat alone	1/30/98
laugh	12/4/97	crawled	4/26/98
baby food	1 yr.	stood with assistance	6 mo.
table food	11 mo.	stood alone	11 mo.
word		took my first step	1 yr.
word was		drank from a cup	10 mo.
kisses	6/20/98	waved good-bye	1 yr.
		clapped my hands	4/1/98
		discovered my feet	1/31/98
		saw my hand	11/1/97

What You Need to Get Started:

4 photos per page
12-month calendar: blank
Adhesive
Card stock: blue; green; red; teal; yellow
Craft punch: star
Decorative-edged scissors: cloud; scallop; zigzag
Markers: 0.5 mm black liner
Pencil
Scissors
Stickers: assorted
Templates: oval; rectangle

How do I create calendar pages?

Making a scrapbook from a calendar is a wonderful way to keep a record of the special events that happen every day. Later, because you took the time to write it down on your calendar, you will be able to remember when and what happened and make certain that it is also recorded in your journal or scrapbook. Combined with favorite photos, it becomes a mini scrapbook to look at from year to year.

School Memories

Here's How to Create September:

1. Refer to Technique 6 on page 46. Crop selected photos as desired.

2. Refer to Technique 2 on page 38. Adhere photos onto coordinating card stock. Using scissors, cut the card stock ¼" larger than the photo on the sides and bottom and ⅞" larger on the top. Cut the card stock ⅜" larger than the oval photo on four sides, creating a rectangle. Using the decorative-edged scissors, cut the card stock ¼" larger than two remaining rectangle photos all around.

3. Refer to Technique 7 on page 48. Punch a star in each corner of the oval photo's card stock frame. Punch stars along the wide edge of the rectangle photo's card stock frame.

4. Refer to Technique 1 on page 36. Arrange and adhere photos onto the blank page.

5. Refer to Technique 11 on page 55. Carefully place the stickers onto the photo page as desired. Carefully place stickers onto the calendar page that coordinate with the recorded events.

6. Using the marker, add journaling to the photo page.

Here's How to Create May:

1. Refer to Technique 6 on page 46. Crop selected photos as desired.

2. Refer to Technique 2 on page 38. Adhere photos onto coordinating card stock. Cut the card stock ¼" larger than the photos all around.

3. Refer to Technique 1 on page 36. Arrange and adhere photos onto the blank page.

4. Refer to Technique 11 on page 55. Carefully place the stickers onto the photo page as desired. Carefully place stickers onto the calendar page that coordinate with the recorded events.

5. Using the marker, add journaling to the photo page.

Design Tip:

Use the calendar to record the small day-to-day events, such as your child's first word, the day you collected flowers, dance recitals, etc.

Interactive Pop-up Pictures

picture pop-up

materials

Album: expandable spine

Cardboard: lightweight

Cording: coordinating

Double-sided fusible web

Fabric: coordinating cotton print; coordinating cotton
solid; white cotton; assorted coordinating scraps (8)

Photo transfer paper

Quilt batting: lightweight

general supplies & tools

Glue gun and glue sticks
Iron/ironing board
Marker: disappearing fabric
Measuring tape
Scissors: fabric; pinking shears

instructions

1. Measure album cover. Add 2" to height and width measurements and cut two pieces from cotton print fabric for front and back album covers.

2. Center and lay front cover on right side of one fabric piece and mark placement using disappearing fabric marker.

3. Enlarge **Seasons Patterns** at right and on page 106 to desired size for album cover. Refer to General Instructions for **Fusible Appliqué** on page 21. Trace outer patterns onto paper side of fusible web. Iron fusible web to back side of white fabric following manufacturer's instructions.

4. Copy photographs onto photo transfer paper at a copy center, following manufacturer's instructions. Reduce or enlarge as necessary to fit traced patterns.

5. Position photo transfers over traced patterns and iron onto white fabric. Cut out patterns, trimming them ⅛". Remove paper backing and iron onto front cover fabric piece.

6. Cut quilt batting to fit front and back covers. Hot-glue batting to top side of front and back covers.

7. Lay front and back fabric pieces face down. Center and lay covers on top of fabric, batting side down. Mark spine holes. Wrap and hot-glue fabric edges to inside of covers.

8. Cut cardboard into two pieces, ⅛" smaller than inside covers. Cut cotton fabric into two pieces, 1" larger than cardboard pieces. Lay cardboard onto fabric. Wrap and hot-glue fabric edges to inside of cardboard. Hot-glue fabric-covered cardboard to inside front and back

covers to hide all raw edges. Cut out spine holes. Hot-glue cording around edges of front and back covers.

9. Trace seasonal motifs onto paper side of fusible web. Cut around patterns. Iron motifs to back sides of fabric scraps and cut out.

10. Remove paper backing and iron patterns as shown in photograph onto solid cotton fabric. Cut out motifs using pinking shears and leaving a ⅛"-wide border. Lay appliquéd motifs over photo transfers and hot-glue top edge of motifs to cover. Lift motifs to reveal photographs underneath.

11. Reassemble album.

Seasons Patterns

Seasons Patterns (cont.)

Picture Pop-up

Verse:

God made a world out of his dreams,

Of magic mountains, oceans, and streams.

Prairies and plains and wooded land,

Then paused and said, "I need someone to
   stand . . .

On top of the mountains, to conquer the seas

Explore the plains and climb the trees.

Someone to start out small and grow

Sturdy, strong, like a tree" and so . . .

He created boys, full of spirit and fun. . . .

— Author Unknown

baby bundle

materials
Cardstock: coordinating colors (3)
Decorative paper: baby theme
Die-cut shape: diaper pin
Stickers: ¾" alphabet

general supplies & tools
Adhesive
Craft knife
Marker: fine point black
Ruler: metal-edge
Scissors: craft; decorative edge

instructions

1. Cut decorative paper to fit album page using craft scissors. Adhere paper to album page.

2. Enlarge **Envelope & Heart Patterns** at right and trace onto different colors of cardstock. Cut out shapes. Slit mark on envelope with a craft knife

3. Score and fold envelope as shown on pattern.

4. Adhere heart to top flap of envelope as shown on photograph on opposite page.

5. Cut out a ⅛" section from one side of die-cut pin. Adhere pin to heart. Draw slits on heart with black marker so pin appears pinned to heart.

6. Cut photograph to fit inside of envelope using decorative edge scissors. Use alphabet stickers for child's name and birth date and attach to inside envelope flaps.

7. Use alphabet stickers for desired message and attach to second cardstock paper. Cut around message using decorative edge scissors. Adhere message to third cardstock paper. Cut paper. Adhere message and envelope to album page.

Envelope & Heart Patterns

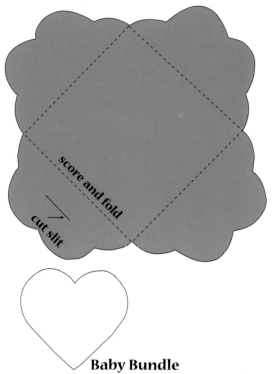

score and fold

cut slit

Baby Bundle

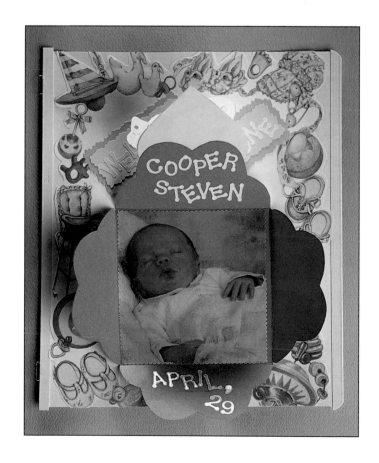

2. Cut ⅛ off all sides of second sheet of cardstock using second pair of decorative edge scissors. Fold paper in half to form card.

3. Open card. Measure and mark 2" in from each side of card at center fold. Make two vertical slits at marks, extending 1" above and below center fold, using a craft knife and ruler. Score between ends of slits using a craft knife and ruler as shown in **Diagram 1** on opposite page. Slowly fold card so slit section pops up.

4. Cut ⅛ from sides and 1¼ from top and bottom edges of a third sheet of cardstock using second pair of decorative edge scissors. Fold paper in half and adhere over top of folded card, making certain not to adhere center section where pop-up is located.

5. Enlarge **Cake, Candle, & Balloon Patterns** on opposite page. Trace onto desired colors of cardstock. Use one balloon to trace onto photograph. Cut out shapes and photograph using craft scissors.

6. Adhere cake layers together. Adhere frosting over top of each layer. Adhere flames to candles and adhere candles to cake. Adhere decorated cake to front of pop up section.

7. Stamp a balloon using birthday theme stamp and pigment ink pad. Apply embossing powder over stamped design following manufacturer's instructions. Heat and cool.

8. Attach balloons above cake to inside of card using 3-D sponges and adhere.

9. Use stickers to embellish inside and outside of card and album page as desired.

Circles can be used to make balloons. Just draw in the string and add a stem. Highlight the curve of the balloon with a scrap of white paper.

happy birthday

materials
Cardstock: coordinating (6)
Embossing powder: clear
Pigment ink pad: coordinating bright variegated
Sponges, 3-D self stick: ⅛ diameter x ¼" thick (3)
Stamp: birthday theme
Stickers: birthday theme

general supplies & tools
Adhesive
Craft knife
Heat tool
Ruler: metal edge
Scissors: craft; decorative edge (2)

instructions
1. Cut one sheet of cardstock to fit album page using decorative edge scissors. Adhere paper to album page.

Cake, Candle, & Balloon Patterns

Diagram 1

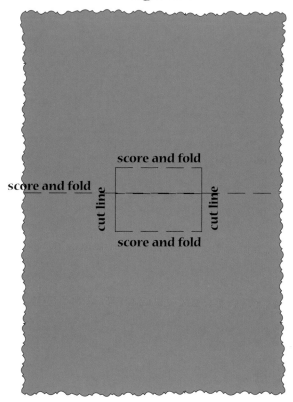

Happy Birthday

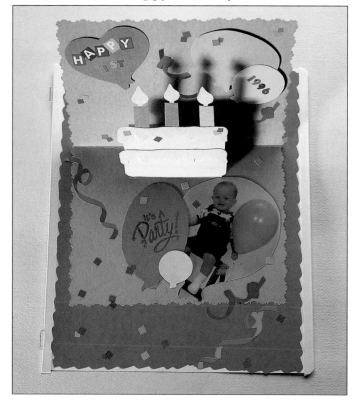

Make a pop-up gumball machine. Cut out circles of all sizes and colors to look like gumballs and some to look like coins. Cut photographs into circles, too. Include the childhood verse, "Bubblegum, bubblegum, in a dish. How many pieces do you wish?"

daddy's coat

materials
Cardstock: coordinating (4)
Decorative paper: coordinating (2)
Medium-weight paper: coordinating

general supplies & tools
Adhesive
Craft knife
Paper punch: round
Pen: point .03 black
Ruler: metal edge
Scissors: craft; decorative edge

instructions
1. Cut one sheet of decorative paper to fit album page using craft scissors. Adhere paper to album page.

2. Enlarge **Daddy's Coat Patterns** below and trace onto cardstock. Trace tie onto second sheet of decorative paper. Cut out shapes.

Daddy's Coat Patterns

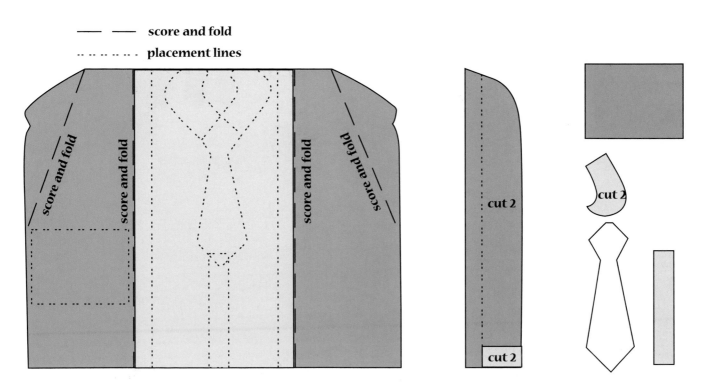

3. Refer to General Instructions for **Scoring** on page 18. Score and fold coat as shown on pattern.

4. Refer to photograph on opposite page. Adhere cuffs to sleeves. Adhere sleeves to back of coat. Adhere pocket to left inside flap of coat. Adhere shirt to inside of coat. Adhere collar, placket, and tie to shirt. Adhere assembled coat to album page.

5. Draw buttons on placket, and draw stitching lines around cuffs, lapels, pocket, collar, and placket using black pen. Write desired message on right inside flap of coat.

6. Punch six "buttons" from cardstock using round paper hole punch. Adhere buttons to front right flap of coat.

7. Cut a 7" x 2½" strip from medium-weight paper. Fold strip into three 2¼" squares. Fold remaining ¼" under. Cut photos slightly smaller than each folded square using decorative edge scissors. Adhere photos to folded squares. Adhere ¼" fold to inside of pocket.

Daddy's Coat

sunflower pocket

materials
Cardstock: coordinating
Stickers: ¾" alphabet; decorative

general supplies & tools
Adhesive
Craft knife
Markers: extra fine point; medium point
Ruler: metal edge
Scissors: decorative edge

instructions
1. Refer to General Instructions for **Scoring** on page 18. Score and fold sides and bottom of cardstock paper, ¾" from edges, as shown on **Diagram 1** on page 112, using a craft knife and ruler. Cut 4½" off top of paper using decorative edge scissors.

2. Adhere folded edges of paper to album page, creating a pocket. Use alphabet and decorative stickers to embellish pocket as desired. Draw

Diagram 1

halloween

materials
Cardstock: coordinating (3)
Stickers: Halloween theme

general supplies & tools
Adhesive
Pen: point .03 black
Scissors: craft

instructions
1. Cut a sheet of cardstock to fit album page. Adhere paper to album page.

2. Enlarge **Tombstone Pattern** on opposite page and trace onto cardstock, using different colors for fronts and backs of tombstones. Trace tombstones onto photographs. Cut out all.

3. Cut three 1" x ⅛" strips from cardstock. Fold strips in half and adhere to back of tombstones and album page. Align photographs with tombstones and adhere to album page.

4. Use pen to write epitaphs on tombstones and stickers to embellish album page as desired.

Tombstone Pattern

 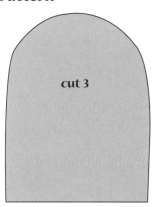

cut 3   cut 3

Halloween

school lunch

materials
Cardstock: "food" colors (9); trunk colors (3)
Decorative paper: coordinating (2)
Stickers: ¾" alphabet; decorative; stripes

general supplies & tools
Adhesive
Marker: fine point black
Scissors: craft; decorative edge

instructions
1. Cut one sheet of decorative paper to fit album page using craft scissors. Adhere paper to album page.

2. Enlarge **Food Patterns** and **Lunch Box Patterns** on page 114 and trace onto cardstock, using different colors for inside and outside of lunch box. Cut out.

3. Refer to photograph above. Adhere inside lunch box and inside lid shapes to inside of lunch box. Cut two

⅛" x 2" strips from cardstock. Fold strips in half and adhere to inside of box and lid for hinges. Adhere latch to lunch box.

4. Cut a 3" square from second sheet of decorative paper for napkin. Fold as shown in **Diagram 1** and adhere to inside of lunch box.

5. Adhere leaf and stem to apple. Write teacher's class and year on apple using black marker. Adhere chocolate chips to cookie. Adhere apple and cookie to inside of lunch box.

6. Cut class photo to fit inside lid of lunch box using decorative edge scissors.

7. Adhere bread to crusts. Cut two ⅛" x 2" strips from cardstock. Fold strips in half and adhere to inside of bread for hinges.

8. Cut two ¼" x 1" strips. Fold strips in half and adhere to cheese and lettuce, and to lettuce and meat for hinges.

9. Adhere individual photographs to cheese, lettuce and meat. Adhere meat to inside bottom slice of bread. Close sandwich and adhere to album page.

10. Use alphabet, decorative, and stripe stickers to embellish album page and lunch box as desired.

Food Patterns

cut 2

cut 3

cut 7

Lunchbox Patterns

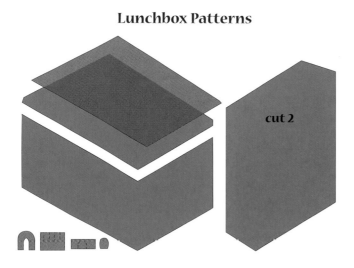

cut 2

Diagram 1

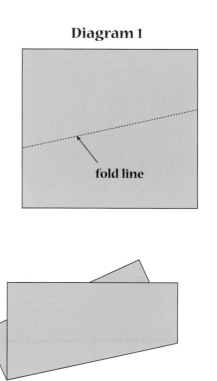

fold line

School Lunch

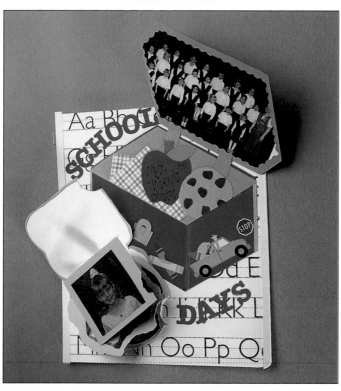

holiday stocking

materials
Cardstock: coordinating (6)
Decorative paper: coordinating (2)
Grosgrain ribbon: ⅛"-wide coordinating
Stickers: Christmas theme

general supplies & tools
Adhesive
Craft knife
Marker: fine point
Scissors: craft; decorative edge

instructions
1. Cut one sheet of decorative paper to fit album page using craft scissors. Adhere paper to album page.

2. Enlarge **Holiday Stocking Patterns** on page 116 and trace stocking, cuff, "Ho," tree, crayon, gingerbread boy, and train patterns onto cardstock, using different colors for trains. Cut out shapes, cutting one train slightly smaller than other. Slit designated mark on cuff using a craft knife.

3. Trace heel pattern onto second sheet of decorative paper and cut out. Adhere heel to stocking.

4. Adhere edges of stocking and cuff to album page. Do not adhere centers or top edge of stocking.

5. Cut three 2" squares from cardstock using decorative edge scissors. Adhere squares to album page. Adhere "Ho" to squares.

6. Trace gingerbread boy, crayon, and tree shapes onto photos. Cut out photos, slightly within cutting line, using craft scissors. Adhere photos to cardstock shapes.

7. Adhere train shapes together. Write "Christmas" and year on train using marker.

8. Cut ribbon into four equal lengths. Adhere one end of each ribbon to back of shapes. Place opposite ribbon end through slit on stocking cuff and adhere in place. Gently stuff stocking with shapes.

9. Attach stickers to form garland across bottom of stocking cuff.

Holiday Stocking Patterns

cut 3

cut 2

cut line

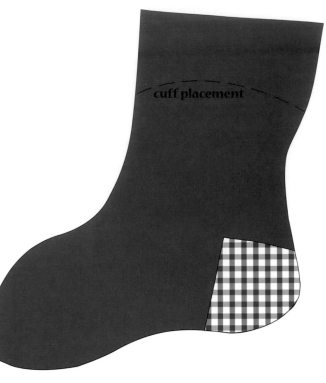

cuff placement

Holiday Stocking

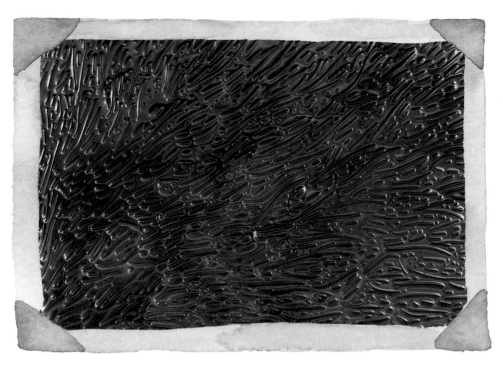

fold-out pets

Passion for Pets

materials
Cardboard: heavy
Copper tooling foil: 36 gauge
Decorative paper: coordinating
Handmade papers: coordinating

general supplies & tools
Adhesive
Embossing tool
Glue gun and glue sticks
Newspapers: small stack
Scissors: craft; old or tin snips

instructions
1. Cut two pieces of cardboard to desired size of album cover using craft scissors.

2. Cut copper foil ⅛" larger than cardboard using old craft scissors.

3. Refer to General Instructions for

Tradition See page 46

Lay copper on newspapers. Press desired pattern onto copper using embossing tool.

4. Color embossed copper pieces as desired. Hot-glue copper to cardboard, folding and wrapping excess copper to back of cardboard as shown in **Diagram 1**, to form front and back album covers. Snip corners, if needed.

5. Cut handmade and decorative papers slightly smaller than album cover using craft scissors. Overlap decorative papers ¼" and adhere together to create a continuous page, to desired length. Gently tear handmade papers into a variety of widths. Mix papers and adhere to back of decorative paper page.

6. Fold one end of handmade paper side of page under ¼" and adhere, decorative paper side down, to inside of front album cover. Gently fold page, accordion-style, to create album pages. Fold end of last page under ¼" and adhere, decorative paper-side down, to inside of back album cover. If necessary, adhere additional decorative and handmade papers together for even distribution of pages.

Diagram 1

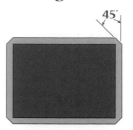
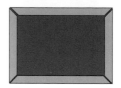

pet pages

materials
Colored pencils or pens
Handmade papers: coordinating
Lightweight paper: white
Magnetic sheet
Stickers

general supplies & tools
Adhesive
Craft knife
Scissors: craft

Note: *All text for photo pages was typed on a computer using whimsical fonts and printed on various hand-made papers. The papers were then gently torn from around the text.*

The subject of all pictures was cut out from photographs using craft scissors. Small areas were cut out from photographs using a craft knife.

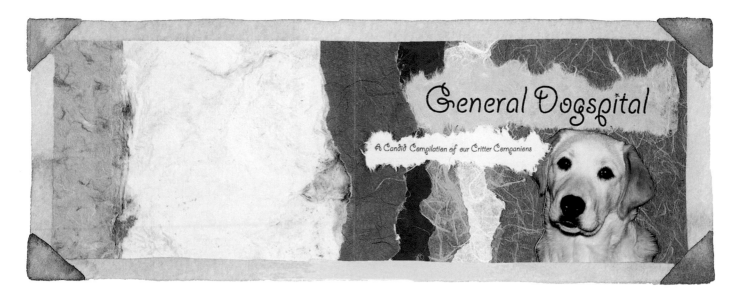

title page

instructions

1. Select a creative title and subtitle for page. Print titles on different handmade papers. Gently tear paper from around titles and adhere to page.

2. Cut out pet from photograph and adhere to page.

critter quiz

instructions

1. Create questions and fun facts that evoke memories of a pet. List multiple choice answers for each question and fact. Print questions and facts with multiple choice answers on handmade paper. Gently tear or cut paper from around words, leaving a ¼" margin all around.

2. Fold left margin at ¼" mark on each paper to create hinges. Adhere hinges to page.

3. Print letters of correct answers. Gently tear or cut paper from around letters. Adhere letters to album page, under corresponding questions and facts papers.

4. Use photographs and stickers to embellish album page as desired.

pet profile

instructions

1. Create a profile of fun and interesting facts and memories about a pet and its personality. List date of birth, identifying features, how the pet became a family member, etc. Print profile on handmade paper and gently tear paper from around profile. Adhere profile to album page.

2. Use close-up action photographs to embellish album page as desired.

More title ideas:
Dogs of Our Lives
The Guiding Dog
All My Critters
Pet Passion

tradition

instructions

1. Create a game from a family tradition such as "dress up." Print story of tradition on handmade paper. Gently tear paper from around story and adhere to page.

2. Adhere photograph to magnetic sheet and cut out.

3. Refer to small photograph on page 117. Draw items of clothing, such as a hat, vest, socks, or bandanna, to fit on pet photo using lightweight white paper and black pen. Color clothing with colored pencils or pens. Adhere clothing to magnetic sheet and cut out.

4. Cut an 8½ x 3¾" rectangle from a sheet of handmade paper. Fold as shown in **Diagram 1** to form an envelope. Adhere sides of envelope together. Adhere envelope to album page. Stuff envelope with clothing and pet magnets.

5. Use photographs depicting the tradition and stickers to embellish album page as desired.

Diagram 1

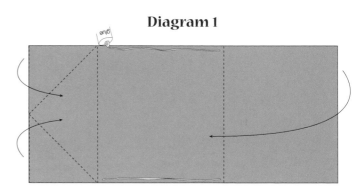

Add depth to a dark photograph by mounting it on a light-colored piece of paper, creating a silhouette effect.

shane game

instructions

1. Create a "concentration" game involving pets and critters. Cut an equal number of pairs of photographs or drawings of pets into square game pieces, or make two color copies of **Critters** below at a copy center and cut out.

2. Make appropriate number of symbols for top and bottom game pieces, or make color copies of **Symbols** provided below and on page 122. Adhere top and bottom symbols to magnetic sheet, making certain magnetic polarities match, and cut out.

3. Adhere back side of bottom game pieces in rows on album page. Adhere pet photographs/drawings to bottom side of top game pieces and place on top of bottom game pieces.

4. Print story and rules of game on handmade paper. Gently tear paper from around story and adhere to one side of album page.

5. Use photographs and stickers to embellish page.

Critters & Symbols

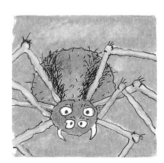

Symbols

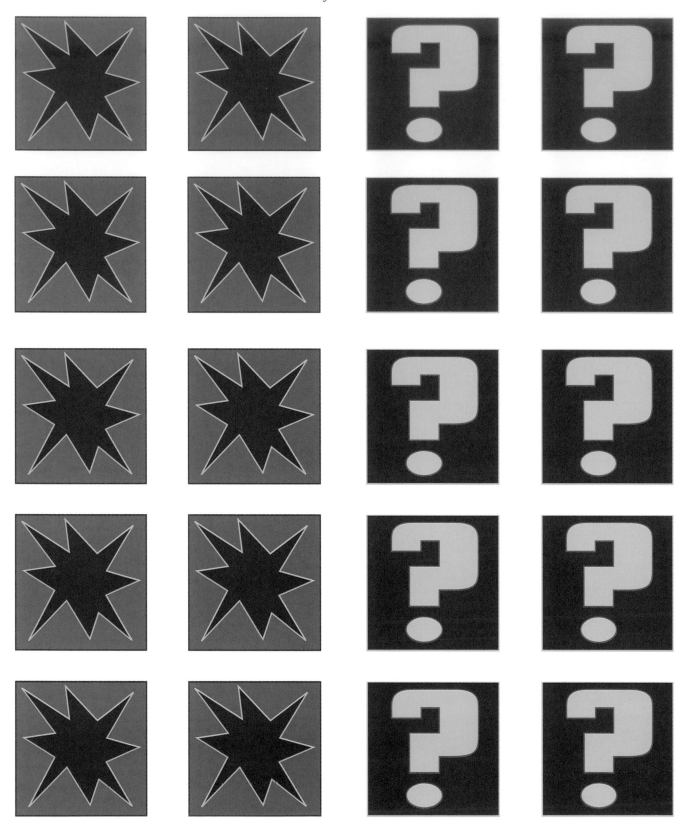

Baby in Black & White

baby book

materials
Design materials: fabric, lace,
ribbon, trims, etc.
Liquid gloss: polymer medium
white
Paper: watercolor

general supplies & tools
Adhesive
Cardboard
Craft knife
Paintbrush
Ruler: metal edge
Scissors: craft; fabric

instructions
1. Design cover using desired
ribbons, laces, trims, fabrics, and
such. Tack design materials
together and adhere to cardboard.

such. Tack design materials together and adhere to cardboard. Make a color copy of cover design at a copy center, reducing or enlarging to desired size. Trim color copy, if necessary, to fit top front cover using a craft knife and ruler.

2. Apply eight coats of gloss to color copy, allowing gloss to dry 30 minutes between coats. Allow final coat to dry 24 hours.

3. Soak coated paper in water until paper becomes soft enough to rub off. Remove all paper and rinse clean. Color remains with gloss forming a film. Let dry.

4. Cut watercolor paper same size as colored film.

5. Apply a coat of gloss to watercolor paper and adhere to bottom of colored film. Gently rub top of colored film to remove air bubbles and to seal edges, forming a cover.

6. Position cover on front of album and apply two coats of gloss, making certain edges are covered and sealed. Allow gloss to dry 24 hours.

7. Embellish as desired.

baby pages

Technique: Color small details on black-and-white photos or photo copies using pigment pens. Gently color details and immediately blot with paper towel to lighten color if desired.

general supplies & tools
Adhesive
Iron/ironing board
Pencil
Scissors: fabric

fabric photo mat

materials
Double-sided fusible web
Fabric: patchwork

instructions
1. Apply fusible web to back of fabric following manufacturer's instructions.

2. Cut fabric to fit album page. Cut out patches in fabric.

3. Lay fabric on album page and mark placement for photographs. Adhere photographs to album page.

4. Remove paper backing from fabric and iron onto album page, making certain iron does not touch photos.

ribbon flowers

materials
Ribbon: white organza; self-adhesive, coordinating colors and widths

instructions
1. Adhere photograph to album page.

2. Cut organza ribbon to fit over top of photograph.

3. Cut self-adhesive ribbons to form desired border and design around photograph and on album page. Adhere ribbons around photograph and to album page, making certain organza ribbon is secured over top of photo.

Take a photograph of the child each year, beginning at birth, with a stuffed animal to see how much the child has grown.

great-grandma

materials
Ribbon
Marker: fine point black

instructions
1. Adhere photo to album page.

2. Cut ribbon to form desired border around photo. Adhere ribbon to album page.

3. Label album page and draw decorative motifs using black marker.

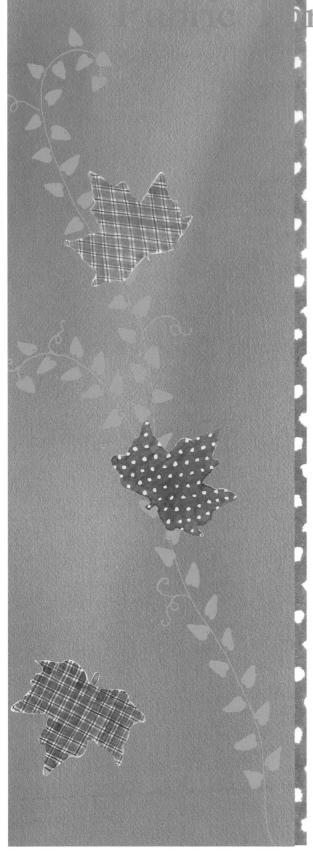

seasons

materials

Cardboard: lightweight

Cardstock

Dimensional fabric paint: coordinating (3)

Double-sided fusible web

Fabric: coordinating for cover; coordinating scraps (4)

Quilt batting: lightweight

general supplies & tools

Adhesive
Iron/ironing board
Pencil
Ruler
Scissors: craft; fabric

instructions

1. Lay album flat on work surface and measure. Cut a piece from quilt batting. Add 2" to height and width measurements and cut a piece from fabric for album cover.

2. Measure spine. Add 1½" to width and cut two strips from fabric. Adhere strips to inside spine, using an edge of a ruler to press fabric under metal ring plate.

3. Adhere quilt batting to album cover. Lay fabric wrong side up and center album over fabric. Wrap and adhere excess fabric to inside of binder, turning top and bottom edges under enough to fit up against edges of metal ring plate.

4. Cut cardboard into two pieces ¼" smaller than inside covers. Cut fabric into two pieces 1" larger than cardboard pieces. Lay fabric wrong side up and center cardboard on fabric. Wrap and adhere fabric edges to inside of cardboard. Adhere fabric-covered cardboard to inside front and back covers to hide all raw edges.

5. Refer to General Instructions for **Fusible**

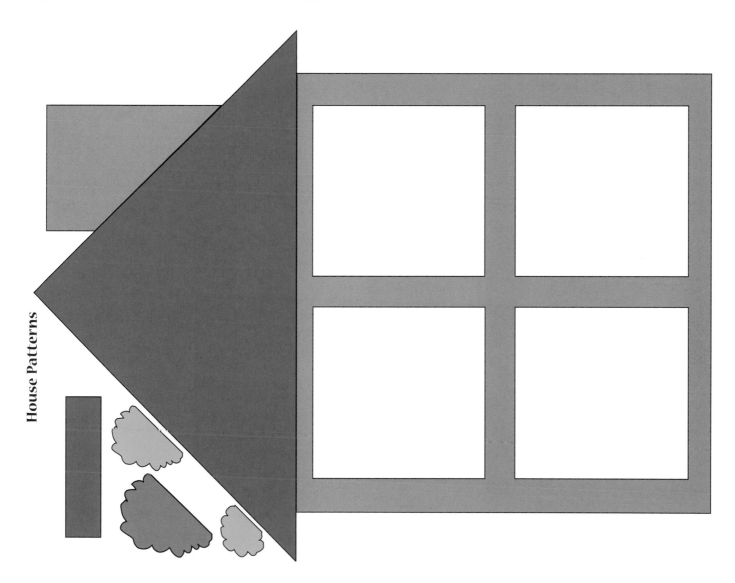

House Patterns

Appliqué on page 21. Reduce or enlarge **House Patterns** on page 127 and trace onto paper side of fusible web. Cut around motifs. Iron motifs to back sides of fabric scraps. Cut out motifs.

6. Remove paper backing from house motif and iron onto cardstock. Cut out house and windows using a craft knife and metal edge ruler.

7. Trim photographs to fit behind window openings and adhere in place. Adhere house to album cover. Cover house with a pressing cloth to avoid damaging photographs and fuse chimney to album cover. Fuse roof and shrubs to album cover.

8. With a decorative stitch, outline all edges of house pieces and shrubs and around edge of front cover using dimensional fabric paint. Allow paint to dry thoroughly.

valentine

materials
Cardstock: coordinating (3)
Decorative paper: coordinating (2)
Double-sided fusible web
Fabric: coordinating
Photo frames (2)

general supplies & tools
Adhesive
Craft knife
Iron/ironing board
Markers: fine tip black; metallic gold
Ruler: metal edge
Scissors: craft; decorative edge

instructions
1. Iron fusible web to back side of fabric following manufacturer's instructions. Remove paper backing and iron fabric to album page. Trim excess fabric from edges of album page using a craft knife and ruler.

2. Reduce or enlarge **Heart Patterns** below and on opposite page. Trace desired number of large and small hearts onto cardstock and decorative paper. Cut out hearts using decorative edge scissors. Trace medium hearts with lettering onto cardstock and trace over lettering using a black marker. Cut out medium hearts using craft scissors.

3. Center and trace frame opening onto photographs. Draw a ¼"-thick line around traced opening using a metallic gold marker.

4. Adhere photographs to photo frames. Adhere photo frames and hearts to album page.

Heart Patterns

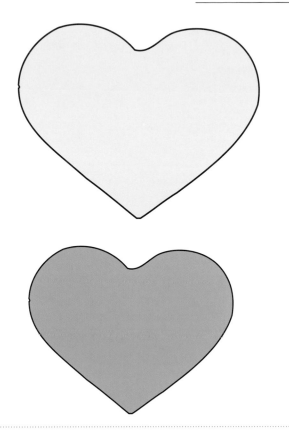

bunny hop

materials
Acrylic paint: coordinating
Cardstock: coordinating (2)
Double-sided fusible web
Fabric: coordinating
Felt: coordinating
Ribbon: ⅛"-wide coordinating (5)

general supplies & tools
Adhesive
Craft knife
Iron/ironing board
Ruler: metal edge
Scissors: fabric; decorative edge
Stylus

instructions
1. Iron fusible web to back side of fabric following manufacturer's instructions. Remove paper backing and iron fabric to album page. Trim excess fabric from edges of album page using a craft knife and ruler.

2. Refer to General Instructions for **Fusible Appliqué** on page 21. Reduce or enlarge **Bunny Pattern** on page 130. Trace five bunnies onto paper side of fusible web. Cut around bunnies. Iron bunnies to felt and cut out using fabric scissors.

3. Cut one cardstock ⅛" larger than photograph using decorative edge scissors. Cut second cardstock ¼" larger than photograph. Center and adhere cardstocks together. Adhere photograph to cardstock.

4. Make a decorative dot pattern around border of photograph using stylus tip and acrylic paint.

5. Remove paper backing from bunnies and iron onto album page. Tie ribbons into small bows and adhere to bunnies.

6. Adhere photographs to album page.

Bunny Pattern

This bunny could also be used on a page dedicated to the family's pet rabbit.

pumpkin patch

materials
Cardstock: coordinating (3)
Double-sided fusible web
Fabric: coordinating Halloween prints (3)

general supplies & tools
Adhesive
Iron/ironing board
Marker: fine point black
Pencil
Scissors: craft; pinking shears

instructions
1. Iron fusible web to back side of one fabric following manufacturer's instructions.

2. Cut fabric ¼" smaller than album page using pinking shears. Remove paper backing and iron fabric to album page.

3. Reduce or enlarge **Pumpkin Patterns** on page 132 and trace onto photos. Cut out photos using craft scissors.

4. Trace pumpkins onto two colors of cardstock. Cut out pumpkins ⅛" larger than cutting line.

5. Refer to General Instructions for **Fusible Appliqué** on page 21. Trace pumpkins and center pumpkin sections onto paper side of fusible web. Cut around pumpkins and sections. Iron pumpkins and center sections to back sides of remaining fabrics and cut out using fabric scissors. Remove paper backing and iron center pumpkin sections to pumpkins. Iron pumpkins to cardstock.

6. Adhere photographs to cardstock pumpkins.

7. Reduce or enlarge **Star & Moon Patterns** on opposite page and trace to cardstock and cut out using craft scissors.

8. Draw a decorative line around photographs, fabric pumpkins, stars, and moon using a black marker.

9. Adhere photographs, fabric pumpkins, stars, and moon to album page.

Star & Moon Patterns

pretty package

materials
Cardstock: coordinating (2)
Double-sided fusible web
Fabric: coordinating Christmas prints (2)

general supplies & tools
Adhesive
Craft knife
Iron/ironing board
Marker: fine point black
Paper punch
Ruler: metal edge
Scissors: craft; fabric; decorative edge

instructions
1. Iron fusible web to back side of one fabric following manufacturer's instructions. Remove paper backing and iron fabric to album page. Trim excess fabric from edges of album page using a craft knife and ruler.

2. Refer to General Instructions for **Fusible Appliqué** on page 21. Reduce or enlarge **Inside & Outside Package Patterns** on page 132. Trace outside package onto one cardstock and trace inside package onto paper side of fusible web. Cut out outside package using craft scissors. Cut around inside package. Iron inside package to back side of second fabric and cut out using fabric scissors. Remove paper backing and center and iron to outside package.

3. Cut four squares from second cardstock. Cut photographs ¼" smaller than squares and adhere to squares. Adhere photo squares to package. Adhere package to album page.

4. Trace gift tag onto cardstock and cut out using decorative edge scissors. Outline gift tag and draw lettering using a black marker. Punch hole in end of gift tag. Adhere gift tag to package.

Pumpkin Patterns

Inside & Outside Package Patterns

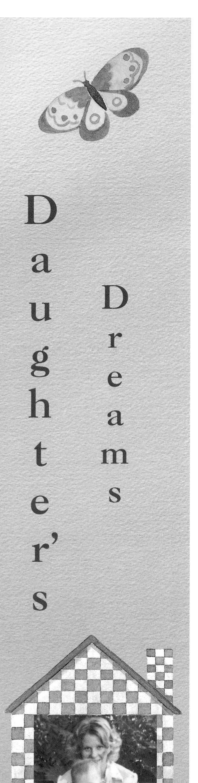

to my daughter

materials

Album: expandable spine
Buttons: ⅜"–¾" assorted coordinating (4)
Colored pencil: coordinating
Double-sided fusible web
Fabric: light-colored broadcloth;
    coordinating cotton; assorted
    coordinating scraps
Photo transfer paper: 8½" x 11"
Yarn: coordinating cotton crochet

general supplies & tools

Glue: fabric
Iron/ironing board
Measuring tape
Pressing cloth

Angel House   See page 137

Scissors: fabric
Sewing machine
Thread: coordinating

instructions

1. Measure an opened, flat album. Add ⅛" to height measurement and 11" to width measurement and cut piece from cotton fabric.

2. Press sides of short ends under ¼" and stitch a hem. With right sides together, fold short ends back 5¼". Stitch along top and bottom, from A to B, as shown in **Diagram 1**. Clip corners and turn right side out.

3. Turn remaining top and bottom edges under ¼" and stitch from B to B as shown in **Diagram 2**. Press.

4. Copy houses from **Angel House Artwork** on opposite page onto photo transfer paper at a copy center, following manufacturer's instructions. Reduce or enlarge as necessary.

5. Iron photo transfers onto broadcloth following manufacturer's instructions. Remove transfer while still hot.

6. Apply double-sided fusible web to back of broadcloth following manufacturer's instructions. Use a pressing cloth over top of photo transfers to prevent damage to transfers.

7. With a ⅛" margin, cut out each house.

8. Refer to General Instructions for **Fusible Appliqué** on page 21. Reduce or enlarge **Shapes Patterns** on page 137. Trace two hearts, stars, and flowers, and draw one rectangle for title box onto paper side of fusible web. Cut around motifs. Iron motifs to back sides of fabric scraps. Cut out motifs.

9. Enlarge, center, and transfer **Daughter Verse** at right to title box using colored pencil.

10. Remove paper backing and arrange houses, motifs, and title box on front of album cover as desired. Lay pressing cloth over cover and iron pieces in place.

11. Draw stitch lines around inside edges of houses, motifs, and title box using colored pencil.

12. Cut two 2⅛" lengths and one 7" length from yarn. Knot one end of 2⅛" lengths and glue knotted end to center of each flower. Wrap and glue yarn in a spiral around knot. Tie 7" length into a bow with tails and glue to upper left corner of title box. Glue button on center of bow. Glue remaining buttons on lower right side of title box.

Diagram 1

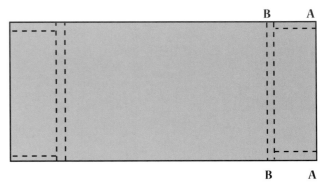

Diagram 2

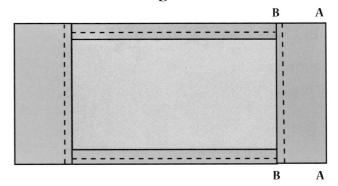

Daughter Verse   Enlarge 145%

Angel House Artwork

Angels live with God, and sometimes they come to visit. They help love grow, and sometimes they can even about angels never. What do you think? Angels have pretty names like Sistina and Turia. Some people say you become one when you die, but maybe we are all angels now. What do you think? —Tatiana, age 8

Dreams

Wishes

Memories

Angel House   See page 63

Butterfly Kisses   See page 63

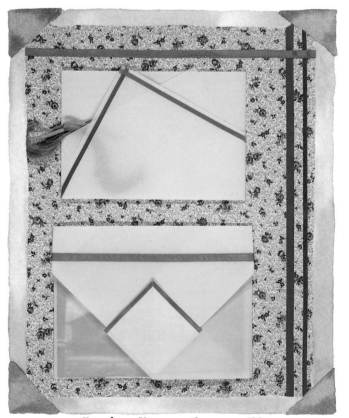

Envelope Keepers See page 139

Family Tree See page 140

Shapes Patterns

4. Sew through button holes on ceramic button using needle and thread. Knot at back of button and glue to center of color copy. Adhere color copy to album page.

butterfly kisses

materials
Double-sided fusible web
Colored pencil: coordinating
Fabric: coordinating cotton

general supplies & tools
Adhesive
Cardboard: lightweight
Craft knife
Iron/ironing board
Pencil
Scissors: craft; fabric

instructions
1. Make a color copy of **Butterfly Artwork** on page 138 at a copy center, reducing or enlarging to desired size for album page. Cut out butterfly using a craft knife.

2. Reduce or enlarge **Butterfly Pattern** on page 132. Trace pattern onto cardboard and cut out for template.

3. Position template over each photograph and trace around template. Cut out photographs using craft scissors.

4. Apply double-sided fusible web to back of fabric following manufacturer's instructions. Measure and cut fabric to fit album page. Remove paper backing and iron fabric to album pages.

5. Arrange and adhere photographs and butterfly artwork to album pages as desired.

6. Draw stitch lines around photographs and artwork using colored pencil.

angel house

materials
Button: coordinating ceramic

general supplies & tools
Adhesive
Craft knife
Needle: hand-sewing
Ruler: metal edge
Thread: coordinating

instructions
1. Make a color copy of **Angel House Artwork** on page 135 at a color copy center, reducing or enlarging if necessary, to fit album page. Trim blank edges from around artwork using a craft knife and ruler.

2. Carefully cut around top, right side, and bottom of doors. Fold and crease left side of doors open.

3. With doors open, position and glue photographs to back of color copy. Cut photograph to fit top left frame on color copy and adhere in place.

Butterfly Artwork

Today we would do well
to take a moment to dream
of lighthearted and sweet
beautiful things
like butterflies and daffodils
and birds that sing.

Butterfly Pattern

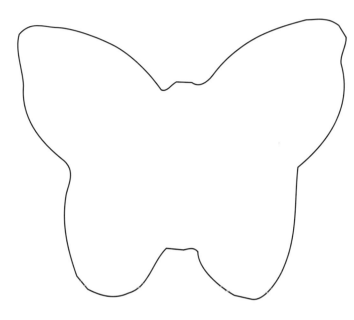

envelope keepers

materials
Embossing tool
Fabric: coordinating print
Ribbon: ⅛"-wide coordinating; ¼"-wide coordinating
Stencils: assorted as desired
Vellum paper: 11" x 17" white (2)

general supplies & tools
Adhesive
Craft knife
Iron/ironing board
Ruler: metal edge
Scissors

instructions
1. Press fabric. Make a color copy of fabric at a copy center, reducing or enlarging to desired size for album. Trim color copy, if necessary, to fit album page using a craft knife and ruler. Adhere color copy to album page.

2. Cut ¼"-wide ribbon into two lengths to fit across top and side of album page. Cut ⅛"-wide ribbon to fit across side of album page. Adhere ribbons in place as shown in photograph on page 136.

3. Fold right edge of one sheet of vellum paper to left edge as shown in **Diagram 1-A** on opposite page. Measure 4" from fold and fold again as shown in **B**. Measure 2¼" from upper left corner and fold to right as shown in **C**. Measure 2½" from upper right corner and fold to left as shown in **C**. Insert right end into fold of left end as shown in **D**.

4. Unfold envelope and position top flap, right side down, over stencil and rub embossing tool around edges of stencil. Stencil around inside edges of top flap.

5. Cut ⅛"-wide ribbon to fit edges of front flap of envelope. Adhere ribbons to envelope, ⅛" from edge, overlapping at top point.

6. Trim remaining sheet of vellum to 11" square and fold in half diagonally as shown in **Diagram 2-A** on page 140. Mark triangle into thirds along base and fold left corner over as shown in **B**. Fold right side over in same way as shown in **C**. Points and folds should meet. Fold back half of upper point as shown in **D**. Open small triangular section and flatten as shown in **E**. Fold down upper flap and insert into opened section as shown in **F**.

7. Position envelope flap right side down over stencil and gently but firmly press embossing tool around edges of stencil. Stencil across top edge of envelope flap.

8. Cut ¼"-wide ribbon to fit across top flap. Adhere ribbon to flap, slightly below embossed pattern.

9. Adhere envelopes to album page and tuck mementos inside.

Diagram 1

A

B

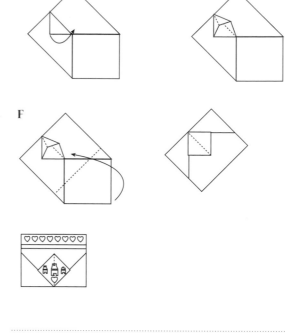

D (cont.)

E

F

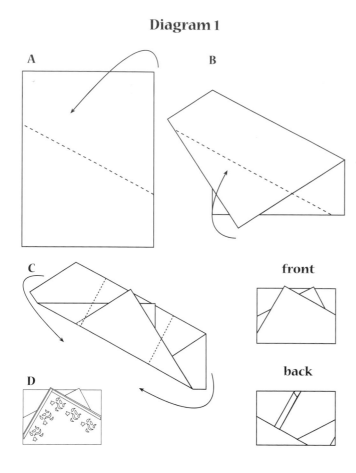

C

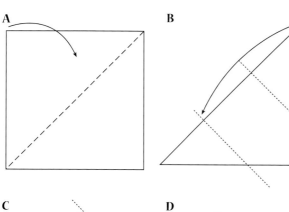

front

back

D

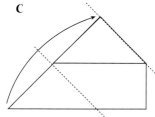

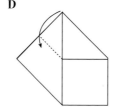

Diagram 2

A

B

C

D

family tree

materials
Pigment pen: coordinating

general supplies & tools
Adhesive
Craft knife
Ruler: metal edge

instructions
1. Make desired number of color copies of **Family Tree Fruit** below and **Family Tree Artwork** on opposite page at a copy center, reducing or enlarging to desired size for album page.

2. Cut copy of family tree to fit album page using a craft knife and ruler. Adhere copy to album pages.

3. Write one family member name on each fruit using a pigment pen. Cut out, arrange, and adhere in order of pedigree.

Family Tree Fruit

Family Tree Artwork

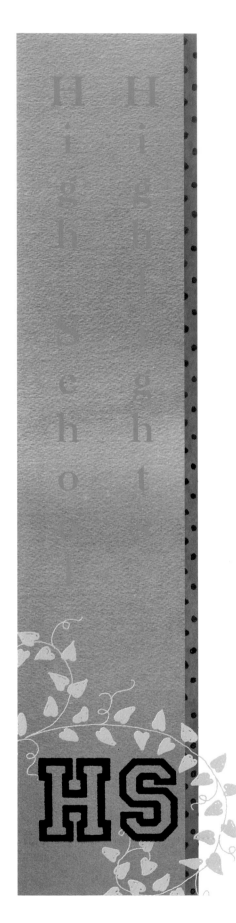

high school days

materials

Binder: 3-ring
Charms or jacket pins (with pin cut off): assorted
Letterman's jacket emblems

general supplies & tools

Glue gun and glue sticks

instructions

1. Order name, year, and school insignia emblems from local letterman's jacket distributor.

2. Hot-glue emblems to front of binder as desired.

3. Hot-glue charms or pins to school insignia emblem.

alternate instructions

1. Cover binder with desired color fabric as instructed for **Seasons** Steps 1–4 on page 126. Order desired school emblem.

2. Cut the school letter out of cardboard and batting. Cover cardboard and batting letter with felt in the school color. Wrap and glue felt to back of cardboard.

3. Hot-glue letter and emblem to front of binder as desired.

high school pages

materials

Acrylic paints
Cardstock
Glitter
Paper: white transfer
Pens: pigment
Stickers

general supplies & tools

Adhesive
Craft knife
Marker: black permanent
Paintbrushes
Paint dishes
Paper towel
Pencil
Ruler: metal edge
Scissors: craft

instructions

1. Enlarge desired **Page Art** on pages 147–149 at a copy center, using colored cardstock of choice.

2. Depending upon pages selected, either cut out photo openings using a craft knife and ruler; trace photo slots onto transfer paper, transfer onto photographs, and cut out using craft scissors; or, cut photographs as desired to create a collage.

3. Use pigment pens or acrylic paints to color pattern pages. If painting, place three drops of paint into paint dish. Fill dish two-thirds full of water. Add additional drops of paint if deeper color is desired. Dip brush in paint then dab on paper towel to remove excess water. Allow paint to dry thoroughly. Place page under heavy object over night to avoid paper curl.

4. Adhere photographs to pattern pages.

5. Embellish pages with stickers and glitters as desired.

6. Label photographs and write narrative using a permanent marker.

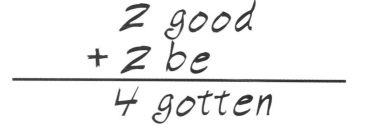

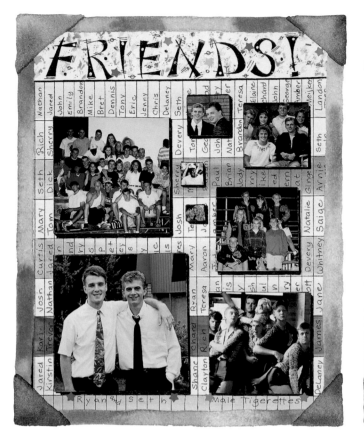

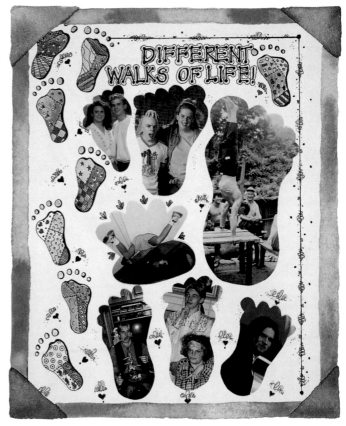

Page Art

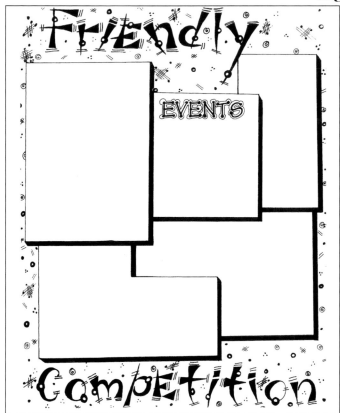

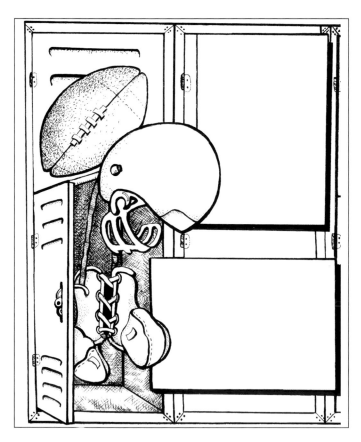

Page Art

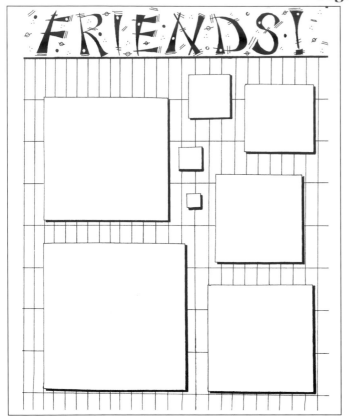

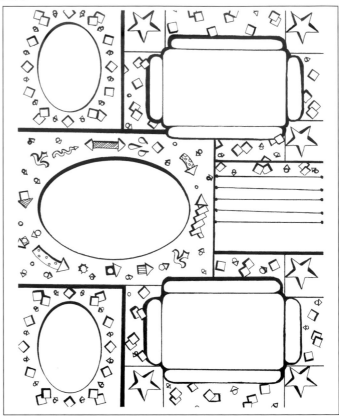

Page Art

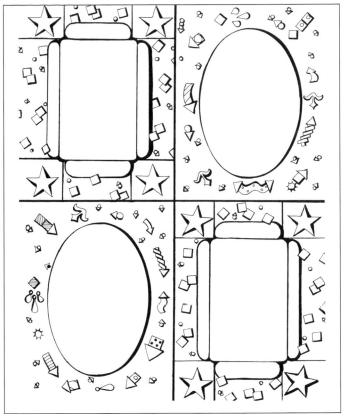

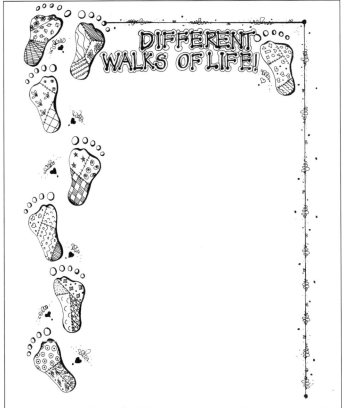

Weddings Are Forever

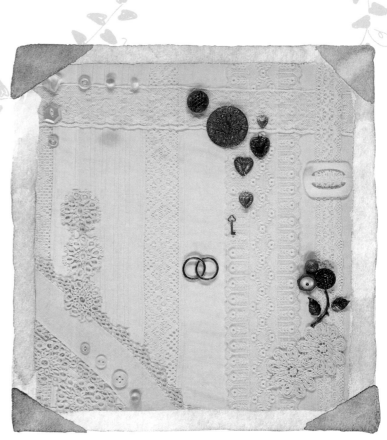

wedding album

materials
Album: expandable spine
Cardboard: lightweight
Embellishments: assorted buttons, buckles, charms, tatted pieces
Fabric: coordinating broadcloth
Gown: antique christening
Lace: assorted flat antique
Quilt batting: lightweight

general supplies & tools

Glue gun and glue sticks
Needle: hand-sewing
Scissors: fabric
Sewing machine
Straight pins
Thread: coordinating

instructions

1. Disassemble album. Measure front and back covers. Add 3" to height and width measurements and cut two pieces from gown and two pieces from broadcloth fabric.

2. Overlap one piece of gown on one piece of fabric ¼" and pin together for front. Sew two rows of stitches, ¼" apart, using sewing machine. Repeat process for remaining gown and fabric pieces for back.

3. Embellish front cover with assorted buttons, buckles, charms, laces, and tatted pieces as desired. Tack all embellishments to cover using needle and coordinating thread.

4. Cut quilt batting to fit front and back covers. Hot-glue batting to top side of front and back covers.

5. Lay front and back fabric pieces face down. Center and lay covers on top of fabric, batting side down. Wrap and hot-glue fabric edges to inside of covers.

6. Wrap spine/page guard with lace and hot-glue to secure. Hot-glue lace over raw edges of inside binding folds on front and back covers. Cut holes in binding pieces for metal connectors to fit through.

7. Cut cardboard into two pieces, ⅛" smaller than inside covers. Cut fabric into two pieces, 1" larger than cardboard pieces. Lay cardboard onto fabric. Wrap and hot-glue fabric edges to inside of cardboard. Hot-glue fabric-covered cardboard to inside front and back covers to hide all raw edges.

8. Reassemble album.

wedding pages

general supplies & tools

Adhesive
Craft knife
Embossing tool
Light box
Ruler: metal edge
Scissors: craft; fabric
Stencil
Tape: drafting

weddings past

instructions

1. Make a color copy of **Antique Document** on page 152 at a copy center, reducing or enlarging if necessary, to fit album page. Trim color copy, if necessary, using a craft knife and ruler. Adhere color copy to album page.

2. Adhere photographs to album page as desired.

Antique Document

which said Messuages or Dwellinghouses Closes Lands & hereditau
piece or parcel of Land called the roughpiece containing by estimat
Acre be the same more or less, One other piece or parcel of Land
or parcels of Land & hereditaments and premises are situate lying
er Ground AND ALSO One Barn and One Close called the Barn
Barn containing by estimation One Acre be the same more or
or less, One other Close called the Pingle containing by estima
estimation One acre and an half be the same more or less, O
or less, One other Close or parcel of Land called the Top
is and hereditaments are situate standing lying and being at
re mentioned now are or late were in the tenure and occupation
Undertenants Together with all and singular the houses Out
lls waters watercourses Trees woods Underwoods hedges Ditches
and Appurtenances whatsoever to the said Messuages Dwellingho
wise appertaining Or accepted reputed taken and known as part p
parcel thereof **To have and to hold** the said Messuages
or intended to be hereby bargained and sold with their Appurten
to the full end and term of
said Thomas Flinn and George Flinn to
the intent and purpose that by virtue of these presents an
ofession of the premises aforesaid with the Appurtenances And m
tance thereof to him and his heirs To and for such Uses Estates
ded to bear date the day next after the day of the date hereof and
d White of the other part by their several additions therein
als the Day and Year first above written.

cordially invited

materials
Cardstock: coordinating
Lace paper

instructions
1. Cut cardstock to fit album page using a craft knife and ruler. Adhere cardstock to album page.

2. Adhere lace paper at an angle to album page. Trim excess paper from edges of page using craft scissors.

3. Adhere invitations to album page as desired.

Make a color photocopy of completed album cover for excellent background paper for the rest of the photo pages.

generations

instructions
1. Make color copies of **Photo Surrounds** on page 154 at a copy center, reducing or enlarging to desired size for album page. Cut out photo surrounds using a craft knife and ruler. Cut out inside ovals and around flowers using a craft knife.

2. Position photographs in ovals and adhere to back of photo surrounds.

3. Position album page right side down over stencil on light box and tape page in place. Gently but firmly press around edges of stencil using embossing tool. Remove tape.

4. Adhere photo surrounds to album page as desired.

Photo Surrounds

Poetry & Lace Photo Surround

Verse:

A relationship is placing one's heart and soul in the hands of another while taking charge of another in one's soul and heart.

— Kahlil Gibran

4. Position photographs in openings and adhere to back of photo surround. Adhere photo surround to center of album page.

5. Glue lace around photo surround, leaving a space between photograph and lace same width as ribbon.

6. Cut four lengths from ribbon, two to fit vertically and two to fit horizontally on album page, using fabric scissors. Lay ribbons in space between photo surround and lace and adhere to album page using a small amount of craft glue in corners. Cut ribbon ends at an angle.

poetry & lace

materials
Cardstock: coordinating
Glue: craft
Lace: antique flat
Paper punch: decorative corner
Ribbon: coordinating

instructions
1. Make a color copy of **Poetry & Lace Photo Surround** on page 154 at a copy center, reducing or enlarging to desired size for album page.

2. Cut cardstock to fit album page using a craft knife and ruler. Adhere cardstock to album page. Punch top corners of photo surround using decorative paper punch.

3. Cut out center openings of photo surround using a craft knife and ruler.

art of marriage

instructions
Make a color copy of **Marriage Artwork** on page 151 at a copy center, reducing or enlarging if necessary, to fit album page. Trim color copy, if necessary, using a craft knife and ruler. Adhere color copy to album page.

garter photo corners

materials

Lace: 1"-wide gathered
Photo corners: clear
Ribbon: ¼"-wide coordinating

instructions

1. Cut lace into four equal lengths to fit diagonally around each corner of photograph. Wrap lace around corners and adhere to back of photograph.

2. Cut ribbon into four equal lengths to wrap around top edge of lace corners. Adhere ribbon to back of photograph.

3. Place clear photo corners on photograph and adhere to album page.

victorian house

instructions

1. Make a color copy of **Victorian Surround** on page 158 at a copy center, reducing or enlarging if necessary, to fit album page. Trim photo surround, if necessary, and cut out photograph openings using a craft knife and ruler.

2. Position photographs in openings. Trim photographs to reduce bulk from overlapping. Adhere photographs to back of photo surround.

3. Adhere photo surround to album page.

Verse:

Love for the joy of loving, and not for the offering of someone else's heart.

— Marlene Dietrich

Marriage Artwork

The Art of Marriage

A good marriage must be created.

In the art of marriage the little things are the big things...

It is never being too old to hold hands.

It is remembering to say "I love you," at least once each day.

It is never going to sleep angry.

It is having a mutual sense of values and common objectives.

It is standing together facing the world.

It is forming a circle of love that gathers in the whole family.

It is speaking words of appreciation and
demonstrating gratitude in thoughtful ways.

It is having the capacity to forgive and forget.

It is in giving each other an atmosphere in which each can grow.

It is finding room for things of the spirit.

It is a common search for the good and the beautiful.

It is not only marrying the right partner,
It is being the right partner.

Wilferd A. Peterson

Victorian Surround

antiquity

materials
Album: expandable spine
Cardboard: lightweight
Charm: coordinating
Embroidery ribbon: 4mm
    coordinating; 13mm coordinating
Lace: ¼"-wide flat; 1½"-wide flat;
    medallions (4)
Leaf stems: velvet (2)
Organza ribbon: 24mm
    coordinating
Stamens: beaded (2)
Wire-edge ribbon: ⅝"-wide
    coordinating

general supplies & tools
Adhesive: solid; spray
Craft knife
Scissors: craft; fabric

instructions

1. Disassemble album. Measure front and back covers. Add 3" to height and width measurements and cut two pieces from fabric using fabric scissors.

2. Spray top of front and back covers with adhesive. Center and lay covers on wrong side of fabric pieces. Wrap and adhere fabric edges to inside of covers. Cut out spine holes using a craft knife.

3. Cut cardboard into two pieces, ⅛" smaller than inside covers, using craft scissors. Cut fabric into two pieces, 1" larger than cardboard pieces. Center and lay cardboard on wrong side of fabric pieces. Wrap and adhere fabric edges to inside of cardboard. Adhere fabric-covered cardboard to inside front and back covers to hide all raw edges. Adhere ¼"-wide lace around edges of fabric-covered cardboard.

4. Adhere 1⅛"-wide lace around top edges of front cover. Adhere 4mm embroidery ribbon over edge of lace.

5. Enlarge **Oval Pattern** on page 161 at a copy center, to desired size for photograph (300% for original size). Trace oval onto cardboard and photograph and cut out using craft scissors. Spray cardboard with adhesive and adhere photograph to cardboard. Adhere photograph to center of album cover.

6. Adhere lace medallions around photograph. Adhere velvet leaves, beaded stamens, and charm to top of leaves as shown in photograph.

7. Refer to a ribbon embroidery instruction guide to do the following ribbonwork: a) make three freeform flowers using wire-edge ribbon; b) make three pencil flowers using 13mm embroidery ribbon; c) make one spiral rosetta using organza ribbon.

8. Adhere spiral rosetta on top of leaves and stamen as shown in photograph. Adhere freeform flowers and pencil flowers around spiral rosetta as desired.

9. Reassemble album.

Before cutting photos — photocopy!

family quilt

materials

Button: small
Double-sided fusible web
Embroidery floss: coordinating
Embroidery ribbon: 4mm
    coordinating;
    13mm coordinating
Fabric: assorted coordinating
    calico print scraps;
    white cotton, pressed
Lace: assorted flat scraps
Organza ribbon: 9mm
    coordinating;
    18mm coordinating
Photo transfer medium

general supplies & tools

Adhesive: fabric
Craft knife
Iron/ironing board
Needle: hand-sewing
Pencil
Ruler: metal edge
Scissors: fabric

instructions

1. Make a copy of photo and copies of **Quilt Patterns** below at a copy center, reducing or enlarging to desired size to fit album page.

2. Trace quilt pattern pieces onto paper side of fusible web. Cut around pattern pieces. Iron pattern pieces to back sides of fabric scraps. Add ¼" to all sides of pattern pieces and cut out.

3. Remove paper backing from fusible web and fuse pattern pieces to white cotton fabric, overlapping as necessary.

4. Transfer copy of photograph onto cotton fabric using photo transfer medium and following manu-facturer's instructions. Enlarge, center, and trace **Oval Pattern** below onto fabric photo. Cut out fabric photograph. Adhere to center of "quilted" fabric.

5. Cut lace pieces to fit seams of "quilted" fabric and to fit around photo. Adhere lace to quilted fabric

6. Refer to an embroidery stitch guide to make the following stitches: randomly stitch lazy daisy petals along lace seams using a hand-sewing needle and two strands of embroidery floss.

7. Tie 4mm embroidery ribbon into a bow and glue to top center of oval, cascading ribbon tails around top portion of photo.

8. Refer to a ribbon embroidery stitch guide to do the following ribbonwork: a) make two freeform flowers using 13mm embroidery ribbon; b) make two gathered petals using 9mm organza ribbon; c) make six folded petals using 18mm organza ribbon.

9. Adhere folded petals in circle at top center of photo. Adhere button to center of petals. Adhere gathered petals on each side of petal flower. Adhere freeform flowers on each side of gathered petals.

10. Adhere "quilted" fabric to album page. If necessary, trim edges using a craft knife and ruler.

Quilt Patterns & Oval Pattern

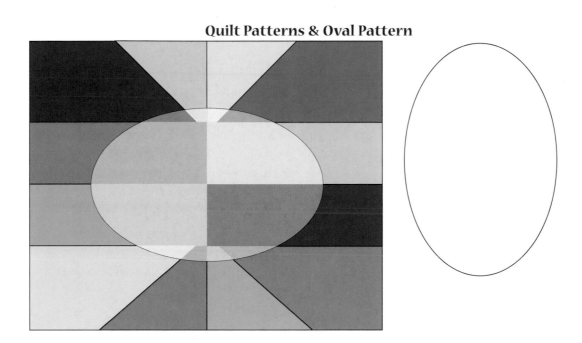

organdy envelope

materials

Cardboard: lightweight
Embroidery ribbon:
    7mm coordinating (2);
    13mm coordinating
Fabric: coordinating organza
Organza ribbon: 18mm
    coordinating;
Paper doily: 8" square
Picot-edge ribbon: ⅛"-wide
    coordinating
Spray paint: coordinating
Trim: coordinating eyelash

general supplies & tools

Adhesive: solid; spray
Craft knife
Pencil
Ruler: metal edge
Scissors: craft; fabric

instructions

1. Spray album page with spray paint. Let dry.

2. Spray album page with adhesive. Lay organza fabric over top and press to secure to album page. Trim excess fabric from edges of album page using a craft knife and ruler.

3. Adhere one 7mm embroidery ribbon around edge of album page. Adhere eyelash trim around edge of album page on top of embroidery ribbon.

4. Make a copy of **Small Oval Pattern** on opposite page at a copy center, reducing or enlarging to desired size. Trace two ovals onto cardboard and cut out using craft scissors.

5. Center and trace two ovals on photographs. Cut out.

Spray back of photographs with adhesive and adhere to cardboard ovals.

6. Refer to a ribbon embroidery stitch guide to do the following ribbonwork: a) make ⅛" box pleats along 13mm embroidery ribbon; sew a running stitch ⅛" from edge of ribbon; b) gather ribbon to fit around photographs; c) make three pencil flowers using one 7mm embroidery ribbon; d) make three baby rosettes using second 7mm embroidery ribbon.

7. Adhere ruched ribbons to edge of ovals. Cut two lengths from picot-edge ribbon to fit around outside edge of ovals. Adhere ribbon to top of ruched ribbons on ovals.

8. Cut three lengths from 18mm organza ribbon. Fold each ribbon as shown in **Diagram 1 (A–B)** and secure with adhesive. Cut three smaller lengths from 18mm organza ribbon and wrap a ribbon around each folded ribbon as shown in **C**, securing at back, to form a bow as shown in **D**. Adhere bow to center top of ovals. Set remaining bow aside.

9. Adhere baby rosettes in center of pencil flowers. Adhere one pencil flower to center top of each oval.

10. Cut 18mm organza ribbon into desired lengths for hangers. Fold ribbons in half and adhere raw ends to back of ovals. Adhere ovals to album page.

11. Fold paper doily into envelope as shown in **Diagram 2 (A–E)**. Adhere three corners together.

Adhere remaining pencil flower to top of envelope flap.

12. Cut 18mm organza ribbon into desired length for envelope hanger. Adhere hanger to album page. Adhere envelope to album page at base of hanger. Adhere remaining organza bow to top of hanger.

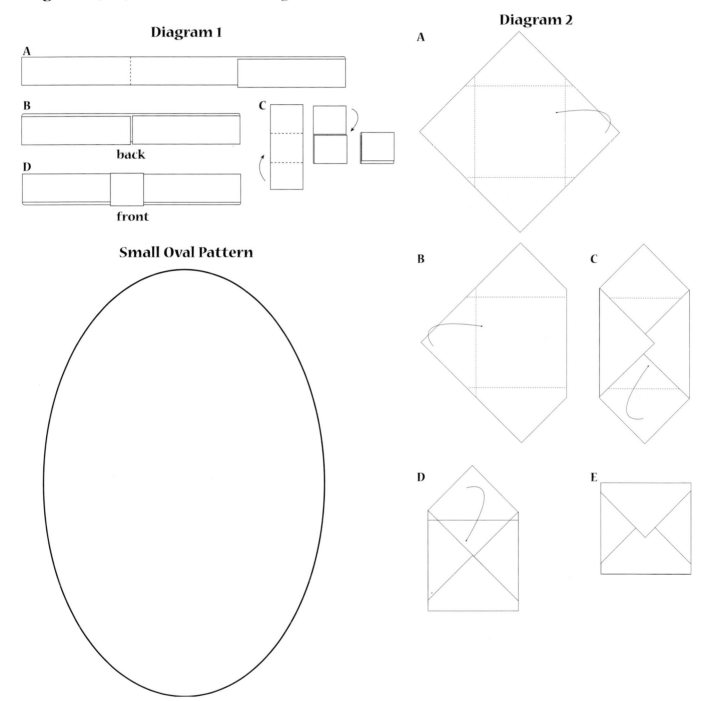

Diagram 1

Diagram 2

Small Oval Pattern

wedding vows

materials

Acrylic paints: coordinating (3)
Beads: coordinating seed (27)
Buttons: small (2)
Cardboard: lightweight
Cardstock: coordinating
Embroidery ribbon: 4mm
    coordinating;
    5mm coordinating (2);
    7mm coordinating (2)
Lace: ⅝"-wide flat
Trim: coordinating
Woven ribbon: 1½"-wide green
Wire-edge ribbon:
    ⅝"-wide coordinating (2);
    ⅞"-wide coordinating (2);
    1½"-wide coordinating

general supplies & tools

Adhesive; solid; spray
Craft knife
Paint roller brush: small
Pen: gold
Pencil
Ruler: metal edge
Scissors: fabric; decorative edge
Sponge
Transfer paper

instructions

1. Paint album page using a small roller brush and one color of paint. Apply remaining colors of paint, one at a time, using a sponge. Allow paint to dry.

2. Make a copy on cardstock of **Oval with Verse** on opposite page at a copy center. Cut out oval using decorative edge scissors and leaving a ⅛" border. Color decorative border around oval using a gold pen.

3. Spray cardboard with adhesive. Adhere photographs to cardboard and cut out using a craft knife and ruler. Adhere photographs to album page.

4. Adhere lace around photographs, mitering corners. Adhere trim on top of lace at edge of photographs.

5. Transfer desired number of leaves onto green ribbon using **Leaf Pattern** on opposite page and transfer paper. Trace over transfer lines with a gold pen and cut out leaves using fabric scissors. Adhere leaves to album page as desired.

6. Cut 5mm embroidery ribbon into desired length to cascade across top of photographs. Randomly tie knots in ribbon and knot ribbon ends. Adhere ribbon to album page.

7. Refer to a ribbon embroidery instruction guide to do the following ribbonwork: a) stitch one ruched ribbon flower using ⅞"-wide wire-edge ribbon; b) stitch one multi-petal flower with tucks using ⅝"-wide wire-edge ribbon; c) stitch one double ruffle rosette using 1½"-wide wire-edge ribbon; d) fold and stitch three pansies using ⅝"-wide wire-edge ribbon with 7mm embroidery ribbon for centers; e) make desired number of pencil flowers using 4mm and 7mm embroidery ribbons; sew three seed beads in center of each pencil flower.

8. Adhere flowers to album page as shown in photograph. Adhere buttons in center of folded multi-petal flower and double ruffle rosette.

Leaf Pattern

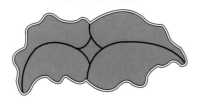

Oval with Verse   Enlarge 125%

L et me dwell in the light of thine eyes, Let me find a sweet home in thy heart! For my soul like a wild bird flies, To linger wherever thou art—As night gives place to the day, And darkness before the sun flies, So my sorrows will all melt away, When I live in the light of thine eyes.

grandma's fan

materials
Acrylic paints: coordinating (2)
Cardboard: lightweight
Charms: coordinating (3)
Cording: ⅛"-wide coordinating
Double-sided fusible web
Embroidery ribbon: 13mm coordinating
Fabric: coordinating; lace
Organza ribbon: 5mm coordinating;
    9mm coordinating;
    18mm coordinating, green;
    24mm coordinating
Picot-edge ribbon: ⅛"-wide coordinating
Spray paint: coordinating
Wallpaper: coordinating print

general supplies & tools
Adhesive: archival; fabric; spray
Iron/ironing board
Marking pen
Paint brush: large flat
Pencil
Sealer: matte spray
Scissors: craft; decorative edge; fabric

instructions
1. Spray album page using light coat of spray matte sealer. Let dry. Spray album page with light coat of adhesive. Let dry. Lay lace fabric over top of album page and lightly spray lace and album page using spray paint. Lift lace and let painted album page dry.

2. Mix water with each acrylic paint in a 3:1 ratio. Wash painted album page with each. Let dry.

3. Make a copy of **Fan Patterns** at right and on opposite page at a copy center, reducing or enlarging to desired size to fit album page. Trace fan blade, frame, and two ovals onto cardboard and cut out with craft scissors. Set ovals aside for Step 7.

4. Trace seven blades (one next to the other) onto cardboard to form complete fan. Trace seven blades onto back of wallpaper using fan blade template. Spray back of wallpaper with spray adhesive and cut out blades. Attach paper blades to cardboard fan. Trim fan edge with decorative edge scissors.

5. Cut picot-edge ribbon into eight lengths for spokes of fan. Adhere ribbon to fan using fabric glue. Adhere completed fan to album page. Adhere large charm to bottom of fan.

6. Trace frame onto fusible web, adding ⅛ to inside cutting line. Cut out traced frame from fusible web, leaving center uncut, and fuse to fabric. Add ⅛ to outside cutting line and cut out traced frame from fabric. Spray cardboard frame with adhesive. Place sprayed side of frame onto fused web. Clip curves on fabric. Wrap fabric to back of frame and secure using fabric glue.

7. Trace oval from center of cardboard frame onto two photographs. Enlarge oval by ⅛ and trace onto third photograph and cardboard. Cut out oval photographs and cardboard oval using craft scissors. Spray adhesive onto photographs and adhere to cardboard ovals.

8. Refer to a ribbon embroidery instruction guide to do the following ribbonwork: a) make nine folded petals using 13mm embroidery ribbon and adhere three petals to top backside of each small oval and to top backside of frame; b) make eight folded petals using 18mm organza ribbon and adhere four petals each to top backside of small ovals; c) make twelve folded petals using green organza ribbon and adhere three petals each to backside of small ovals and,

rather than gluing ends flat on remaining six petals, pinch and glue ends, cutting off excess tails and adhering to front of frame for leaves; d) make five folded petals using 24mm organza ribbon and adhere to back of petals on frame; e) make three pencil flowers using 9mm organza ribbon and adhere one flower to front of each small charm and to front of frame; f) make one pencil flower using 5mm organza ribbon and adhere to front of frame; g) make one circular ruffle using 13mm embroidery ribbon and adhere to front of frame.

9. Cut cording into two lengths to fit around front edge of each small oval. Adhere cording to ovals. Adhere one small charm with pencil flower to each small oval.

10. Adhere small ovals to album page. Adhere large oval to back of frame. Adhere frame to album page.

Fan Patterns

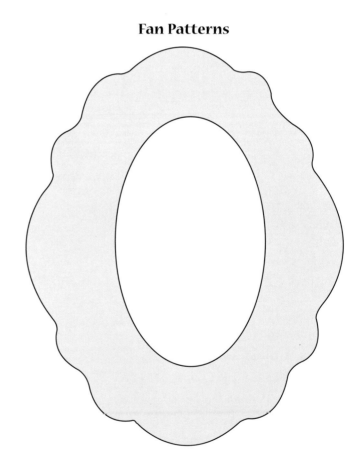

Fan Patterns (cont.)

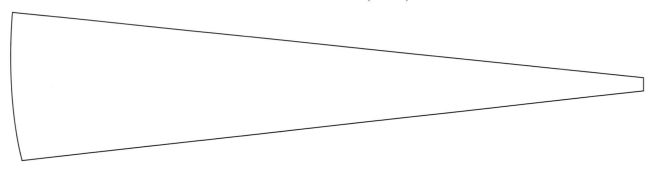

fuchsia frames

materials

Acrylic paint: coordinating
Buttons: small assorted (3)
Dowel: ⅛" x 36"
Embroidery ribbon: 4mm
    coordinating; 13mm coordinating
Fabric: coordinating moiré
Lace: ¼"-wide flat
Ribbon: ⅞"-wide coordinating (3);
    1½"-wide coordinating
Stamens

general supplies & tools

Adhesive: solid; spray
Craft knife
Paintbrush
Ruler: metal edge
Scissors: fabric

instructions

1. Apply spray adhesive to album page. Center and adhere fabric to album page. Let dry. Trim excess fabric from edges of album page using a craft knife and ruler.

2. Adhere lace around edge of album page.

3. Cut dowel to create frames for photos as shown in photograph. Paint dowel pieces with paint and let dry. Adhere photographs to album page. Adhere dowel pieces around photographs.

4. Refer to a ribbon embroidery stitch guide to do the following ribbonwork: a) make three fuchsias using one ⅞"-wide ribbon, two using second ⅞"-wide ribbon, two using remaining ⅞"-wide ribbon, and one using 1½"-wide ribbon; b) make three freeform flowers using 13mm embroidery ribbon.

5. Randomly tie knots on a length of 4mm green embroidery ribbon and cascade ribbon across top of photo frames. Adhere to album page at knots.

6. Adhere ribbon flowers to album page as desired above photo frames. Adhere buttons in centers of freeform flowers.

trellis

materials

Cardboard: lightweight
Embroidery ribbon: 7mm coordinating
Fabric: lace netting
Organza ribbon: 24 mm
    coordinating (2);
    18 mm coordinating, green
Paper cutouts
Spray paint: coordinating

general supplies & tools

Adhesive: solid, spray
Craft knife
Ruler: metal edge

instructions

1. Paint album page using spray paint.

2. Spray album page with adhesive. Lay lace netting over top and press to secure to album page. Trim excess netting from edges of album page using a craft knife and ruler.

3. Cut embroidery ribbon into desired number of lengths to fit across album page in a trellis pattern as shown in photograph. Adhere ends of ribbons to album page.

4. Spray cardboard with adhesive. Adhere photographs to cardboard and cut out using a craft knife and ruler. Slip photographs under and over trellis and adhere in place.

5. Cut green organza ribbon into two lengths. Twist ribbons into stems and adhere to album page.

6. Refer to a ribbon embroidery instruction guide to do the following ribbonwork: a) stitch three free form flowers using one 24mm organza ribbon; b) stitch three free form flowers using second 24mm organza ribbon and three using 18 mm organza ribbon; c) fold and stitch twenty-six folded leaves using remaining 18 mm green organza.

7. Assemble all flowers in the following manner: place flower inside one leaf and secure with adhesive; place end of leaf inside a second leaf and secure with adhesive; place end of second leaf inside a third leaf and secure with adhesive. Adhere flowers and leaves to album page.

8. Embellish album page with paper cutouts as desired.

9. Adhere remaining embroidery ribbon around edges of album page.

Verse:
    Those who bring sunshine to the lives of others cannot keep it from themselves.

        — Sir James M. Barrie

sister's favorite

materials
Beads: coordinating seed (3)
Buttons: small (2)
Cardstock: coordinating
Charms
Embroidery ribbon: 4mm
    coordinating (2);
    13mm coordinating (4)
Fabric: sheer
Lace: ⅛"-wide flat
Wrapping paper: coordinating

general supplies & tools
Adhesive
Craft knife
Ruler: metal edge
Scissors: fabric; decorative edge

instructions

1. Adhere wrapping paper to album page. Trim excess paper from edges of album page using a craft knife and ruler.

2. Place a thin layer of adhesive around edges of album page. Lay sheer fabric over top and adhere to album page. Trim excess fabric from edges of album page. Adhere lace around edges of album page.

3. Adhere photographs to cardstock, leaving 1" between photographs. Cut out photographs on card-stock using decorative edge scissors and leaving a ¼" border. Adhere photographs to album page as desired.

4. Refer to a ribbon embroidery instruction guide to do the following ribbonwork: a) stitch two pansies using one 13mm embroidery ribbon; b) fold and glue five folded petals using second 13mm embroidery ribbon; c) stitch three freeform flowers using third 13mm embroidery ribbon; sew seed beads in center of one flower; fold remaining flowers in half; d) stitch one pencil violet using fourth embroidery ribbon; e) stitch three pencil violets using 4mm embroidery ribbon.

5. Cut second embroidery ribbon into desired lengths to cascade around photographs. Randomly tie knots in ribbons. Tie charms onto ribbons as desired. Adhere ribbons around photographs as desired.

6. Adhere ribbon flowers in corners of photographs, on top of cascading ribbons. Adhere folded petals in a circle on corner of one photograph. Adhere buttons in center of 13mm pencil violet and folded petal flower.

Use new or antique victorian-looking frames to create quick photo frames to decorate old family photographs. Place the frames upside down on a copy machine set "darker" and copy. Trace the copy onto a fine quality piece of paper, using a brown or black pigment pen. Cut out the frame and place it on a patterned background paper.

days gone by

materials

Acrylic paints: coordinating colors (2),
    copper, gold
Cardboard: lightweight
Charms: coordinating
Decoupage medium: matte
Double-sided fusible web
Fabric: coordinating tapestry
Leaf: fabric
Paper: coordinating decorative
Photo album: 3-ring binder
Photo mat: pre-cut
Ribbon: ¾"-wide coordinating wire-edge ombré; 1½"-wide
    coordinating wire-edge ombré

general supplies & tools

Adhesive
Iron/ironing board
Paintbrush
Pencil
Scissors: craft; fabric
Sponge

instructions

1. Paint photo album with two light coats of decoupage medium mixed 1:1 with water. Let dry.

2. Lightly sponge several layers of acrylic paint on album, beginning with darkest coordinating color and finishing with copper and gold. Let dry.

3. Paint two more layers of decoupage medium thinned with water over sponged album. Let dry.

4. Highlight fabric leaf with copper and gold paints. Paint edge of leaf and edge of photograph gold.

5. Adhere 1⅛"-wide wire-edge ribbon down left side of album, ⅛" from edge. Wrap ends around to inside of cover and secure.

6. Cut tapestry fabric 1" larger than photo mat. Cut fusible web same size as mat. Mark opening with pencil and cut out using fabric scissors.

7. Following manufacturer's instructions, adhere fusible web to photo mat. Remove paper backing and adhere fabric to mat.

8. Cut out opening in fabric, leaving a 1" border. Clip around opening every 1" and to within ⅛" of mat. Fold flaps to wrong side of mat opening and secure with adhesive.

9. Cut cardboard same size as photo mat. Adhere decorative paper to cardboard and then adhere photograph, making certain photograph placement fits photo mat opening. Adhere mat and photo boards together. Place under a heavy object until adhesive is thoroughly dry.

10. Wrap and adhere ¾"-wide ombré ribbon around left side of photo mat, securing at back of mat. Adhere fabric leaf in top left corner of mat. Tie ¾"-wide ombré ribbon into a bow with tails. Adhere bow on top of leaf, cascading tails as desired. Adhere charms to leaf and bow. Adhere embellished photo mat to album cover.

textured pages

Follow instructions for each page in this section or obtain color photo copies, enlarged to desired size, of the textured pages provided on pages 178–181.

Use a craft knife and ruler to carefully cut out photographs on copies, leaving photo openings. Place personal photographs behind photo openings and

little sister

materials
Acrylic paints: coordinating; gold
Embellishments: coordinating
Paper: handmade ovals
Stencils: coordinating; decorative edge

general supplies & tools
Adhesive
Paintbrushes
Paper towels
Scissors: craft
Sponges: 1"–2"-wide, sea

instructions
1. Mark pattern on edge of marbled paper using a decorative edge stencil. Cut pattern edge.

2. Stencil design on handmade paper oval using coordinating acrylic paint and sponge. Load sponge with paint (or mixture of paints). Dab excess paint onto paper towel to avoid seepage under stencil. Softly pat stencil in an up-and-down motion over stencil. Remove stencil and let paint dry.

3. Stencil design on marbled paper.

4. Paint edges of marbled paper, photograph, and embellishments using gold paint.

5. Adhere paper oval to stenciled, marbled paper. Adhere photograph to paper oval. Adhere stenciled, marbled paper to a sheet of sponged paper. Adhere embellishments as desired.

Say "thank you" to a special teacher by making up an album chronicling the school year.

pansy border

materials
Acrylic paints: coordinating; gold
Cardstock: coordinating
Charms (4)
Clipart border
Colored pencils: soft-leaded
Greeting card: coordinating
Grosgrain ribbon: ⅛"-wide coordinating
Photo mounts: gold corner (4)
Wire-edge ribbon: ¾"-wide coordinating

general supplies & tools
Adhesive
Glue gun and glue sticks
Paintbrushes
Scissors: craft
Toothpicks: round

instructions

1. Make a photo copy of a clipart border design using brown tones at a copy center. Cut out one side of design to form a decorative corner border.

2. Lightly color details on border design using colored pencils. Repeat, building light layers of color. Do not work in one heavy layer.

3. Paint background area of border design and a ⅛"-wide border around photograph using acrylic paint.

4. Cut desired motifs from greeting card.

5. Paint edges of motifs, border, and photograph, and add detailing on border design using gold paint. Lightly dot gold paint around design areas using toothpicks.

6. Adhere corner border design and photograph to cardstock.

7. Cut a length from wire-edge ribbon 2" longer than length of album page. Gently pull wires to remove from ribbon edges. Adhere ribbon to left edge of cardstock.

8. Cut four 4" lengths from wire-edge ribbon. Shape each ribbon into a fan and secure with a dot of hot glue. Adhere fans to corners of photograph. Hot-glue charms to ribbon fans.

9. Cut three lengths from grosgrain ribbon to fit across top, bottom, and right side of cardstock. Adhere ribbons to cardstock.

10. Attach photo corners to corners of cardstock. Adhere cardstock to album page.

For a 50th wedding anniversary, send a scrapbook page to friends of the couple. Have them include a photo and write down a memory.

train

materials
Cardboard: lightweight
Embellishments: coordinating
Paper: coordinating color; patterned paper using plastic wrap and watercolors
Silhouette pattern

general supplies & tools
Adhesive
Craft knife
Masking tape
Newspapers
Paintbrush
Ruler: metal edge

instructions

1. Place silhouette pattern face up on colored paper and tape edges together.

2. Cut out silhouette pattern from colored paper using a craft knife and newspapers as a pad. If there are openings at center of pattern, cut these first and cut outside edges last.

3. Thin adhesive to a brushable consistency. Brush on backside of colored silhouette, brushing from center to outside edges.

4. Adhere silhouette to patterned paper. Surface may be lightly sponged with a damp cloth to remove excess adhesive.

5. Cut out center of sponged paper, using a craft knife and ruler, to create a ⅛"-wide frame. Adhere frame to patterned paper.

6. Adhere photograph to leftover sponged paper. Trim paper to a ⅛" border around photograph. Adhere photograph to patterned paper.

7. Adhere embellishments to patterned paper as desired.

ship

materials
Cardboard: lightweight
Gold leafing
Gold leafing adhesive
Paper: coordinating color; patterned paper using plastic wrap and watercolors
Photo mounts: gold corner (4)
Silhouette pattern

general supplies & tools
Adhesive
Craft knife
Masking tape
Newspapers
Paintbrush
Ruler: metal edge

1. Repeat **Train** Steps 1-4 above using silhoutte pattern.

2. Cut two ⅛"-wide strips of marbled paper to fit across top and bottom of remaining sheet of patterned paper. Adhere strips to patterned paper.

3. Adhere gold photo mounts in corners of patterned paper.

4. Cut cardboard ¼" larger than photograph. Adhere photograph to cardboard.

5. Cut leftover marbled paper into a ¼-wide frame to fit around photograph. Adhere frame to cardboard. Adhere framed photograph to patterned paper as desired.

6. Apply gold leafing to corners of framed photograph following manufacturer's instructions.

dear friends

materials
Acrylic paint: gold
Cardstock: coordinating
Leaves: velvet (3)
Paper: sponged
Photo corners: decorative (4)
Postcard: coordinating
Ribbon: ⅛-wide coordinating
Stickers

general supplies & tools
Adhesive
Craft knife
Hot glue gun and glue sticks
Paintbrush
Waxed paper

instructions
1. Enlarge postcard to desired size for album page at a photocopy center.

2. Cut a decorative opening in postcard using a craft knife.

3. Lay postcard on waxed paper and outline opening with a bead of hot glue. Let adhesive dry and then paint glue with gold acrylic paint. Outline details on postcard, if desired. Remove waxed paper.

4. Paint edges of postcard, leaves, and stickers by loading paintbrush with gold acrylic paint and using a scraping motion. Let dry for one hour.

5. Center and adhere photograph over opening on back side of postcard. Adhere postcard to sponged paper. Adhere stickers and leaves to postcard.

6. Tie ribbon into a bow and adhere to postcard.

7. Adhere sponged paper to cardstock for album page. Adhere decorative photo corners to album page.

A scrapbook makes a priceless gift for a best friend's birthday. Gather photographs of times shared throughout the years. Include event tickets or programs from concerts, plays, games, and other activities that friends attended together. Write about favorite past-times and experiences that should not be forgotten.

special delivery

materials
Acrylic paints: brown, gold
Cardstock: light colored (1), dark colored (2)
Charms: coordinating (3)
Envelope: decorative coordinating
Paper cut-outs: decorative coordinating
Ribbon: ⅛"-wide coordinating; ⅜"-wide coordinating

general supplies & tools
Adhesive
Paintbrush
Paper towels
Scissors: paper edgers

instructions
1. Trim one dark-colored cardstock to 7" x 10" and other to 3⅛" x 5⅛" using paper edgers.

2. Crumple envelope and carefully tear edges for a tattered appearance. Smooth envelope and brush with clean water to dampen.

3. Add one drop of brown acrylic paint to one tablespoon of water. Stir with paintbrush until water and paint are well mixed. Brush onto envelope, allowing paint-stained water to sink into broken areas of envelope. Immediately blot with paper towel. Repeat process as desired.

4. Adhere ⅛"-wide ribbon down left side of light-colored cardstock.

5. Load paintbrush with gold acrylic paint and paint edges of all pieces of cardstock and paper cut-outs in a scraping motion. Drybrush broken areas on envelope and on small dark colored cardstock with gold acrylic paint. Allow paint to dry for approximately one hour.

6. Adhere large dark-colored cardstock to light-colored cardstock, and adhere envelope to cardstock, positioning as desired.

7. Adhere ⅛"-wide ribbon across tops of cardstock. Tie ⅛"-wide ribbon into a bow and adhere to envelope.

8. Adhere photograph to small dark-colored cardstock and position in envelope. Secure with adhesive. Adhere paper cut-outs inside envelope.

9. Adhere charms in top corners of photograph and on knot of bow.

Honor a family heritage by displaying a family crest (if available), the meaning of the surname, a map of the country where the family originated, photographs or postcards of that country or people, and important holidays or events that may still be passed on through the family that originated in the old country.

3. Layer and adhere decorative tissue paper over top of cardstocks.

4. Tear random shapes from oriental lace paper. Randomly and sparingly apply adhesive to layered tissue paper and press lace paper onto layered tissue paper. Set several torn pieces aside.

5. Apply adhesive to back of photograph and adhere to layered paper. Adhere remaining torn pieces of lace paper around photograph.

6. Tie ribbon into a bow and adhere at bottom of photograph.

oriental lace

materials
Acrylic paint: gold
Cardstock: black, white
Paper: oriental lace; decorative tissue
Photo: hand-tinted (see **Hand-tinting Photographs** on page 16.)
Ribbon: ¾"-wide coordinating

general supplies & tools
Adhesive
Paintbrush
Scissors: paper edgers

instructions
1. Trim white cardstock to 8¼" x 10¾" using paper edgers.

2. Paint two coats of gold acrylic paint on side of white cardstock. Center and adhere gold-painted cardstock to black cardstock.

mother & daughter

materials
Acrylic paint: coordinating, brown, gold
Cardstock
Leaf: fresh, natural

Paper: white ; oriental
Ribbon: ¼"-wide
Rosettes: coordinating (8)

general supplies & tools
Adhesive
Paintbrush
Paper edgers

instructions
1. Crinkle white paper and carefully tear edges for a tattered appearance. Smooth paper and brush with clean water to dampen.

2. Add one drop of brown acrylic paint to one tablespoon of water. Stir with paintbrush until water and paint are well mixed. Brush onto paper, allowing paint-stained water to sink into broken areas of paper. Immediately blot with paper towel. Repeat process as desired. Adhere crinkled paper to cardstock.

3. Adhere ribbon to left side of cardstock.

4. Trim photograph using paper edgers and adhere to crinkled paper.

5. Paint underside of leaf with acrylic paints. Press oriental paper onto leaf and gently smooth paper with fingers from center to outside edges, pressing paint and image into paper. Lift paper and let dry to touch. Trace around outside edge of leaf print with paintbrush and clear water. Reload paintbrush with water as necessary. Gently tear leaf print from paper at dampened edge. Allow edges to dry.

6. Thin adhesive with water and apply to backside of leaf print. Adhere leaf print to crinkled paper, overlapping edges onto photograph.

7. Adhere rosettes to top corners of photograph and randomly to leaf print.

Little Sister Art

Mother & Daughter Art

Pansy Border Art

Train Art

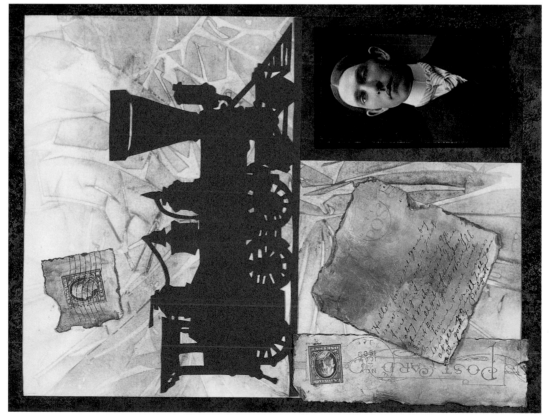

Ship Art

Dear Friends Art

Special Delivery Art

Oriental Paper Art

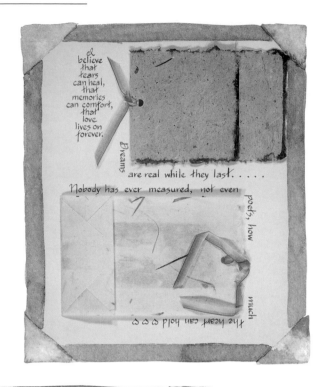

Sentimental Journey

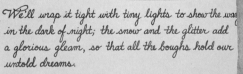

sentimental pages

instructions

Turn favorite greeting cards into photo mats. Use adhesive tape to attach photographs to mats.

Place photographs inside small paper books and envelopes.

Write a favorite message, poem, or thought using a coordinating calligraphy pen.

for giving, for sharing...

laughter...

for it now-they are

Our affections

Keep love in your life my child
If you would have perfe

The face of all
the world changed
when first I heard
the footsteps
of your souls.

Those Who
Hear Not
The Music

Think The
Dancers
Mad.

DESTINY

Some reckon
time by stars,
And some by
hours;
Some measure
days by dreams,
And some by
flowers;
My heart alone
records
All our days
and hours.

VANESSA ANN COLLECTIBLES

You are a part of lovliness to me

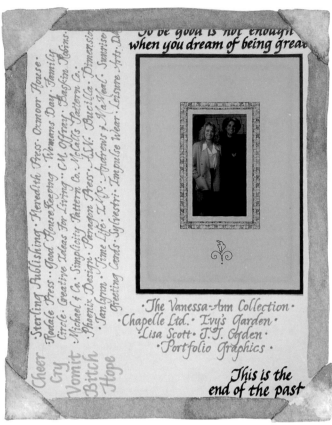

My friend, you are an inspiration to me.

Happiness
is not
a state to
arrive at,
but a
manner
of
traveling.

other covers & bindings

angel cover

materials

Binder: 3-ring
Foam board: 3" x 5"
Greeting card: coordinating
Paper: decorative, coordinating, 12" x 12"; translucent,
　　　Japanese, 24" x 36"

general supplies & tools

Craft knife
Glue: découpage
Marker: permanent
Paintbrush
Pencil
Scissors: craft
Sponge: small

instructions

1. Using craft scissors, cut out artwork from card.

2. Dilute découpage glue in a 1:1 ratio with water. Apply glue to binder cover.

3. Apply translucent paper to binder cover and gently press with damp sponge. Let project dry thoroughly. Repeat process once more.

4. Using craft knife, cut design to correspond to artwork from foam board, if desired. Apply glue to foam board. Wrap foam board with small piece of decorative paper.

5. Using pencil, write saying on scrap piece of decorative paper. Using desired color of permanent marker, write saying.

6. Glue decorative pieces and artwork to binder cover.

celestial insights cover

materials

Book with blank pages: 9¼" x 9"
Charms
Greeting card: coordinating
Paper: handmade, 8" x 9"; 10¼" x 6"

general supplies & tools

Adhesive
Paintbrush
Pantina green
Pen: calligraphy
Scissors: craft

instructions

1. Adhere 8" x 9" handmade paper diagonally across front cover of book. Tear and adhere 10¼" x 6" handmade paper to cover portion of 8" x 9" handmade paper.

2. Wrap paper around back binding of book, and fold piece over top edge of book to inside front cover. Adhere to secure.

3. Using craft scissors, cut out artwork from card. Glue artwork over 8" x 9" paper on lower right corner of book.

4. Using paintbrush and pantina green, apply over charms to antique. Adhere charms on front of book as desired.

5. Using calligraphy pen, write saying on 8" x 9" handmade paper.

Save anything from private thoughts to favorite family recipes to much loved photographs in this scrapbook. Match the greeting card to the subject.

simple appliqué cover

materials
Album: cardboard, ring binder
Double-sided fusible web
Fabric: muslin; coordinating cotton; assorted
    coordinating scraps

general supplies & tools
Iron/ironing board
Markers: permanent #05 black
Ruler
Scissors: fabric

instructions
1. Measure an opened, flat album. Add 1" to height and width measurements and cut piece from muslin fabric. Cut two pieces of muslin ⅛" smaller than inside cover.

2. Measure and cut a strip of cotton fabric 2⅛" wider and 1" longer than spine.

3. Tea-dye muslin, cotton and fabric scraps. Press fabrics after tea-dying

4. Refer to General Instructions for **Fusible Appliqué** on page 21. Reduce or enlarge **Simple Shapes Pattern** on page 188. Trace motifs onto paper side of fusible web. Cut around motifs. Iron motifs to back sides of fabric scraps. Cut out motifs.

5. Apply fusible web to back side of muslin cover, cotton spine, and inside cover pieces. Refer to **Diagram 1** below. Remove paper backing and iron muslin onto album cover, wrapping edges to inside of cover. Iron cotton spine fabric in place, wrapping ends to inside of cover and clipping as necessary to fit around ring hardware. Iron inside cover pieces to inside front and back covers to hide raw edges.

6. Iron motifs onto front and back cover as shown in photo.

7. Draw stitch lines around edges of motifs and spine fabric using a black permanent marker.

Diagram 1

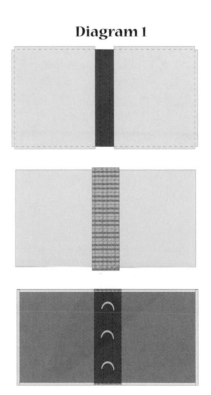

Simple Shapes Pattern

paper around left end of text papers for binding and punch holes as in Step 2.

4. Using textile ink, randomly stamp buildings on wire-edge ribbon and around top and bottom edge of scrapbook cover.

5. Using alphabet stamps, stamp book title on top center of journal cover.

6. Thread ribbon through holes and tie into a bow.

home sweet binding

materials
Cardstock: coordinating, 8½" x 11"
Paper: corrugated; medium-weight text
Ribbon: 1½"-wide coordinating wire-edge
Stamps: alphabet, small buildings
Textile ink

general supplies & tools
Paper punch
Scissors: craft, fabric

instructions
1. Using craft scissors, cut cardstock paper in half.

2. Punch two holes in left end of both pieces of cardstock, ¼" from edge and 1" from top and bottom edges.

3. Cut text paper to 8¼" x 5". Evenly fold corrugated

string binding

materials
Cardboard: lightweight
Paper: corrugated; medium-weight text
Thread: binding

general supplies & tools
Adhesive

Awl
Craft knife
Mallet
Needle
Ruler: metal edge

instructions

1. Trim medium-weight text paper to desired page size using a craft knife and ruler.

2. Trim lightweight cardboard to fit as a cover around text papers. Trim corrugated paper same size as cardboard. Adhere corrugated paper to top side of cardboard cover.

3. Measure and mark width of spine on inside cover and gently score. Fold cover to fit around text paper.

4. Mark the position of binding holes. Top and bottom holes should be ⅜" from top and bottom edges and 1" from spine edge. Two remaining holes should be spaced equal distances in between top and bottom holes. Pierce holes with an awl and mallet.

5. Thread needle and knot end of thread. Turn book face down and insert needle up through text paper and out at second hole from right, hiding knotted string end inside text pages. Bring needle around spine to front of book and up again through same hole. Tightly pull thread. Continue stitching as shown in **Diagram 1 (A–L)**.

6. Return to original hole and bring needle around stitching as though picking up a thread. Pull thread tightly into a knot.

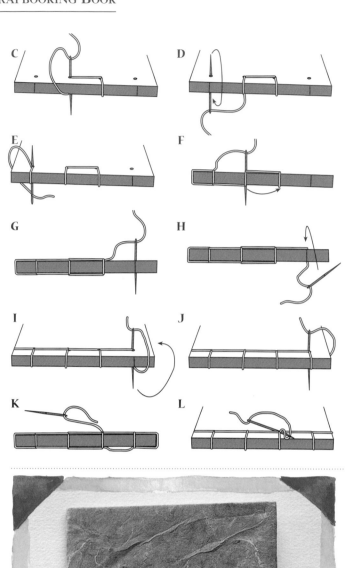

Diagram 1

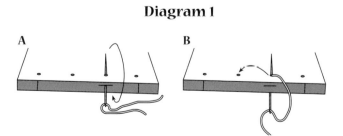

flutter binding

Diagram 1

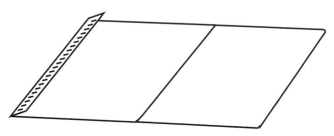

materials
Cardboard: lightweight
Paper: handmade textured; medium-weight text

general supplies & tools
Adhesive
Craft knife
Ruler: metal edge

Diagram 2 **Diagram 3**

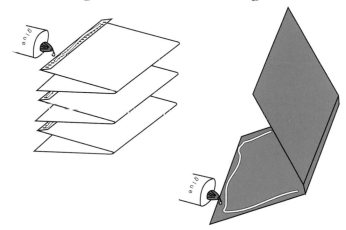

instructions
1. Trim lightweight cardboard to desired book size using a craft knife and ruler. Trim handmade textured paper ¾" larger than cardboard. Trim medium-weight text paper same height as cardboard and ½" wider than width of cardboard.

2. Apply adhesive to one side of cardboard and adhere handmade textured paper to cardboard, wrapping and adhering excess edges to back side of cardboard, to form book cover. Fold book cover in half.

3. Measure ½" from one short end of text paper and score. Fold scored edge up to form a flap as shown in **Diagram 1**. Repeat process for desired number of pages.

4. With flap side of paper facing down, fold opposite end of paper over to meet folded edge and crease in half. Repeat process for remaining papers.

5. Stack folded papers with flaps facing upward. Apply adhesive to flap on bottom paper and adhere next paper in stack to adhesive flap as shown in **Diagram 2**. Repeat process for remaining papers.

6. Adhere edge of bottom paper and top flap to inside edges of book cover as shown in **Diagram 3**.

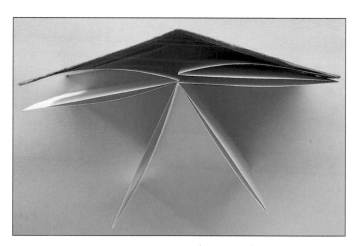
Flutter Binding (top view)

Receipt Book Binding (top view)   See page 118

2. Fold small cardboard piece in half lengthwise. Apply adhesive to inside of cardboard and adhere to spine of one stack of papers as shown in **Diagram 2** for center section of book.

3. Fold one short end of large cardboard pieces over ⅛". Apply adhesive to inside of ⅛" sections and adhere to spines of remaining stacks of papers, making certain one cardboard piece faces up for front cover and one faces down for back cover, and all folded edges of papers are at top.

4. Open center section to middle and place face down on work surface. Pierce two holes ⅛" from top and bottom edges using an awl and mallet. Thread cording through holes as shown in **Diagram 3**.

5. Close center section and place between front and back covers as shown in **Diagram 4**. Open to middle of front and back sections and place face down on work surface. Pierce two holes through all sections ⅜" from top and bottom edges. Thread heavyweight thread through holes and tightly tie into a knot.

6. Close sections into a book. Tie cording into a knot at spine. Knot ends together as shown in **Diagram 5**. Decorate cover as desired.

receipt book binding

materials
Cardboard, lightweight : 3" x 3¼", 3¼" x 8½" (2)
Cording
Paper: 6¼" x 15" medium weight text (30)
Thread: heavyweight

general supplies & tools
Adhesive
Awl
Craft knife
Mallet
Needle
Ruler: metal edge

instructions
1. Fold papers in half lengthwise. Make three stacks of ten papers. Fold each stack in half, short end to short end, and crease fold as shown in **Diagram 1**.

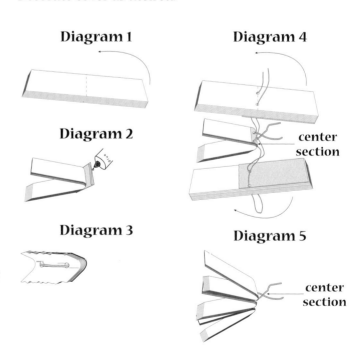

Diagram 1

Diagram 2

Diagram 3

Diagram 4

center section

Diagram 5

center section

3. Trim one sheet of paper ⅜" larger than cardboard. Thin adhesive with water 1:1 and brush onto paper. Center and adhere outside cover to paper. Turn book over and gently smooth paper, wrapping excess paper to inside of cover.

4. Trim one sheet of paper ¼" smaller than inside cover. Brush adhesive onto paper. Adhere paper to inside of cover to cover raw edges.

5. Trim remaining papers ⅛" smaller than cover. Stack papers and lay on opened inside cover.

6. Pierce binding holes in center of spine using an awl beginning and ending 1" from top and bottom edges.

7. Thread cording through needle and sew a double running stitch down and back up through binding holes as shown in **Diagram 1 (A–E)**. Twist end of cording around top inside stitch and secure with

flower paper binding

materials
Cardboard: heavy-weight
Cording: ⅛"-wide coordinating
Paper: handmade flower (8)

general supplies & tools
Adhesive
Awl
Craft knife
Needle: large-eyed
Ruler: metal edge

instructions
1. Trim cardboard to desired book size using a craft knife and ruler.

2. Mark desired width for spine on inside cover and score.

Diagram 1

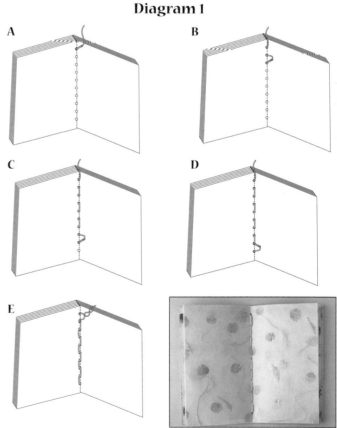

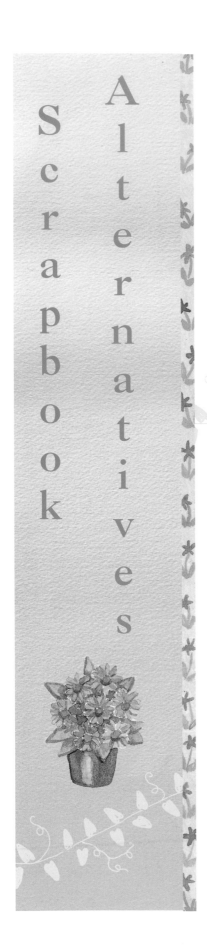

japanese cookbook

materials
Book with blank pages: 9" x 5¾"
Cardstock: 2 sheets
Chop sticks: 1 set
Die-cut: decorative, large

general supplies & tools
Glue: craft
Pen: fine-point, permanent

instructions
1. Adhere cardstock to front and back covers of book, wrapping edges to inside covers.

2. Glue decorative die-cut on front of book.

3. Refer to **"Recipe" Pattern** at right. Using pen, write Japanese characters on front of book, or substitute words in the language of the country the food originates from.

4. Glue chopsticks onto front of book.

"Recipe" Pattern

お料理の本

treasure box

materials

Acrylic paint: coordinating
Buttons: silver orb, 1⅛"-wide (4)
Cardstock: coordinating
Cigar box: 7" x 8½"
Greeting cards: 4–5
Oil pastel crayons: coordinating (2)
Photographs: 1–2
Stickers

general supplies & tools

Acrylic gesso
Acrylic spray sealer
Craft knife
Glue: craft; industrial-strength
Markers: medium-point, permanent (2)
Paintbrush
Paper towels
Pencil
Plastic wrap
Toothbrush

instructions

1. Apply acrylic gesso to inside and outside of box.

2. Using acrylic paint, basecoat outside of box.

3. Using a square piece of plastic wrap crumpled into a ball, dip into acrylic paint and wipe excess onto paper towel. Randomly sponge onto top and sides of box.

4. Using toothbrush and acrylic paint, splatter top and sides of box.

5. Refer to **Diamond Pattern**. Using cardstock and craft knife, cut out pattern.

6. Using diamond pattern and oil pastel crayons, draw diamonds onto all four sides of box. Brush off excess oil pastel.

7. Using marker, draw lines around diamond patterns. Repeat process with different color marker.

8. Arrange greeting cards, photographs, and stickers as desired onto box. Using pencil, trace around each, then remove. Apply thin layer of craft glue to back side of cards and photographs. Reposition onto cigar box lid. Attach stickers as desired. Spray box with sealer.

9. Using industrial-strength glue, position and glue buttons to bottom corners of box.

Diamond Pattern

A box decorated and filled with tea and pastry recipes and tea party pictures is a sweet bridal shower gift!

special awards

Clip newspaper articles pertaining to school events (or use programs from school plays, school bulletins, or award certificates) and create a collage. Copy collage at a copy center. Mount photos on copy as desired.

Devery Ferrin

DESERET NEWS 10

STANDARD EXAMINER FUNDRAISER RACE 5 K

ST. GEORGE MARATHON 1993 10TH PLACE

ST. GEORGE MARATHON
October 2, 1993
Marathon Foto

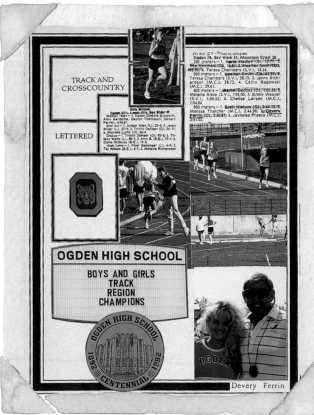

Devery Ferrin

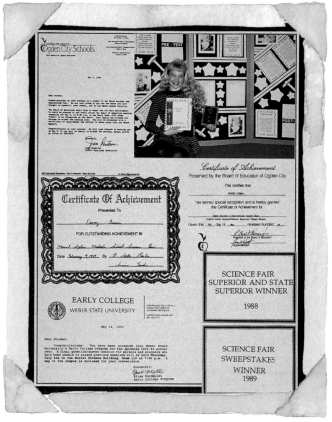

Certificate of Achievement
Presented by the Board of Education of Ogden City

SCIENCE FAIR SUPERIOR AND STATE SUPERIOR WINNER 1988

SCIENCE FAIR SWEEPSTAKES WINNER 1989

Sara Vanessa Buehler

PRESIDENT'S
LEADERSHIP
COUNCIL
SCHOLARSHIP

LEADERSHIP

Senior Officers

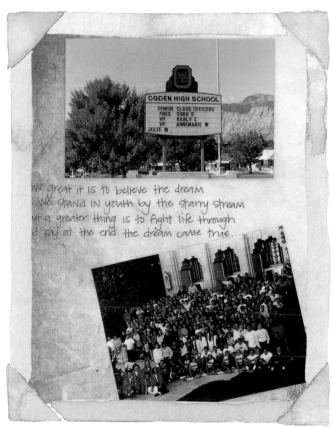

OGDEN HIGH SCHOOL

how great it is to believe the dream
as we stand in youth by the starry stream
but a greater thing is to fight life through
and say at the end the dream came true.

memories shadow box

materials

Acrylic paint: coordinating (2)

Brads: ¾" metal (4)

Embellishments: framed photograph;
    greeting cards; dried flowers; doily;
    buttons; charms

Glass: ⅛" thick, 12¾" x 10½"

Hinges: (2)

Magnets: ¾" diameter (2)

Paper: wrapping

Wood: ¼"-thick plywood, 13" x 12½";
    ¾"-thick plywood, 9" x 18"; block, 1" square

general supplies & tools

Acrylic gesso

Clamps: large (4)

Chisel

Crackle medium

Glue: découpage, antique finish; hot glue gun
    and glue sticks; wood

Paintbrush

Pencil

Router

Sandpaper: medium-grit

Scissors: craft

Stain: fruitwood

Table saw

Instructions

1. Using table saw, cut two 1⅛" x 12½" pieces for shadow box sides, two 1⅛" x 10" pieces for shadow box sides, and one 11" x 12½" piece for shadow box back, from ¼" plywood.

2. Using clamps and wood glue, glue sides and back of shadow box together. Check to make certain all pieces are squared. Let glue dry thoroughly. Using medium-grit sandpaper, sand all edges of box.

3. Cut two 2" x 16" and two 2" x 14" pieces from ¾" plywood for frame. Miter corners at 45° angle.

4. Using clamps and wood glue, glue frame pieces together. Check to make certain all pieces are squared.

5. Using router, cut ¼"-wide x ⁵⁄₁₆"-deep groove around inside edge of frame for glass placement. Using a chisel, remove round corners.

6. Using craft scissors, cut wrapping paper to fit inside shadow box back.

7. Apply acrylic gesso to inside of shadow box and frame.

8. Using acrylic paint, basecoat inside of shadow box and frame.

9. Apply crackle medium to frame. Using acrylic paint, apply topcoat, in contrasting color, to frame.

10. Apply stain to inside of shadow box and frame.

11. Sand all edges of frame for antique appearance.

12. Using antique finish découpage glue, découpage wrapping paper to inside shadow box back.

13. Attach shadow box to frame with hinges.

14. Place and secure glass in frame using one brad in each corner of frame.

15. Using wood glue, glue one magnet to frame. Glue other magnet to 1" square wood block. Glue block to box side with magnet side up, touching magnet on frame.

16. Using craft scissors, cut front from greeting card. Trim card as desired. Using hot glue gun and glue stick, embellish shadow box as desired.

Pictured at right is a variation on the theme of this shadow box. Gather momentos from a special outing and save them in a green shadow box.

framed box

materials
Brads: ¾" metal (8–12)
Fabric: low pile velvet, 13"–19" square (2)
Frame, with 10⅛" x 12⅛" opening for lid
Glass: ⅛" thick single strength, to fit frame
Grosgrain ribbon: coordinating 2"
Mat board: 13"–18" square
Wood moulding: similar to, but wider than
    frame moulding

general supplies & tools
Craft knife
Glue: craft, industrial strength epoxy, wood
Hammer
Ruler
Saw
Scissors: craft
Spray adhesive
Stain: to match frame
Staple gun and staples

Instructions
1. Using ruler, measure outside edges of frame to be used for a lid to determine box size. Add a little to each box side measurement to allow for mitered corners, depending on moulding shape. (The rabbet of the moulding must be slightly larger than outside edges of

the lid so the lid will sit in the rabbet of the box moulding.)

2. Using these measurements and allowing for miters, cut the moulding into four pieces of the correct length using saw. Miter corners at 45° angle. Cut the moulding so that the rabbet edge is upright and the front face of the moulding is the side of the box.

3. Using wood glue, secure moulding pieces together to form box sides. Strengthen as needed with brads.

4. Stain both sides of moulding to finish box sides. Let dry.

5. Cut mat board to same dimension as outside edges of box sides. Cut one piece of fabric to dimension of mat board. Adhere to one side of mat board using spray adhesive. Secure edges using a fine bead of craft glue. Cut remaining piece of fabric one inch larger on all sides than dimensions of mat board. Place fabric face down on a flat surface. Coat plain side of mat board with spray adhesive. Center mat board with sprayed side down on larger piece of fabric. Wrap and secure fabric edges to previously covered side of mat board using a fine bead of craft glue.

6. Staple covered mat board to bottom edges of box sides with raw edges of fabric meeting the wood.

7. Position frame face down on a flat surface. Run a very fine continuous bead of industrial strength epoxy along rabbet. Place glass in frame, forming a lid. Allow epoxy to dry.

8. Fold grograin ribbon in half and secure ends together with craft glue. Center and glue raw ends of ribbon to inside edge of one short side of lid so ribbon protrudes from lid for a handle.

9. Place lid to rest in rabbet of moulding box.

flower girl

materials
Paper: handmade floral
Pressed dried flowers and leaves
Ribbon: ⅛"-wide coordinating (3)

general supplies & tools
Adhesive
Craft knife

instructions
1. Carefully peel up small floral pieces in handmade paper using a craft knife.

2. Slip photograph under floral pieces and adhere to paper. Adhere floral pieces to photograph.

3. Hold ribbons together as one and tie into a bow around dried flowers and leaves. Adhere flowers to paper. Frame as desired.

between each. Use a torn sheet of paper as stencil and deepest color of paint to create ragged edge sponging effect. Stamp over sponging using deepest color of paint and three or four different rubber stamps. Draw details with fine line metallic marker. Punch holes along sealed side of envelope to match binder.

stamped envelope

Turn a manilla envelope into a scrapbook page that can also hold loose phototgraphs. Choose three colors of acrylic paint. Sponge on each color separately, drying

designed by Pauline Locke

Chapter 4:
Family Scrapbooking Fun

The scrapbook page ideas in this chapter are ideal for children and their creativity.

Punches, torn edges, and school pictures, along with lots of art supplies is the way to involve the younger family members.

Cut out lots of different-sized circles, rectangles, squares, squiggles, strips, and triangles from various bright-colored scraps. This gives everyone a variety of choices. If a white background is used, the possibilities for color combinations are unlimited. Glue the white card stock onto a bright background for a splash of color.

● White and yellow card stock for background:
　1. Cut white card stock smaller than yellow and glue onto yellow.

Theme page idea: Take photos of the children while they are "collaging." Have them make extra collaged pages without photos so that you can place new photos of each child on their very own page.

● Circle template • Bright-colored solid and patterned paper scraps:
　1. Cut out a variety of shapes.
　2. Trace several circles and cut out.
　3. Glue shapes and circles onto background in collage, reserving a few to overlap onto photos.

● Photos:
　1. Crop photos as desired and glue photos onto background.

● Green lowercase sticker lettering:
　1. Place lettering on individual paper shapes and glue shapes onto background.

SCRAPBOOK PARTY WITH DADDY

This page will be priceless because of dad's involvement. It will work best with a variety of supplies, such as colored papers and stickers. These are the types of supplies that dad and the children can easily use.

★ White card stock (2) for backgrounds
  • Removable tape:
  1. Lay card stock side by side and tape together on the back side.

★ ⅛"-wide bright-colored strip stickers:
  1. Place one sticker ¼" from edges of backgrounds.

★ Bright-colored solid papers:

1. Cut strips of paper in varying widths and glue onto backgrounds. O*ption: Cut curvy edge on one side of strip for variation.*

★ Circle and oval templates • Photo-safe pencil • Photos:

1. Trace circles and ovals onto some photos and crop.
2. Crop remaining photos as squares, rectangles, and vignettes.
3. Glue photos onto background.

★ Black, uppercase sticker lettering

• Bright-colored circle stickers:

1. Place lettering on background.
2. Place stickers on background as desired.
3. Remove tape from background and cut down center between pages, separating any art that is glued onto both backgrounds.

Tip: Use photos whose subject matter is "dad with the children" for this project.

Theme page idea: Take photos of the children and dad doing scrapbook pages. This will make a great project for the next time dad and the children make scrap-book pages together.

WE LOVE TO DO ART PROJECTS AT GRANDMA'S

Theme page idea: Take photos of the children while they are being creative and use the same supplies on the new scrapbook page that they were using in the photos.

Young children love any involvement with the adults in their family. The key to doing this page with children is the inclusion of many supplies, such as origami folding paper in great colors, watercolored tissue, colored dots, and artwork stickers. Children are creative and will do amazing projects with provided art supplies.

▲ Pink card stock for background

▲ Photos:
   1. Crop photos as desired.

▲ Decorative-edged scissors • Origami and tissue papers:
   1. Cut paper slightly larger than photos. *Option: Tear one edge and cut remaining edges.*
   2. Glue photos onto paper. *Note: If papers are not acid-free, they may need to be sprayed with buffering spray before gluing photos.*
   3. Glue photos and paper onto background.

▲ Colorful markers • Stickers • Colored papers:
   1. Decorate background as desired.

▲ Black uppercase sticker lettering:
   1. Place lettering on page.

WE LOVE TO DO ART PROJECTS AT GRANDMAS

BY Camille

Tip: Allowing the words to be spread throughout the page adds interest and makes excellent use of space.

Connor

The rainbow background is an artwork project that children will enjoy working on. Use current photos of the child and have them write their name and age on a piece of paper to include on the scrapbook page.

■ White card stock (2) for background •
Removable tape:
  1. Lay card stock side by side and tape together on the back side.

▢ ⅛"-wide blue and yellow strip stickers:
  1. Cut strips at a diagonal ½" to 1" shorter than length of page.
  2. Place strips as shown on scrapbook pages.

■ Solid paper scraps in rainbow colors:
  1. Cut ½" squares in a variety of colors and glue onto backgrounds, creating a mosaic rainbow. *Option: If* *younger children are working on this page, you may want to cut the squares in advance.*

■ White card stock • Blue marker:
  1. Have child write name and age.
  2. Cut out name and age.

■ Photos:
   1. Crop photos as desired.

■ Blue/white polka-dot, blue/white stripe, and yellow/blue geometric patterned papers:
   1. Cut papers in various shapes for matting photos, name, and age.
   2. Glue photos, name, and age onto shapes. *Option: Double- and triple-mat some of the photos.*
   3. Glue photos, name, and age onto background.
   4. Remove tape from background and cut down center between pages, separating any art that is glued onto both backgrounds.

Theme page idea: Create mosaic theme designs that would go along with a photo, such as an ocean made from cloud and blue shades of papers, for a family beach trip.

Tip:
When doing a two-page layout, remember not to place any important elements that will be cut and separated, such as the middle of your subject's face.

KEVIN, MATTHEW, AND DADDY

This is a quick and simple, yet attractive page, using the leaf patterned paper for the background. There is no need for a punch or additional papers for this page, making it quite economical.

✦ Autumn leaf

patterned paper for background

✦ Circle and oval templates
  • Photo-safe pencil
  • Photos:
    1. Trace circles and ovals onto photos and crop.
    2. Glue photos onto background.

✦ Yellow uppercase sticker lettering:
    1. Place lettering on background.

Tip: Crop photos large and use two to three so that background can be seen and the page will not be too busy.

so many choices

This is an easy page to make and an excellent opportunity to use some of your paper scraps. Children will want to help make this page. They love to tear the paper pieces and punch out the pumpkins and leaves.

▼ Pale gold card stock for background

▼ Green plaid and green with dots patterned papers:
  1. Tear out six to seven irregular shapes from papers.
  2. Tear one long strip from green with dots paper.
  3. Glue strip onto bottom of background.

▼ Photos:
  1. Crop photos as desired.

▼ Metallic gold paper:
  1. Cut paper slightly larger than photos and glue photos onto paper.
  2. Glue photos and remaining torn shapes onto background. *Option: Tuck some edges of torn shapes under photos, and allow other edges to overlap onto photos.*

▼ Apple punch • Dk. gold, orange, and

peach paper scraps:
  1. Punch seventeen apples for pumpkins and glue onto background.

▼ Small oak leaf punch • Green paper:
  1. Punch seven leaves and glue onto background.

▼ Green lowercase sticker lettering:
  1. Place lettering on page.

Spencer's Artwork

BY Spencer
age 9

Children love to draw when they are young. Give them supplies and let them draw to their heart's content. Remember to have them sign their "masterpieces" and write their age on a separate piece of card stock. Their writing and how old they were at the time will be looked upon as a treasure when they are older.

- Red and white card stock for background:
  1. Cut white card stock smaller than red card stock. Glue white card stock onto red card stock.

- Bright-colored markers • White card stock:
  1. Have child create artwork; write name and age.
  2. Cut around artwork, name, and age. Glue onto background.

- Photos • Photo-safe pencil • Oval template:
  1. Trace an oval onto one photo and crop.
  2. Crop remaining photos in squares and rectangles.

- Green leaf and yellow/white checkered patterned papers:
  1. Cut leaf paper slightly larger than photos and glue photos onto paper.
  2. Cut checkered paper ⅜" larger than name and age. Glue name and age onto paper.
  3. Glue photos and name onto background. *Option: A photo could be double-matted with checkered paper to add interest.*

- Rainbow and various-sized iridescent dot stickers:
  1. Place stickers on background as desired.

A tie-dyed style background, music and brightly patterned papers, sticker lettering, and gold stars show off this budding musician following in grandpa's footsteps.

OFF TO SCHOOL!

Maternelle "Roule"

Kevin Age 3

Neuilly-sur-Seine, FR

OFF TO SCHOOL

Going off to school is certainly a day to remember, along with a backpack that weighs almost as much as the child. This is a good layout if you are short on time and it may be used for a variety of subjects.

✎ Alphabet patterned paper for background

✎ Photo:
  1. Crop photo as desired.

✎ "Off To School" patterned paper:
  1. Cut out title.

✎ Corner punch • Green and yellow paper:
  1. Cut green paper ¾" larger than photo and punch corners.
  2. Cut green paper ¼" larger than "Off To School." Glue "Off To School" onto green paper.
  3. Cut yellow paper ¼" larger than photo. Glue photo onto yellow paper and double-mat onto green paper.

✎ Black marker • School supplies, ¼"-wide alphabet strip and theme book strip stickers:
  1. Place alphabet strip down right side of background.
  2. Place school supplies stickers around photo. Glue photo and "Off To School" onto background.
  3. Write child's name, age, school, and city on theme book strip and place on background.

Tip: Having the child write their name and age allows
them to see their development over the years.

Each school year, children bring home packets containing school pictures. This is a great opportunity to use one photo for each year and place it in a scrapbook of achievements. Down the road, they will look through this book and cherish the chronicled years.

Tip: You will want the child's face and personality to be the emphasis here. When selecting the background, choose a subdued and rich color. Take a close look at the photo and see what the dominant colors are. We chose a pine green in a deep rich tone. The brick color was selected because it is subdued in tone. Forest green and gold were selected to use with the pine green and brick colors, and to add additional interest.

★ Pine green card stock for background

★ Individual school photo:
   1. Crop off white border from photo.

★ ⅛"- wide metallic gold strip stickers:
   1. Cut two strips at an angle with one slightly longer than the other.
   2. Place strips down right side of background.

★ Black marker • Brick-colored paper:
   1. Have child write name and age on paper. Cut out name and age.
   2. Cut brick paper ¼" larger than photo and glue photo to paper.

★ Decorative-edged scissors • Forest green card stock • Metallic gold medium-point pen:
   1. Cut card stock ¼" larger than brick-colored paper and photo.
   2. Randomly dot card stock and glue to background.

★ Metallic gold paper:
   1. Cut paper slightly larger than name and age. Glue name and age onto paper.
   2. Glue name, age, and photo onto background.

Quick and Economical

When time and money are limited, here are some ideas that will allow you to create priceless scrapbook pages.

Although you may have different subject matters than those presented, you can adapt any of these pages to your particular theme.

Pride & Joys

You will have photos that need a very special scrapbook page, such as this one of the grandchildren. Look for a dominant color which appears in several places in the photo to make your paper and lettering choices.

◆ Black card stock for background

◆ Photo:
   1. Crop photo as desired.

◆ Black with dots, red/white polka-dot, and red/white striped patterned papers:
   1. Cut black paper ¼" larger than photo and glue photo onto paper.
   2. Cut polka-dot paper larger than black.

   3. Cut striped paper larger than polka-dot.
   4. Glue striped paper, polka-dot paper, and photo onto background as shown on scrapbook page.

◆ Opaque red pen • ⅛"-wide red strip and ⅛"-wide black/white strip stickers
   • Decorative sticker lettering:
   1. Draw a dotted line border around outside of striped paper.
   2. Place strips on background.
   3. Place lettering on background.

TWINKLE TWINKLE LITTLE STAR

Tip:
Instead of purchasing all of the star punch sizes, perhaps you could borrow from friends and loan some of yours to them in exchange.

A nursery rhyme inspired this layout to use a precious baby photo which becomes the "star" on this page. Use a photo of the baby lying peacefully that can be cradled in the moon. This photo was enlarged in order for it to be the right proportion.

★ Purple with stars patterned paper for background

★ Photo:
   1. Vignette photo.

★ Matte metallic silver paper • Moon Pattern:
   1. Enlarge Moon Pattern 200% and photocopy onto white card stock.
   2. Cut out moon and place on silver paper. Trace moon onto paper and cut out. Set scraps aside to use for punching stars.
   3. Glue moon and baby onto background.

★ Large, medium, and small star punches:
   1. Punch stars from silver paper scraps and glue onto background.

★ Opaque metallic silver medium-point pen:
   1. Write baby's name, birth date, birth weight on background.
   2. Add any quotes, such as "Twinkle twinkle little star . . ." under the moon.

Moon Pattern

Enlarge 200%

Annual Cookie Party

When putting together a page such as this, shoot lots of step-by-step action photos during the process, such as mixing the ingredients, baking the cookies, and all the rest of the fun children have right up to licking the bowl! To get all of the steps on the page, some photos were vignetted, which allowed space for the baking stickers. Use your imagination on this type of scrapbook page, since children like to be in the kitchen cooking hot dogs, grilling hamburgers, popping popcorn, making candy, or anything else involving one another and doing something fun.

- Cream card stock for background

- Photos:
    1. Crop photos as desired and glue photos onto background.

- Red/white polka-dot patterned paper:
    1. Cut one 1" strip of paper and glue strip onto top of background.

- Black and blue uppercase sticker lettering:
    1. Place lettering on background, mixing letter colors.

- Baking-themed stickers:
    1. Place stickers on background.

that's what friends are for!

Use a number of photos on this scrapbook page, show some of the background, and note locations on the map. A favorite phrase for this group of friends and the title for this page is "that's what friends are for.

◆ Map patterned paper or color copy of map for background

◆ Photos:
   1. Crop photos as desired. Glue photos onto background, allowing some photos to extend off edge of paper.
   2. Trim off edges that extend beyond background.

◆ Iridescent star stickers:
   1. Place stars on map background to pinpoint places where friends in the photos live.

◆ ⅛"-wide red strip stickers:
   1. Place strips around edge of background.

◆ Green lowercase sticker lettering
   • Red wide-tip marker:
   1. Place lettering on background.
   2. Outline words as shown on scrapbook page.

Tip: If the photos are too small, enlarge them by making color copies.

The Money Pit

This was a fun page to design. The photo was taken for the family's Christmas card, which was sent to family and friends. The photo is triple-matted in different colors to make it stand out. A patterned theme paper with tools was selected because it related to the building of a home. It is one of those quick and easy pages you might be looking to do.

▼ Cinnamon card stock for background

▼ Photo:
1. Crop photo as desired.

▼ Camel, green, and silver papers:
1. Cut camel paper larger than photo and glue photo onto paper.
2. Cut green paper larger than camel paper and double-mat photo onto green paper.
3. Cut silver paper larger than green paper and triple-mat photo onto silver paper.

▼ Tool patterned paper:
1. Cut paper, if necessary, to fit width of background, allowing same size margin on top and bottom of triple-matted photo.

2. Glue paper and photo onto background.

▼ ⅛"-wide metallic copper strip stickers:
1. Place strips as shown on scrapbook page.

▼ Metallic silver uppercase sticker lettering (2 sizes):
1. Place lettering on background.

▼ Paper money and coins stickers:
1. Place stickers on background.

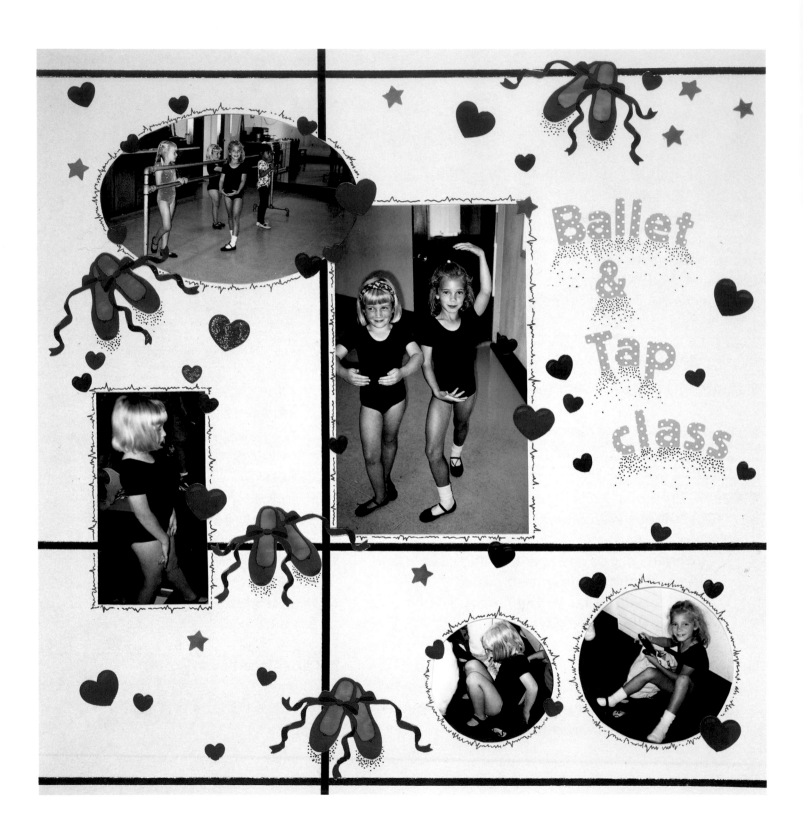

Ballet & Tap Class

If your child has a particular interest or hobby, such as an art class, dancing class, gymnastics, Scouts, 4-H, or other, take a camera to class and start shooting from the beginning of the class to the end. You will have a story photographed in picture form. This makes a great page and a memory your child will never forget.

♥ Pink card stock for background

♥ ⅛"- silver metallic strip stickers:
   1. Place strips on background as shown in scrapbook page.

♥ Circle and oval templates • Photo-safe pencil • Photos:
   1. Trace circles and ovals onto some photos and crop.
   2. Crop remaining photos into rectangles.
   3. Glue photos onto background.

♥ Pink/white polka-dot upper- and lowercase sticker lettering • Iridescent hearts and ballet shoes stickers:
   1. Place lettering, hearts, and ballet shoes on background.

♥ Black medium-point and cranberry fine-point markers:
   1. Draw black dots under letters and shoes to give the hint of a shadow as shown on scrapbook page.
   2. Draw cranberry zigzag border around photos.

IT'S TIME TO HAVE A BABY

Of course, not in the dogs' eyes, since they will definitely slip down the ladder in importance! This is another quick page for a busy family. This page consists of enlarging and color copying a photo, double-matting it, and adding some stickers.

- Dog bone patterned paper for background

- Photo or enlarged color copy:
  1. Crop photo as desired.

- Black and tan papers:
  1. Cut black paper larger than photo and glue photo onto paper.
  2. Cut tan paper larger than black paper and double-mat photo onto paper.
  3. Glue photo onto background.

- Dog accessory stickers:
  1. Place stickers on black paper.

- Black uppercase adhesive lettering:
  1. Place lettering on background.

Napa & Sonoma

If you go into a well-stocked scrapbook store, you will see unbelievable choices of paper colors, not only the solid shades, metallics, and glossies, but also patterned papers of heathers, theme motifs, and much more. A grape-colored solid paper was used for this background since it was fitting to the subject of vineyards.

Tip: Sometimes it is difficult to determine what shade of paper you will want to use with a photo or group of photos. Line up several colors on the table and lay photos from the same grouping on top of each color to see which colors look best with the photos. Keep in mind when you are at the scrapbook store to look for wonderful colors, even the unusual, because at some point in time, you will probably find a need for that special color or pattern purchased six months ago.

✦ Grape card stock for background

✦ Photos:
  1. Crop photos as desired and glue photos onto background.

✦ Decorative-edged scissors • Light plum mulberry patterned paper:
  1. Cut two photo corners for each photo with decorative inside edge as shown on scrapbook page.
2. Glue photo corners onto photos.

✦ Fleur-de-lis punch • Matte metallic gold paper:
  1. Punch nine fleurs-de-lis and glue onto background.

✦ Gold upper- and lowercase sticker lettering:
  1. Place lettering on background.

Napa & Sonoma

234

Christmas Kissing Booth

This is a family Christmas Card and it makes a great page in a scrapbook. Glue the photo onto a background and you have spent little time because it is just about complete with a little extra embellishment. Scrap pieces, such as the matte silver, come in handy so you do not have to buy a whole sheet.

- Red card stock • Red/black plaid patterned paper for background:
  1. Cut plaid paper smaller than card stock and glue onto card stock.

- Matte metallic silver paper:
  1. Cut rectangle from paper and glue rectangle onto background.

- Photo:
  1. Crop photo as desired and glue photo onto plaid paper.

- "Merry Christmas," holly, gift, and kiss stickers:
  1. Place "Merry Christmas" on silver paper.
  2. Place remaining stickers on background.

235

More *for* Less

These pages look like lots of supplies were needed, but, they use simple design techniques and materials and create such wonderful scrapbook pages. The key is to keep the layouts simple and get more out of your scrapbook supplies whether it is in making your own patterns and cut-outs in place of die-cuts or combining stickers that you already have on hand.

helping Daddy

Raking up and then playing in the piles of leaves is a fun activity to do each fall. Dad had as much fun falling in the leaf piles as the boys did. This is a great page for children and dad to make together.

Tip: When cropping photos, determine the most interesting part of the photo, place the template, and trace.

◆ Wood patterned paper for background

◆ Geometric shapes template • Photo-safe pencil • Photos:
　1. Trace geometric shapes onto photos and crop.
　2. Glue photos onto background.

◆ Maple and oak leaf punches • Gold, greens, oranges, tan, and yellow paper scraps:
　1. Punch a variety of leaves and glue onto photos and background.

◆ Green upper- and lowercase sticker lettering:
　1. Place lettering on background.

MOMMIE'S LIL ANGELS RASCALS

Matthew
NO GIRLS!
KEVIN
KIDS ONLY!
daddy's tools
COMICS

Tip: There are so many great stickers, keep an inventory on hand from which to select. The stickers used on this page were from several different manufacturers and worked well together.

Mommie's Li'l Rascals

You will have pictures like this one, which are priceless and do not come along very often. This was the perfect story to try out some unique stickers that had been collected. The boys look like they are thinking about squirting the dog, building a tree house, scaring the cat, playing with snails and jumping frogs, walkie-talkies, flashlights, and whatever else goes with a summer play day.

Tip: Be creative, try weaving stickers in and out or setting them on top of the letters.

Blue card stock for background

◆ Oval template • Photo-safe pencil • Photo:
   1. Trace an oval onto photo and crop.

◆ Oval template • Green, red, and yellow papers:
   1. Cut a green oval slightly larger than photo and glue photo onto oval.
   2. Cut yellow rectangle larger than oval and double-mat photo onto yellow rectangle.
   3. Cut red rectangle larger than yellow and triple-mat photo onto red rectangle.
   4. Glue photo onto background.

◆ Red uppercase sticker lettering:
   1. Place lettering on background.

◆ Miscellaneous stickers:
   1. Place stickers on background.

RACHEL

This is a simple page to make, yet it looks like a lot of time went into it. This page is successful because of the dynamic contrast of color. This child was dressed in bright pink, setting the color theme for the scrapbook page.

Tip: Keep in mind when you are photographing children that when their clothing is bright, it looks like lots of fun is happening.

- Hot pink card stock for background

- Photo:
  1. Crop photo as desired.

- Decorative-edged scissors
  - Black and white card stock
  - Black uppercase sticker lettering:
  1. Cut white card stock slightly larger than photo with decorative edge. Glue photo onto card stock.
  2. Cut white card stock into rectangles with decorative edge, large enough for lettering. Place lettering on card stock.

3. Cut black card stock slightly larger than photo and white card stock. Double-mat photo onto card stock.
4. Cut black card stock slightly larger than letter rectangles and double-mat lettering.
5. Glue photos and lettering onto background.

- ⅛"-wide black strip and music-themed stickers:
  1. Place strips diagonally on upper right corner of background.
  2. Place stickers on background.

Our First Snowfall

This is a "more with less" page. It was done with just a few supplies, and tells a story that a child can recall as a fun day in the snow with friends. Photos were taken of the group as well as the individual children.

✳ Snowflake patterned paper for background

✳ Photos:
   1. Crop photo as desired.

✳ Decorative-edged scissors • Cloud patterned and white papers:
   1. Cut white paper with decorative edge on bottom larger than photos and glue photos onto paper.
   2. Cut blue paper with decorative edge on bottom larger than white paper and double-mat photos onto blue paper. Save scraps for snowflakes.
   3. Glue photos onto background.

Tip: Remember to take individual pictures at group activities. Give yourself as many choices as possible when shooting photos.

✳ ⅛"-wide metallic silver strip stickers:
   1. Place strips across bottom of photos.

✳ Large and small snowflake punches • Cream, silver, and white paper scraps:
   1. Punch a variety of snowflakes and glue onto background.

✳ White uppercase sticker lettering:
   1. Place lettering on background.

There are times when family fun is hard to coordinate and get everyone together for a vacation, camping, or reunions. So, if for no other reason than that, you should be taking the camera along and shooting lots of photos of all those involved and the activities going on. This page is a great layout for any outdoors, woodsy scrapbook page.

▲ Camping patterned paper for background

▲ Photo:
   1. Crop photo as desired.

▲ Brown plaid patterned, brown, lt. green, and med. green papers • Tree Patterns:
   1. Cut two 2¼"-wide strips from plaid paper. Glue strips at an angle onto background paper as shown on scrapbook page. Trim excess paper from background edges.
   2. Cut med. green paper larger than photo and glue photo onto paper.
   3. Cut brown paper larger than green paper and photo, and double-mat photo onto brown paper.
   4. Glue photo onto background.
   5. Enlarge Tree Patterns 200% and photocopy onto card stock for patterns. Cut out trees.
   6. Trace one small and one large tree onto med. green paper and cut out.
   7. Trace one large tree onto lt. green paper and cut out.
   8. Glue trees onto background.

▲ Brown uppercase sticker lettering:
   1. Place lettering on background.

River
Volleyball

Large Tree Pattern

Small Tree Pattern

Enlarge 200%

Living in a city of parks is the perfect excuse to toss the camera into the backpack when going cycling. With a helping hand and the click of a shutter, everyone was in the shot recording a family play day.

Meet Me At The Top

Tip: Consider titling the scrapbook page, using a statement that goes with what is happening in the photo.

- Contemporary orange/gold plaid patterned paper for background

- Vertical view photo:
  1. Crop photo as desired.

- Pale gold parchment paper:
  1. Cut paper larger than photo and glue photo onto paper.
  2. Glue photo onto background.

- Gold and orange papers • White uppercase sticker lettering:
  1. Cut gold paper in rectangles larger than individual letters. Place letters on rectangles.
  2. Cut orange paper larger than gold and double-mat letters onto orange paper. Glue lettering onto background in a tumbling effect.

IRELAND

When you think of Ireland, you automatically think of green. This young college student went to Ireland with friends and has done enough scrapbooking to understand that saving everything makes for a more interesting story. She brought home bus passes, an airplane ticket stub, and receipts from the hotels. The pictures are great, from the sheep's back ends to the rock coming down from above.

◆ Green plaid patterned paper (2) for background • Removable transparent tape:
  1. Lay card stock side by side and tape together on the back side.

◆ Photos:
  1. Crop photos as desired.

◆ Checkered and green/white polka-dot patterned papers • Lt. green parchment paper:
  1. Cut papers larger than photos and glue photos onto papers.

◆ Ticket stubs, receipts, brochures, or other travel mementos:
  1. Glue photos and travel mementos onto backgrounds.

Note: *Allow some of the background pattern to show between pictures.*

◆ Green uppercase sticker lettering • Lt. pink and green parchment papers:
  1. Cut out rectangles larger than lettering from pink parchment. Place lettering on rectangles.
  2. Cut green parchment larger than pink and double-mat lettering onto green parchment. Glue lettering onto background.
  3. Remove tape from backgrounds and cut down center between pages, separating any elements glued onto backgrounds.

EASTER, EASTER, *EASTER*

This holiday scrapbook page has a panoramic photo view across the top of the page which shows the expanse of the crowd waiting for the Easter Egg Hunt. Combine the panoramic photo with six oval-shaped photos and the story is told in pictures.

Tip: Create your own water-color background page.

◆ Pastel watercolor-style paper for background

   Panoramic photos • Photo-safe tape:
   1. Match smaller photos carefully to make one long photo.
   2. Tape photos together on back side.
   3. Crop top and bottom of photos so they are long and narrow.
   4. Glue photos onto background.

Tip: If you do not have a panoramic camera, you may use your regular camera. Stand at a distance from the panoramic view that you wish to photograph. Photograph at the same level, taking three to four shots by moving the camera horizontally, but not vertically.

◆ Oval template • Photo-safe pencil • Photos:
   1. Trace ovals onto photos and crop. Glue photos onto background.

◆ ⅛"-wide pastel strip and bow stickers:
   1. Place strip across top edge of panoramic photo.
   2. Place bow at an angle on strip.
   3. Place strip along bottom edge of background.

   Bunny, duckling, and egg stickers:
   1. Cut one egg in half with jagged edges. Place egg pieces over duckling as if it is hatching.
   2. Place remaining stickers on background.

◆ Gold uppercase sticker lettering:
   1. Place lettering on page.

Theme page idea: Try the panoramic photo idea with other subjects, such as at a soccer or football game, or other gatherings where there are large groups at a distance.

Graduation

Here is another quick and easy page layout which uses few supplies and turns out quite nicely. It is a clean and masculine design, as well as an effective scrapbook page. This layout will work with many different themes.

★ Army green card stock for background

★ Photos:
   1. Crop photos as desired.

★ Graduation patterned and rust papers:
   1. Cut 5¾"-wide strip from graduation paper. Glue strip at an angle onto background and trim excess from edges.
   2. Cut four ⅛"-wide strips from rust paper. Glue strips at an angle onto background as shown on scrapbook page.

★ Beige parchment paper:
   1. Cut parchment ¼" larger than photos and glue photos onto paper.
   2. Glue photos onto background.

★ Graduation cap die-cuts • Graduation stickers:
   1. Place stickers and glue die-cuts onto background.

★ Black uppercase adhesive lettering:
   1. Place lettering on background. *Note: You may want to place year of graduation on background.*

Family
Christmas Card

If you send out photo Christmas cards, a scrapbook is a great way to keep track of them. The photo on this page was cropped on the diagonal as an oval in order to take in more of the sleigh's detail.

Tip: Keep an eye out at scrapbook or copy stores for unusual papers. Watch out year round for unusual seasonal papers, such as Christmas, Easter, birthday, or other.

✦ Red card stock for background

✦ Christmas patterned paper:
  1. Trim around details such as the bow.
  Option: Paper can be cut into two pieces, as was done with this paper. Ribbons were matched up and an attractive backing was created on which to glue photo.

✦ Oval template • Photo-safe pencil
  • Photo:
  1. Trace an oval onto photo and crop. Glue photo onto Christmas paper.

✦ Opaque gold metallic medium-point marker:
  1. Make squiggly motifs around border of background and around photo.
  2. Randomly dot around motifs.
  3. Glue photo and paper onto background.

✦ Metallic gold uppercase sticker lettering
  • Holly stickers:
  1. Place lettering on background.
  2. Place stickers on background.

Odds and Ends

The following scrapbook pages will take you beyond the store-bought supplies look. Many of the materials are of a unique nature. These pages may take a bit more time because of the extra page accents, but even a beginner can make these by following the step-by-step instructions.

Take photos of a child in one of their favorite outfits against a background that complements their clothing. If a child is particularly fond of school, you could use a school theme, complete with stickers and plaids, to suggest a "back to school" look. Play up the single photo by double-matting the photo with solid colors. Letters are placed on apple stickers to further reflect the school theme.

✎ Red/white small plaid patterned paper for background

✎ Red/white large plaid patterned and red papers:
  1. Cut 1¾"-wide strip from plaid paper and glue strip onto left side of background.
  2. Cut 1"-wide strip from red paper and glue strip along center of plaid strip.

✎ Photo:
  1. Crop photo as desired.

✎ Crayon patterned, red, and white papers:

1. Cut white paper ¼" larger than photo and glue photo onto white paper.

2. Cut red paper ¼" larger than white paper and double-mat photo onto red paper.

3. Cut crayon paper ¾" larger than red paper. Glue crayon paper onto the background at an angle. Trim edge even with page if necessary.

4. Glue photo onto crayon paper.

✎ Apple stickers • Black uppercase sticker lettering:

1. Place individual letters on apples.

2. Place apples on background.

✎ Crayon and school-themed stickers:

1. Place stickers on background.

Butterflies Are Fun

Butterflies, bugs, and other creatures fascinate children, which allows for some great photo-taking opportunities. The background paper with the beautiful butterfly border on one side is perfect for this layout. All you will need are a couple of contrasting patterned papers and an extra sheet of butterfly paper.

♥ Butterfly bordered paper for background

♥ Circle and oval templates • Photo-safe pencil • Photos:
1. Trace circle onto one photo and crop.
2. Trace oval onto one photo and crop.
3. Crop remaining photos as desired.

♥ Decorative-edged scissors • Orange patterned and yellow papers:
1. Cut yellow paper slightly larger than circle and oval photos. Glue photo onto paper.
2. Cut orange paper larger than remaining photos with decorative edge on three sides.
3. Cut orange paper slightly larger than circle photo and double-mat photo onto paper.

Silhouetted photos, bright background, fun bug stickers laminated in a cut-out jar, and a loose-weave fabric cut for a butterfly net complete this unforgettable scrapbook page.

♥ Butterfly bordered paper • Sunflower stickers • Decorative sticker lettering:
1. Cut out three butterflies.
2. Glue butterflies and photos onto background.
3. Place lettering and sunflowers on background.

Tulips and Daffodils

The yellow background and a sunny spring day with flowers as far as the eye can see, makes this bright scrapbook page a family treasure. The upper center photo was cropped long and narrow to look like a panoramic photo. Some photos were vignetted, while others were enlarged and color copied to better see facial expressions.

✦ Yellow card stock (2) for background • Removable tape:
   1. Lay card stock side by side and tape together on the back side.

   Decorative-edged scissors • Oval template • Photos • Red paper:
   1. Enlarge and color copy two photos. Trace ovals onto color copies and cut out.
   2. Cut two ovals slightly larger than photos and glue photos onto paper.
   3. Crop one landscape photo with decorative edge on top.
   4. Crop remaining photos as desired.
   5. Glue photos onto backgrounds.

✦ Floral wreath, leaf, and strip stickers:
   1. Place stickers on backgrounds, using some to frame photos.

Green upper- and lowercase sticker lettering:
1. Place lettering on background.
2. Remove tape from backgrounds and cut down center between background pages, separating any art that is glued onto both backgrounds.

✦ Opaque gold metallic medium-point pen (optional):
1. Draw dot designs on backgrounds.

Tip: You can add extra template sizes to your library by tracing an existing template onto a sheet of paper, enlarging it 50% and copying onto card stock. Cut out the ovals, using a craft knife. You can use the openings or the ovals as your templates.

WE ALL HAD A GREAT DAY!

SHARK ENCOUNTER

HARBOR

A Great Day!

Sometimes you have a group of pictures that are not terribly exciting. It may have been an overcast day and the color in the photos are dull, but this is when stickers, lettering, and paper color comes into play, along with a little creativity on your part. Lay out the photos and see if there is a single color which trickles through all the pictures. This will help to determine a pleasant background to play up the pictures. In this case, the theme was determined, the stickers along with the rope detail were added, and a successful scrapbook page was completed.

▼ Aqua card stock for background

▼ Oval template • Photo-safe pencil • Photos:
   1. Trace ovals onto photos and crop.

▼ Decorative-edged scissors • Gold paper:
   1. Cut rectangles larger than two photos with a decorative edge on one edge. Glue photos onto rectangles.
   2. Glue all photos onto background.

▼ Royal blue uppercase sticker lettering
   • Ship-themed stickers:
   1. Place lettering and stickers on background.

▼ White or cream embroidery floss:
   1. Pierce background for rope.
   2. Cut three equal pieces of floss.
   3. Knot one end of floss pieces together.
   4. Thread floss in and out of pierced background, knotting at intervals. Knot remaining end to secure.

264

CELEBRATE

Look through the photos that you have taken to see if there is a great single picture that you can play up with balloons. Maybe it is a special birthday, anniversary, homecoming celebration, or simply a happy photo.

★ Matte silver paper for background

★ Photo:
   1. Crop photo as desired.

★ Metallic red paper:
   1. Cut paper ¼" larger than photo and glue photo onto paper.

★ Decorative-edged scissors • Metallic blue paper:
   1. Cut blue paper ½" larger than red paper, and double-mat photo onto blue paper.

★ Metallic blue, red, and glossy white card stock • Balloon Pattern:
   1. Cut red card stock ½" to ¾" larger than blue paper and photo. Glue red card stock onto background.
   2. Glue photo onto red card stock on background.
   3. Photocopy Balloon Pattern onto white card stock and cut out.
   4. Trace three balloons onto each color of card stock and cut out.

★ Hologram silver stars:
   1. Place stars on background as desired.

★ Self-adhesive foam dots
   • Red and gray embroidery flosses:
   1. Place one side of dot on wrong side of balloons. Place balloons on background as desired.
   2. Cut six pieces of gray floss in varying lengths to fit the placement of the balloons. Glue one end of floss under each balloon. Allow to dry.
   3. Pull ends of balloons together, wrap and knot with red floss. Glue in place.

★ Red upper-case sticker lettering:
   1. Place lettering on background.

Balloon Pattern

265

Cinderella

This scrapbook page includes some items which are not really what you would think of when scrapbooking comes to mind. Fairy tale character postage stamps found their way into the scrapbook supplies. A favorite fairy tale, starring the child, makes an adorable "happily ever after" scrapbook page.

♥ Blue gray card stock and moiré patterned paper for background:
   1. Cut moiré paper smaller than card stock and glue moiré paper onto card stock.

♥ Oval template • Photo-safe pencil • Photo:
   1. Trace an oval onto photo and crop.

♥ Decorative-edged scissors • Lt. blue paper • Theme postage stamps:
   1. Cut oval with decorative edge slightly larger than photo and glue photo onto paper.

2. Cut paper slightly larger than stamps and glue stamps onto paper. *Note: One stamp could be double-matted onto a contrasting color scrap.*
3. Glue photo and stamps onto background.

♥ Silver uppercase sticker lettering:
   1. Place lettering on background.

♥ Hologram makeup and heart stickers:
   1. Place stickers on background.

Happy Valentine's Day

A romantic page where the photo is enhanced by an oval silver mat glued onto a rectangle of black. Place the picture on an angle, add handwritten notes, die-cut hearts, and rose stickers, and a scrapbook page worthy of the Victorian era is created.

Tip: Whether drawing borders, lettering, or decorative motifs, first practice on a separate sheet of paper until you get a feel for what you want to do.

✦ Red moiré patterned paper for background

✦ Oval template • Photo-safe pencil • Photo:
   1. Trace an oval onto photo and crop.

✦ Old letter patterned paper:
   1. Cut paper into separate letter pieces and glue pieces onto background. Save one piece to overlap onto photo.

✦ Black card stock • Matte silver paper:
   1. Cut paper in an oval ⅛" larger than photo and glue photo onto paper.
   2. Cut card stock rectangle larger than photo and double-mat photo onto card stock.

3. Glue photo onto background at an angle. Trim any mat edges that run off background edges.

✦ Die-cut hearts • Silver hearts and Victorian rose stickers:
   1. Cut through left side of white heart.
   2. Link hearts together as shown on scrapbook page and glue onto background.
   3. Place stickers on background.

✦ Black dual-tipped pen • Silver uppercase sticker lettering:
   1. Draw swirl motif on background and place lettering on motif.

PUTTING ON TIGGER

Which was more fun—putting on the costume, face painting, or assembling the scrapbook page? Capturing a night to remember for a memory collection is what you want scrapbooking to be all about. If you achieve this, that is the end goal for a successful scrapbook page.

■ Candy corn on white patterned paper for background

■ Circle and oval templates • Photo-safe pencil • Photos:
   1. Trace a circle onto one photo and crop.
   2. Trace ovals onto some photos and crop.
   3. Crop remaining photos as desired.

■ Black/orange checkered patterned, orange, and yellow papers:
   1. Cut square larger than circle photo from black/orange checkered paper. Glue photo onto paper.
   2. Cut yellow and orange papers slightly larger than remaining photos. Glue photos onto papers. Note: A *wavy edge may be cut around edge for oval photos.*
   3. Glue photos onto background.

■ Orange uppercase sticker lettering • Candy corn patterned and yellow papers:
   1. Cut yellow paper into squares larger than letters. Place letters on squares at angles.
   2. Cut candy corn paper slightly larger than yellow paper. Double-mat yellow paper onto candy corn paper as shown on scrapbook page.
   3. Glue lettering onto background.

■ ⅛"-wide yellow/orange checkered strip stickers:
   1. Place strips on top and bottom of background.

Here is a great theme page to play up the importance of a child's musical endeavors. A page of sheet music cut smaller than the green background and each corner embellished with a decorative corner punch creates a page celebrating the individual.

- Green card stock and music patterned paper for background
  • Decorative corner punch:
  1. Trim paper on an angle smaller than card stock.
  2. Punch corners of paper and glue onto card stock.

- Photo:
  1. Crop photo as desired.

- Decorative-edged scissors
  • Black and tan papers:
  1. Cut tan paper slightly larger than photo and glue photo onto paper.
  2. Cut black paper with a decorative edge larger than tan paper and double-mat photo onto black paper.
  3. Glue photo onto background.

- Decorative-edged scissors • Medium and small heart

punches • Music patterned, black, green, red, and tan paper scraps • Vase Pattern:
  1. Enlarge 200 % and photocopy Vase Pattern onto white card stock and cut out.
  2. Trace Vase Pattern onto music paper; cut out and fold on dotted lines.
  3. Cut tan paper, with a decorative edge on curved end, slightly smaller than folded paper. Insert tan paper inside folded paper.
  4. Cut black paper slightly larger than folded paper and glue onto background.
  5. Punch seven medium and one small heart from red paper.

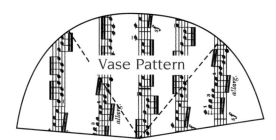

Vase Pattern

Enlarge 200%

6. Glue small heart onto seam of folded paper.

7. Cut out stems for heart flowers and glue onto black vase.

8. Glue medium hearts onto stems and background as shown on scrapbook page.

9. Glue folded paper onto black paper over flower stems.

● Large heart punch • Red paper scraps • Black uppercase sticker lettering:

1. Punch enough hearts for name plus one and glue hearts onto background. *Note: Place two hearts overlapping for one letter.*

2. Place letters on hearts.

Tip: Heart patterns can be made and traced onto red paper if you do not have access to heart punches.

Tip: You may want to have a scrapbook for each child of the family, which could be passed on to them so their spouse and children can see how they spent time as a child.

It's a Boy

This can be a quick page that uses some great paper combinations. The papers consist of stripes, diagonals, and dots, with blue as the dominant color. You can add die-cuts and stickers using the same color combinations for the finishing touch. A combination of photos was used to tell the story.

★ Blue/white polka-dot patterned paper for background

★ Photos:
   1. Crop photos as desired.

★ Blue/yellow/white striped and blue/purple/teal/yellow diagonal striped papers:
   1. Cut papers slightly larger than photos and glue photos onto papers.
   2. Glue photos onto background.

★ ⅛"-wide blue strip and baby-themed stickers:
   1. Place blue strip on bottom of background. Place some of the stickers on center of strip.
   2. Place remainder of stickers on background.

★ "It's A Boy," duck, and diaper pin die-cuts:
   1. Glue die-cuts onto background.

Tip: You may have seen patterned papers in the scrapbooking stores and wonder how to mix and match them. The key is to select patterned papers which have one or more common colors.

I Love the Duck!

You may want to try taking a roll of black-and-white film on occasion and making a scrapbook page that is interesting and different. This was one of those "special shots" which calls for a page of its own, so it was enlarged and color copied to go on this special page.

■ Black card stock and glossy black paper for background:
   1. Cut paper smaller than card stock and glue onto card stock.

■ Oval template • Black-and-white photo:
   1. Enlarge to desired size and color copy photo.
   2. Trace an oval onto color copy and crop.

■ Decorative-edged scissors • Med. gray card stock:
   1. Trace an oval ¼" larger than photo onto card stock and cut out with decorative edge. Glue color copy onto card stock.
   2. Glue color copy and card stock onto background.

■ Decorative-edged scissors • Mickey Mouse punch • Med. gray card stock • Matte silver paper:
   1. Cut 1¼"-wide strip from card stock and paper. Punch out Mickey Mouse every 2". Note: If you turn the paper over and punch out from the wrong side, Mickey will run both directions.
   2. Cut circles and squares around punches with decorative edges.
   3. Glue punches onto background.

■ Metallic silver sticker lettering • Opaque metallic silver medium-point pen:
   1. Place lettering on background.
   2. Draw dots around gray mat as shown on scrapbook page.
   3. Dot around bottom edge of lettering.

At the Cottage

The cottage is so much fun that everyone hates to go home! Remember those extended family traditions by taking lots of photos and making scrapbook pages that show the family members and their activities. This page includes candid and posed shots, along with a landscape shot of the beautiful lake.

▲ Camping motif patterned paper (2) for backgrounds • Removable tape:
  1. Lay card stock side by side and tape together on the back side.

▲ Circle template • Photo-safe pencil • Photos:
  1. Trace a circle onto one photo and crop.
  2. Crop remaining photos as desired.

▲ Blue and green papers:
  1. Cut green paper slightly larger than circle photo and glue photo onto green paper.
  2. Cut blue paper slightly larger than photo and green paper. Double-mat photo onto blue paper.
  3. Cut blue and green papers slightly larger than remaining photos and glue photos onto papers.

  4. Glue photos onto backgrounds.

▲ Moose die-cut:
  1. Glue moose onto background.

▲ Green medium-point marker • Oatmeal-flecked paper • Green upper- and lowercase sticker lettering:
  1. Cut paper into squares larger than lettering and place lettering on squares.
  2. Draw dash and dot border around outside edge of squares. Glue lettering onto backgrounds.
  3. Remove tape from background and cut down center between pages, separating any art that is glued onto both backgrounds.

our new baby

This is a beautiful piece of paper with a busy, overall pattern, which can be difficult to use as a background. When the background is treated with soft, tinted colors and gentle-styled photos, it makes a beautiful page. There is a certain "quietness" here because of the subject and the photos. Soft gold and peach papers surround the photos with some photos double-matted. Lettering and stickers were selected in the same soft, muted baby colors.

◆ Baby-themed patterned paper for background

◆ Oval template • Photo-safe pencil • Photos:
  1. Trace ovals onto two photos and crop.
  2. Crop remaining photos as desired.

◆ Birth announcement or hospital certificates:
  1. Crop as desired and glue onto background.

◆ Soft peach and soft gold papers • Black lowercase sticker lettering:
  1. Trace ovals slightly larger than oval photos and crop. Note: *Oval photos may be double-matted with both colors.*
  2. Cut papers slightly larger than remaining photos for matting. Glue photos onto papers.
  3. Glue photos onto background.
  4. Cut rectangles slightly larger than individual letters from soft gold paper. Place letters on rectangles.
  5. Glue letters onto background.

◆ Baby-themed stickers:
  1. Place stickers on background.

Moving Along

Moving along to more detailed pages does not mean difficult, it means "more" in the way of stickers, pen work, lettering ideas, papers—well, you get the idea!

These pages will take a little more time because they are more detailed, but they will be well worth it.

A large number of children are playing soccer or other sports these days, so why not create a page with photos of your athlete and their team members. Combine the photos and soccer stickers with bright papers for contrast to make a creative page. Use this idea with baseball or softball stickers, or the swim team with fish or other related stickers.

● Blue card stock for background

● Photos:
   1. Crop photos as desired. *Note: One or more photos may be cropped long and narrow like a panoramic shot.*

● Soccer ball patterned and bright yellow papers:
   1. Cut soccer ball paper larger than individual photo and glue photo onto soccer paper.
   2. Cut yellow paper larger than soccer ball paper and photo and double-mat photo onto yellow paper.
   3. Cut yellow strip paper larger than team photo as shown on scrapbook page and frame photo onto yellow paper.
   4. Cut strip of soccer ball paper as shown on scrapbook page.
   5. Cut strip of yellow paper larger than soccer ball paper and glue soccer ball paper on yellow paper.
   6. Glue photos and soccer ball paper onto background.

● Black/white checkered patterned and lime green paper scraps • Black upper case lettering:

  1. Cut checkered paper in squares larger than letters and place letters on paper.

  2. Cut green paper wider than checkered paper and glue checkered paper onto green paper.

3. Glue lettering onto background in tumbled fashion.

● Soccer stickers • Black pen (optional):

  1. Place stickers on background.

Option: Write child's name and age on scrapbook page.

Céline

Usually babies are photographed too far away to see their features and beautiful skin, so try shooting close-ups to create your baby scrapbook page.

✦ Pink parchment paper for background

✦ Oval templates • Photo-safe pencil • Photos:
1. Trace ovals onto some photos and crop.
2. Crop remaining photos as desired.

✦ Gold parchment paper:
1. Cut paper slightly larger than photos and glue photos onto paper.
2. Glue photos onto background.

✦ Floral, initial sticker lettering:
1. Place lettering on page. *Note: Extra letters may be applied to fill up void spaces.*

✦ Opaque silver pen:
1. Draw scroll and dot designs around matted photos and on background.

Summer Memories

These are favorite scrapbook pages, because they hold precious memories. Maybe knowing that this town is where "The Sound of Music" was filmed also has something to do with it. The play money was purchased in a toy store in this city, music-themed paper was cut up, and one of our favorite photos was enlarged.

This layout can be used for any vacation, whether it is in Europe, Asia, Boston, Seattle, or just a few hours away from home. Start with some interesting shots of popular landmarks, always remembering to look for those candid shots that tell the story and keep the memories alive. Watch for unusual items from drug stores, travel agencies, and hotel lobbies you can place on scrapbook pages. It is important to remember that scrapbook pages and the materials placed on them should be of archival quality.

▶ Dk. green card stock for backgrounds
 • Removable tape:
  1. Lay card stock side by side and tape together on the back side.

▶ Music-themed paper:
  1. Cut paper into desired sizes and glue onto backgrounds.

▶ Photos:
  1. Crop photos as desired.

▶ Pale gray marbled paper • Play paper money • Buffering spray:
  1. Spray paper money with buffering spray, if necessary.
  2. Cut paper slightly larger than photos and glue photos onto paper.
  3. Glue photos and paper onto backgrounds.

▶ Coins • Black card stock and gold paper scraps • Decorative-edged scissors • Double-sided tape runner • Plastic page protector:
  1. Cut 2" x 3" rectangle from card stock.
  2. Cut gold paper slightly smaller than card stock with decorative edges and glue onto card stock.
  3. Cut 5" x 7" rectangle from page protector.
  4. Place matted paper and card stock right side down onto center of plastic. Pull edges up tight lengthwise and secure with double-sided tape runner. Fold one end over and secure.

5. Slip coins into front side of packet and secure remaining end in back. Glue coins onto background.

▶ Sticker lettering • Musical note stickers:
  1. Place lettering on background.
  2. Place stickers on background.
  3. Remove tape from background and cut down center between pages, separating any art that is glued onto both backgrounds.

BEACH TRIP

There is something special about taking a picnic lunch and spending the day on the beach. Take lots of photos such as baby on the blanket, in mommy's and daddy's arms, as well as an afternoon "snooze" under the beach umbrella to record the activities of the day.

* Pale aqua card stock (2) for backgrounds:
    1. Lay card stock side by side and tape together on the back side.

* Med. blue and turquoise papers • Wave decorative-edged ruler:
    1. Trace wave edge onto med. blue paper and cut out.
    2. Trace wave edge onto turquoise paper and cut out.
    3. Glue blue paper onto backgrounds, matching edges where pages meet.

* Turquoise upper-case sticker lettering:
    1. Place lettering on backgrounds.

* Blue and aqua medium-point markers:
    1. Draw bubbles coming from the sea animals on backgrounds.
    2. Remove tape from background and cut down center between pages, separating any art that is glued onto both backgrounds.

4. Glue turquoise paper lower than blue paper, matching edges where pages meet.

* Circle and oval templates • Round corner punch • Photo-safe pencil • Photos:
    1. Trace circles and ovals onto some photos and crop.
    2. Crop remaining photos in squares and punch corners.

* Sea horse, fish, dolphin, octopus, and sun die-cuts:
    1. Glue photos and die-cuts onto backgrounds.

Wrigley Field

Adapt this style of layout to any sports event that you or your family attends. The tickets, popcorn, pretzels, and baseball stickers were purchased at the scrapbook store. The bats and giant baseball were cut from patterned papers, while the pennants were cut from white paper.

Option: Cut blue paper larger than one or more photos and glue photos onto paper.

● Large baseball patterned paper:
    1. Cut out baseball.
    2. Glue photos and baseball onto backgrounds.

● Baseball bat patterned and white papers • Baseball, popcorn, pretzel, and ticket stickers • Blue and red medium-point pens:
    1. Cut out baseball bats and glue onto background. *Note: The bats were cut out individually and glued onto the background in a grouping.*
    2. Place stickers on background.
    3. Cut out pennants and glue onto background.
    4. Draw red border around edge of pennant and add blue text in center of pennant.
    5. Remove tape from background and cut down center between pages, separating any art that is glued onto both backgrounds.

● Red/white grid patterned paper for backgrounds • Removable tape:
    1. Lay card stock side by side and tape together on the back side.

● Photos:
    1. Crop photos as desired.

● ¼"-wide blue strip stickers • Blue paper (optional):
    1. Place a strip on one straight edge of each photo.

$1+1=2$ Daniel $_{2+2=4}$

Acknowledge a child's academic achievement with their very own scrapbook page. Even if they do not have any extra special accomplishments, make a page each year to let them feel pride and achievement in learning. This page uses a few apple punches, but relies on an opaque white pen for the decorative elements.

- Black card stock for background

- Circle template • Photo-safe pencil • Photos:
  1. Trace a circle onto one photo and crop.
  2. Crop remaining photos as desired.

- Apple punch • Decorative-edged scissors • Red card stock:
  1. Cut one red card stock circle $\frac{1}{4}$" larger than circle photo. Glue photo onto card stock.
  2. Cut red card stock larger than remaining photos with decorative edges. Glue photos onto card stock.
  3. Punch eight to ten apples from card stock.

- School-themed and black/white gingham papers:
  1. Cut gingham paper square larger than red circle. Double-mat photo onto gingham paper.
  2. Cut gingham paper larger than one photo. Double-mat photo onto paper.
  3. Cut $1\frac{1}{2}$"–2" strip of black/white gingham paper.
  4. Cut strip $\frac{1}{4}$" larger than school-themed paper. Glue school-themed paper onto gingham paper.
  5. Glue paper strip, photos, and apples onto background.

- Pencil • Opaque white pen • White sticker lettering (optional):
  1. Draw white numbers, alphabets, swirls, dots, and borders on background as shown on scrapbook page.
  2. Draw white markings on apples.
  3. Lightly pencil name on background and trace over name with white.
  Note: *Practice name on a separate sheet of paper.*
  Option: *White sticker lettering may be used if you feel uncomfortable writing on the background.*

EASTER EGG

Who can resist a baby or child popping out of an "Easter" egg?
The background paper has a fresh spring-like color of yellow stripes.

◆ Egg Pattern:
   1. Enlarge Egg Pattern 200% and photocopy onto white card stock.
   2. Cut egg from card stock for egg template.
   3. Cut along jagged edges in center of egg for top and bottom eggshell pattern.

   Yellow/white striped patterned paper for background

◆ Photo • Photo-safe pencil:
   1. Place egg template on photo and trace egg. Crop photo and glue onto background.

◆ Lavender paper • Segmented tape
   • Easter grass:
   1. Trace eggshell patterns onto paper and cut out.
   2. Apply tape to back side of bottom eggshell. Line up bottom edge of eggshell with photo edge and press.
   3. Place small amount of Easter grass in eggshell and press, adding extra tape where necessary.
   4. Repeat with top eggshell.

◆ Silver metallic medium-point pen:
   1. Outline jagged edges of eggshells.
   2. Draw decorative border on top and bottom of page.

   EASTER die-cut:
   1. Glue die-cut onto page.

◆ Rabbit punch • Pink paper:
   1. Punch seven rabbits from paper and glue onto background.

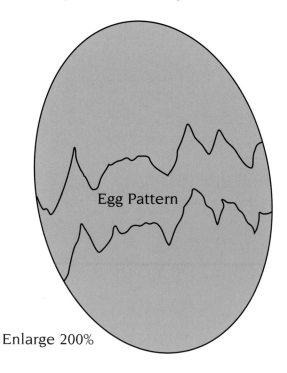

Egg Pattern

Enlarge 200%

294

◆ Diamond punch
  • Cloud patterned paper:
    1. Punch nineteen diamonds from paper and glue onto eggshells.

◆ Circle punch • Pale green paper:
    1. Punch fourteen circles from paper and glue onto eggshells.

◇ Opaque white pen:
    1. Dot an eye on each rabbit.
    2. Draw and color a circle in the center of punched circles.
    3. Dot eggshell with decorative dots.

◆ Butterflies, eggs, and flower stickers:
    1. Place butterflies on die-cut.
    2. Place flowers on egg shells.
    3. Place eggs tumbling down the sides of background.

Tip: When selecting the photo for this page, a child dressed in light pastel or white clothing will look best.

Tip: Tiny flower stickers can be cut from an arch or wreath sticker. Save the greenery for use on another scrapbook page.

Halloween

Holiday theme pages are always fun to do, and each holiday has its own traditional colors and motifs to design around. The vibrancy of colors and the whimsical stickers tell the story of this Halloween party for preschoolers.

★ White card stock (2) for backgrounds:
　　1. Lay card stock side by side and tape together on the back side.

★ Green and yellow medium-point markers:
　　1. Draw two green parallel lines on sides and bottom of backgrounds as shown on scrapbook pages.
　　2. Draw one wavy line through green lines.

★ Circle and oval templates • Photo-safe pencil • Photos:
　　1. Trace circles and ovals onto photos and crop.

★ Bright orange, orange, and yellow papers:
　　1. Cut papers larger than photos and glue photos onto papers.

2. Double-mat two to three photos.
3. Glue photos onto background.

★ "Halloween" die-cut • Halloween theme and star stickers:
   1. Glue die-cut onto background.
   2. Place stickers on backgrounds.

★ Orange and red medium-point markers:
   1. Randomly dot groups of four orange dots with a red dot in the middle on backgrounds.
   2. Remove tape from background and cut down center between pages, separating any art that is glued onto both backgrounds.

Tip: Purchase supplies associated with holidays when you see them, because chances are you will wish you had later on.

Thanksgiving

The annual gathering of Thanksgiving is great fun with lots of turkey and family interaction, especially in the case of the children, whether they are playing with cousins or interacting with the adults. Page layout consists of photos, die-cuts, and pen-drawn designs.

◆ Oatmeal-flecked paper:
  1. Cut paper into rectangle shapes and glue onto background.
  2. Glue photos onto background.

◆ Black fine-point, dk. green medium-point, and brown medium-point markers:
  1. Draw border across top edge of page and around photos as shown on scrapbook page.

◆ Brown and green self-adhesive leaf and acorn die-cuts:
  1. Place leaves and acorns on backgrounds.

◆ Lt. gold card stock (2) for backgrounds:
  1. Lay card stock side by side and tape together on the back side.

◆ Oval template • Photo-safe pencil • Photos:
  1. Trace an oval onto one photo and crop.
  2. Crop remaining photos.

◆ Dk. green sticker lettering • Black fine-tip pen:
  1. Place lettering on background and accent with black dots as shown on scrapbook page.
  2. Remove tape from background and cut down center between pages, separating any art that is glued onto both backgrounds.

First Train Ride

Make scrapbook pages that include "firsts," such as a train ride, pony ride, the slide at the park, or any other firsts. In this case, the train picture is a postcard picked up at the train station.

The photos are surrounded with different shades of green papers, and the backgrounds are pen-dotted. Using one color, such as green, can be very effective when used in a variety of tones and shades.

▼ White card stock (2) for backgrounds
  • Removable tape:
  1. Lay card stock side by side and tape together on the back side.

▼ Circle, oval, and octagon templates
  • Photo-safe pencil
  • Photos:
  1. Trace a circle onto one photo and crop.
  2. Trace an octagon onto one photo and crop.
  3. Trace ovals onto two to three photos and crop.
  4. Crop remaining photos as desired.

▼ Lime green medium-point marker:
   1. Draw single-line border ¼" from background edge.

▼ Leaf green, lt. green, lime green, and med. green papers:
   1. Cut papers larger than photos and glue photos onto papers.
   2. Glue photos onto backgrounds.

▼ Shamrock die-cut
   • Shamrock stickers
   • Coordinating sticker lettering:
   1. Glue die-cuts onto background.
   2. Place stickers and lettering on background.

▼ Green and black medium-point markers:
   1. Decorate backgrounds with lines and dots.
   2. Remove tape from background and cut down center between pages, separating any art that is glued onto both backgrounds.

at the park with cousins

Pole
Patterns

This is a fun page to do because of the opportunity for great photos. The play equipment and children are in bright primary colors and photos were shot close up and at a distance. Photos were taken of the children on the play equipment so that the equipment shapes could be reproduced on the page. Remember to include the sandpile with a sand castle, and of course, a few ladybug and kite stickers.

■ Green card stock (2) for backgrounds • Removable tape:
  1. Lay card stock side by side and tape together on the back side.

■ Circle and oval templates • Photo-safe pencil • Photos:
  1. Trace a circle onto one photo and crop.
  2. Trace ovals onto two photos and crop.
  3. Crop remaining photos as desired.

302

■ Oatmeal-flecked patterned, and blue and yellow papers • Pole, Roof, and Slide Patterns:

1. Cut yellow ovals slightly larger than photos and glue photos onto paper.

2. Cut blue paper with a wavy edge slightly larger than circle photo and glue photo onto blue paper.

3. Enlarge as desired and photocopy Pole patterns on page 302, and Roof and Slide Patterns onto white card stock and cut out.

4. Trace Pole Patterns onto blue paper and cut out.

5. Trace Roof Pattern onto yellow paper and cut out.

6. Glue playground equipment to backgrounds to accommodate cropped photos.

7. Cut oatmeal paper into an irregular shape for sandpile and glue onto background.

8. Glue photos onto background as desired.

■ Yellow lowercase sticker lettering
• Caterpillar, kites, and ladybug stickers:

1. Place sticker lettering on background.

2. Place stickers on background.

3. Remove tape from background and cut down center between pages, separating any art that is glued onto both backgrounds.

303

Best Friends

Since pets are often an important part of the family, it is only natural to make scrapbook pages portraying these special family friends. Various family members and their pet dogs are included on this page along with theme stickers.

♥ Tan card stock for background

♥ Circle and oval templates • Photo-safe pencil • Photos:
 1. Trace circle onto one photo and crop.
 2. Trace oval onto one photo and crop.
 3. Crop remaining photos as desired.

♥ Green/red plaid patterned paper:
 1. Cut paper slightly larger than photos and glue photos onto background.

♥ Dog-themed stickers:
 1. Place stickers on background as desired.

Chapter 5: *Ideas from Brianna*

Brianna Johnson started scrapbooking four years ago when her first child was born. It was such a joy for her to capture moments of life that she never wanted to forget. Instead of keeping a journal, she makes scrapbooks. She has one book for each year of each of her children's lives.

Recently, Brianna started her own professional photography business, which she finds both challenging and rewarding. She is very active and one of her favorite sports is rock climbing.

Brianna, her husband Ryan, and their children Cloe (4), and Gavin (1) all enjoy looking back at their memories again and again because they are recorded in scrapbooks.

• It is important to include some of your own handwritten script in your scrapbooks because it personalizes the memories and your personality shows through.

• Try to write a letter to each of your children each year and put it in the front of their scrapbooks. Write about all that has happened during the past year and what you hope for the next year. It is important to express your feelings about each child. These will be treasured for many years.

• If you have a lot of memorabilia that is hard to put in your scrapbook, but you want it in your book, take a picture of it and make pages from the photographs. Then you can store your memorabilia or throw it away.

• Use extra pictures by cutting out around faces and making a collage page.

• When someone says something humorous, write it down and transfer it onto your pages. It is fun to go back and remember events or situations.

• Create your own backgrounds with scraps of patterned or colored paper.

• It is fun to have young children make a scrapbook page of their own. Give them some extra pictures and supplies and let them be creative. You can put their pages in a book of their "very first scrapbook pages".

• Ribbons are a fun addition to any scrapbook page. Remember that everything in your book does not have to be paper.

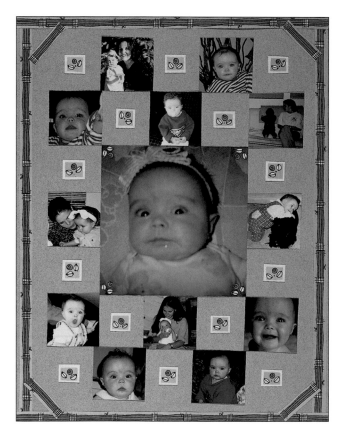

you lift your head
while laying
on your stomach

two months

you laugh
and coo,
especially
at gravity

you smile
when spoken
to

DR. FRANK BROWN

2 MONTH CHECK-UP !!!

YOUR VERY FIRST DOCTOR! HE IS
SUCH A GOOD, GENUINE PERSON.
EACH TIME WE WOULD GO IN FOR
A CHECK UP, HE WOULD SPEND
AT LEAST 15 MINUTES WITH US,
ASKING ME HOW OUR LIVES WERE.
HE ALWAYS HAD GREAT ADVICE
FOR US TOO! WE ARE BLESSED
TO HAVE HIM FOR OUR DOCTOR.

When laying out scrapbook pages, make certain to leave room for journaling. You may think that journaling isn't necessary because you would never forget the event, but remember, your scrapbooks will be passed from generation to generation. The information you supply will be very important to others viewing the pages and is a necessary part of any scrapbook page. Journaling "tells the story". Even a few years can make a difference in what you will remember.

The doctor visits documented here are things a child would never know about if the visits were not recorded. Journaling can be short and simple like the example above left, or a little more detailed as in the examples to the right. Sometimes simple words used to title pages will tell about the subject, as in the above right example of Dr. Frank Brown.

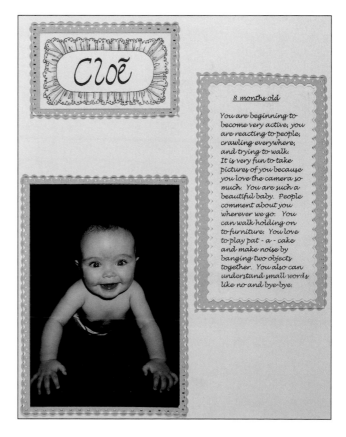

Cloé

8 months old

You are beginning to
become very active, you
are reacting to people,
crawling everywhere,
and trying to walk.
It is very fun to take
pictures of you because
you love the camera so
much. You are such a
beautiful baby. People
comment about you
wherever we go. You
can walk holding on
to furniture. You love
to play pat-a-cake
and make noise by
banging two objects
together. You also can
understand small words
like no and bye-bye.

307

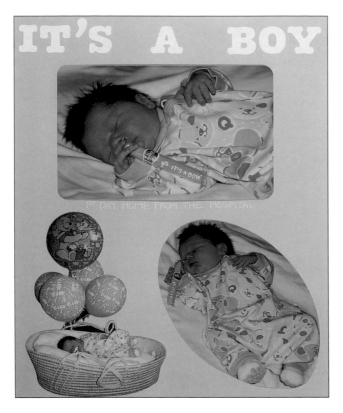

Mix different techniques on a page. Silhouetting and matting are the perfect compliment to each other (above & below).

The jagged edge of the decorative-edged scissors (above) complements the messy hairdo.

Laying out double-page spreads allows you more room to work with a theme. It can also give variety to your album and makes it pleasing to the eye as you flip through.

Double-page spreads can be a continuation as shown above or just two pages with a similar theme as shown on page 15.

MANY TIMES A DANDELION IS A WEED IN THE GREEN, GRASSY SOD. BUT A DANDELION IS A FLOWER DIVINE IN THE HANDS OF A CHILD OF GOD.

24 KARAT CLOÉ

CLOE & UNCLE JOSH · PLAYING IN THE WATER ON A HOT SUMMERS DAY.

To accommodate more than one large photo on a page, consider overlapping or mounting them at angles. Bleeding photos off the page is another idea.

Stationery can be cut apart and used as a frame or as stickers (above).

Crop photos and use them to create fun shapes (below).

Crop photos to match page. The photo (above) is cut straight and complements the pine trees' straight lines.

Rounded corners on the photo (above) add to the soft, curved lines of the cut-out tulips.

Try journaling around cut-out shapes or stickers (above and below).

Just a few well-placed stickers give a little pizzazz to a page (above).

Random stickers are a fun way to accent a theme page (above).

Mats are a great way to tie several pages together (above and below).

316

Stickers can be used in many ways to add variety or a special effect to a page. In the example below stickers are used to accent a photo. The page to the left uses stickers to decorate and draw your eye smoothly from one photograph to the next. The page on the lower left uses a single sticker in conjunction with other cutouts.

On page 318 (upper left) the stickers make a train track border as well as the train and the smoke. This works great with the photos from the park train ride. The page on the upper right uses stickers to help form a border. The double-page spread (below) uses stickers to form the words "Happy Birthday". Stickers can be used to form any word or name for any page. Mix different letter styles in words for a different look. Be creative with stickers, mix-and-match them with punches, mats, stationery, or cutouts.

CLOE AND HER CHRISTMAS CHOO CHOO

HAPPY BIRTHDAY

HAPPY BIRTHDAY

ONE

YEAR

OLD

WHAT A FUN PARTY WE HAD! ALL OF OUR FRIENDS CAME AND WE ATE HOAGIE SANDWICH'S, CHIPS, SALADS AND OF COURSE YOUR BEAR BIRTHDAY CAKE. THERE WAS LOTS OF KIDS SO YOU ALL JUST PLAYED WITH YOUR NEW TOYS & THE BIRTHDAY BALOONS. THE ADULTS JUST ATE AND TALKED FOR HOURS! IT WAS A VERY SPECIAL NIGHT! I THINK WE ALL HAD A GREAT TIME!

I'M ONE

BIRTHDAY PARTY WITH FRIENDS JAN. 21st 1995

CLOE ONE YEAR OLD

Cropping and silhouetting are fun techniques to mix. When cropping, be certain to include things that help tell the story, such as the flags and balloons on these pages.

Remember to use everyday events in your books as well as special events. "Wash day" (above) is a priceless memory.

Be certain to include special pets in your memories. Take pictures of your children with their favorite furry friend (above).

Several snapshots of the same occasion can create a sequential picture (below).

Backgrounds cropped from photos can be cut into other shapes or letters (below).

A child's handprint adds a lovely touch to your page. Paint the hand with acrylic paint, and press it on your page (above).

You can draw attention to a favorite photo by keeping it larger and placing it on a page all its own (above).

MOMMY, DADDY, & CLOÉ
★ JULY 24TH ★
WEBER STATE
FIREWORKS!

HELP PREVENT
FOREST FIRES, NEVER
PLAY WITH MATCHES

SMOKEY

KNOTTSBERRY FARM

SMOKEY & ME

AMIGO AUSTIN

AMIGO HUNTER

AMIGO KADEN

MY THREE AMIGOS

CLOÉ

Keep the focus on your photos with simple backgrounds (below).

Close-up snapshots will help preserve memories of special people (below).

Celebrate special holidays and occasions by remembering to include special friends and extended family members in your photographs and scrapbook pages (above and below).

You loved to go and visit Santa at the mall and tell him all of your wishes that you have for christmas. This year the thing you wanted most of all is was a red jeep and a kitty. Santa asked you if you had been good throughout the year and you said yes, I am always good!

HOLLYDAYS

CHRISTMAS '96
Happy Holidays
GOING TO SEE THE LIGHTS

327

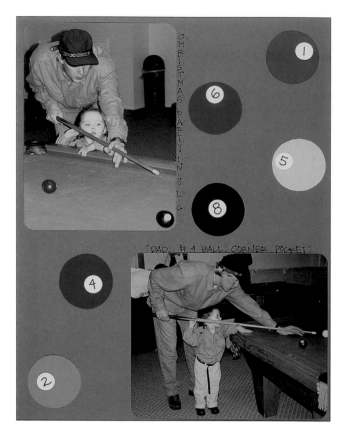

Words as well as photographs can make a unique page. Words can carry special memories about family events (below).

When taking photographs, get close to your subject. Fill the frame so less cropping is necessary (below).

Black and white photographs add variety and interest (above).

Cropping several poses into shapes creates a unique page (below).

Take photos from a variety of angles. The view from baby's feet is a fresh, unique angle (above).

Matting cropped photographs adds a finishing touch (below). Use paper that complements the photos and background.

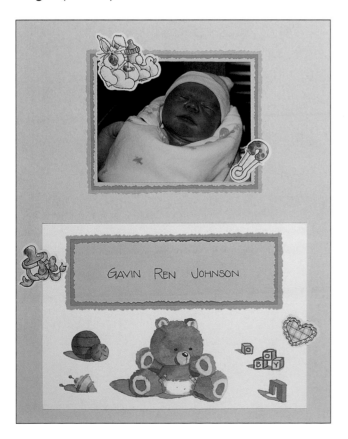

Decorative-edged scissors can add a little spice to a scrapbook page. They can be used to cut mats as well as to crop photos.

For a charming, different effect, try mixing a silhouetted photo with cutouts or stickers (below).

Simple ovals and circles are useful in making faces the focus of attention. Experiment with different sizes (above and below).

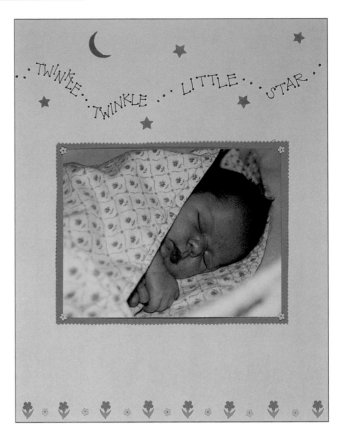

Explore the possibilities of a page where data can be added (below) and you can "track" a child's progress or change.

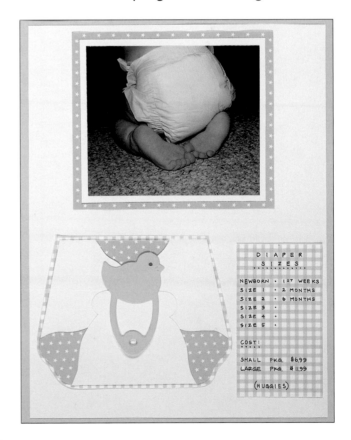

333

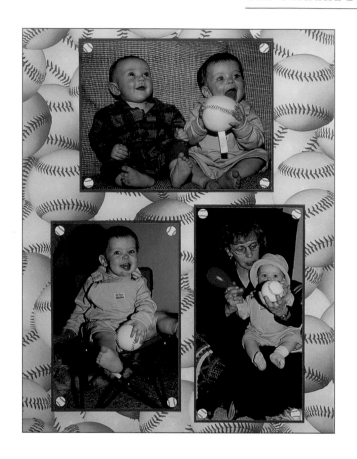

Pages don't need to have dozens of photographs to capture a priceless moment.

Double or triple mats are an easy way to highlight a single photograph (below).

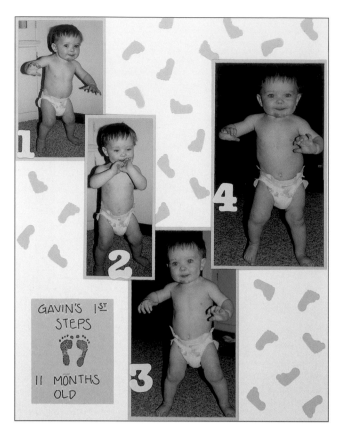

Be certain to have your camera readily available for those once in a lifetime shots (above).

Don't forget to include pages that will bring back fun memories without the use of a photograph (above).

Remember that color is a terrific way to accent your memories. Use black to emphasize the subject (above right), or orange (below) to accent a double-page spread.

Chapter 6: *Ideas from Emily*

A stay-at-home Mom, Emily lives in Ogden, Utah, with her husband and baby boy, Lazarus. She has always enjoyed activities that challenged her creativity, including writing. Growing up in a family of seamstresses, artists, and multitalented people, her life was centered around art.

When Emily was introduced to scrapbooking, it did not take long for her to fall headfirst into a lifelong hobby. She has found a way to express herself and share her memories with family members and friends in the form of photographs and scrapbooks.

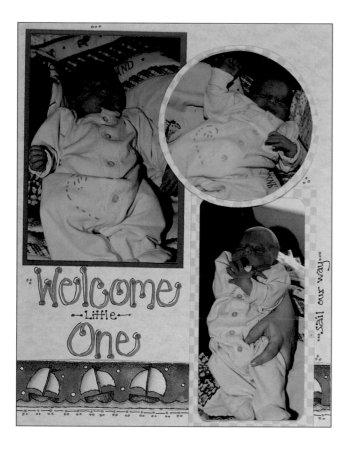

• Patterned papers are quite versatile. They can be used for background papers, making borders, mats for photos or pages, or making cut-out shapes for accents or decorations.

• Cutting out pictures from stationery or patterned papers allows you to make your own stickers.

• Silhouetting a photograph and then using custom-cut objects to go with it or around it will make a unique page.

• Choose mats for photographs that will complement the subject. You may need to try several colors to find just the right one. Double or triple mats will make a photograph really stand out.

Nature provides an endless number of possibilities for fun scrapbook pages. The pea pods (above) could be any vegetable and the stars (below) provide a fun page theme.

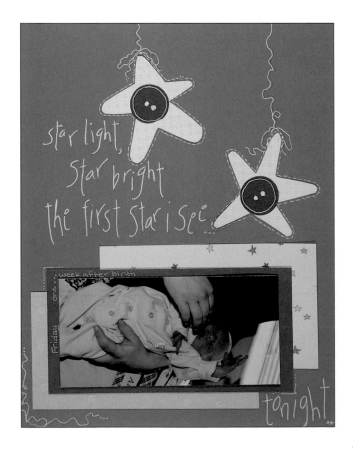

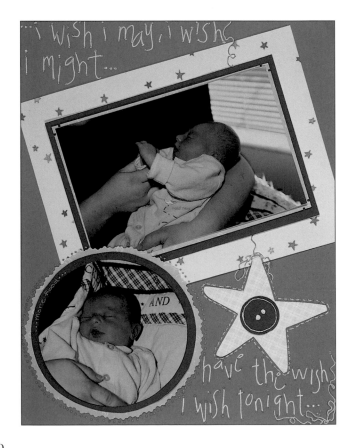

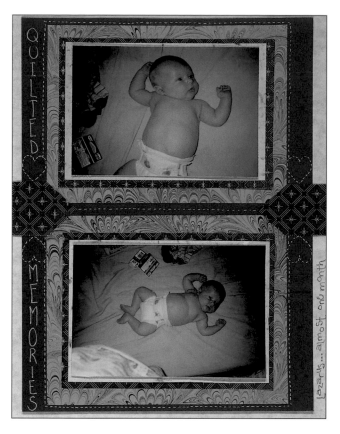

Mats are an inventive way to make a page look quilted (above).

Mats do not have to be cut square. Use other shapes (below) for a unique, look.

Scissors and patterned paper provide all the decoration for these pages.

Mix and match template shapes when cropping photos (below).

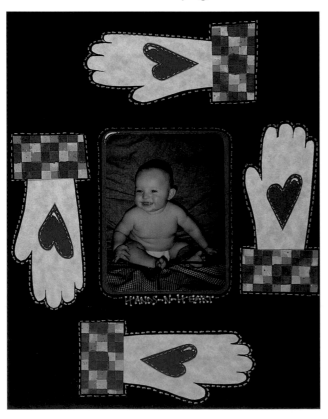

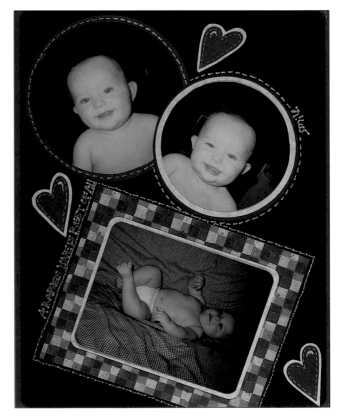

Using colorful patterned paper will add spice and give variety to your pages. The patterned paper on these pages was not only used to mat the photographs, but was also cut into fun shapes to accent and decorate.

Silhouetting a photograph, then adding custom cutouts creates a special effect.

Fine-tipped pens are great tools to add accents, fine lines, and journaling.

Double-page spreads are a fun way to use several photographs of the same occasion or that have a similar theme.

Patterned paper has an unlimited number of possibilities for creating a scrapbook page. Be certain you have a pair of small craft scissors so you can cut details and very small shapes. In the upper-left page, the paper was cut into a pumpkin shape. The photographs were then cropped into the same shape. The same patterned paper worked well for leaves in the adjoining page.

Often, a fun custom shape can be cut from scraps that you already have and eliminates the need to purchase stickers. The horse on the page to the right was cut from scraps of background paper. The mane and saddle were also cut from colored scrap paper. The mat was cut with decorative-edged scissors, which adds a little extra emphasis to the photograph. Save scraps and organize them in colors or patterns for easy reference.

Cutting the mat and cropping the photograph in the same shape as the subject of the photograph makes these pages eye catching and pleasing to look at.

Putting a title on a page (above) will help to bring back memories.

Pens can be used to embellish an entire page (above).

Abstract or geometric shapes are a fun way to add accents to your page (above).

Ants (below) are only one insect that can help embellish the memories of a vacation.

You can use color to emphasize a photograph. Color can also be used to complement the subject of photographs, re-create a season, or convey a feeling or mood.

Bleed a graphic onto two pages (above) for an effective way to tie two pages together.

Use acid-free markers to embellish pages with your personal handwriting (above).

Animals are a favorite to use in decorating scrapbook pages (above). They can be used as an embellishment or as a subject.

Adding a mat or a border is a simple way to finish a page or tie it to another one (below).

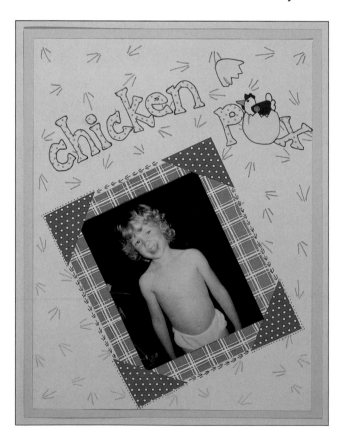

Pastel patterns are mixed and matched in these pages to give them a soft fresh look.

Accent cutouts or create cheerful titles with markers or pens.

A single strip of patterned paper ties the pages together (above).

Hand-cut corners are a unique way to finish off a page (below).

Family events, whether large or small, create memories that should be recorded.

For extra emphasis, try double- or triple-matting photographs with patterned paper.

Including snapshots of your home is a good way to recall memories (above).

Bleeding an element across a background ties a double-page spread together (below).

Decorative-edged scissors were used to cut the foil paper mat (below).

Using a metallic pen for journaling or embellishing adds a little extra flair.

Try different lettering styles to write titles and names (above and below).

The snowflakes (above) have been matted to achieve a fun 3D effect.

To add a little variety, try mounting pictures horizontally on the page (below).

Be creative with lettering. Try a sentence that spans a double-page spread (above).

Holidays provide a great opportunity to be creative. Double-page spreads give you plenty of room to develop the theme and still highlight those special photographs.

Chapter 7: *Ideas from Becky*

Becky Hunsaker started scrapbooking in 1995 after the loss of an infant son. She wanted to do a special book in his memory and also continue the memories with her two other sons. She was instantly hooked and since that times has completed many books, including a 50th anniversary book for her parents, a book for her husband, a grandpa book, a family photo book, and of course, she continues to work on her children's books. She hopes one day to do her own!

Becky works at Memories by Design, where she teaches a Scrapbook Basics class. She likes to create fun, simple pages that do not detract from the photos. She also loves to add simple verses or journal entries to her pages.

Her other hobbies include sewing, reading, bowling, and spending time with her family. She has experienced many emotions through scrapbooking —from the healing of a broken heart to the excitement of learning more about her heritage, to the thrill of hearing the giggles of her boys as they look at their books.

• Find cute graphics from computer clip art programs and print them on different colors of paper. Cut them apart, then stack them together for a layered effect.

• When I back my pictures or use stencil letters, I use the same pattern paper but in different colors.

• Interview your children or a family member and do a page on their answers. For example a "Favorites at Five" page would feature their favorite color, food, friend, toy, etc. This would also work great for a grandparent.

• Make page pockets to store special notes or pictures in. Use a full piece of card stock for the backing. Then cut stationery or another piece of card stock in half and glue it on three sides to the back piece. This creates a pocket to store special things in. I like to do this for school memorabilia, such as notes from teachers, report cards, or hand-drawn pictures.

• It is interesting to find different ways to use punches. Make a face with the circle punch and use a leaf or scallop punch for the hair. Cut the heart punch in half to make leaves for a flower.

• Stickers can be used to make borders. Place stickers across or down to make an edge to a page.

• Make color copies of blankets, scout badges, kids' pictures, etc., to add to pages. These can be used as backgrounds or just cut out to add accents.

Colored paper scraps created the background (above) to match the photograph.

This black-and-white photo is complemented by a handmade paper mat (above).

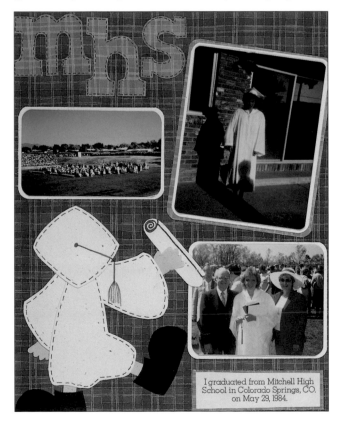

Each of the these photographs were taken at different times, but they complement each other wonderfully in this delightful double-page spread (above).

Stationery can be cut out and used as a border (above), or cut out and used as a picture frame (below).

Die-cuts are a playful way to decorate and come in a variety of shapes to coordinate with any page.

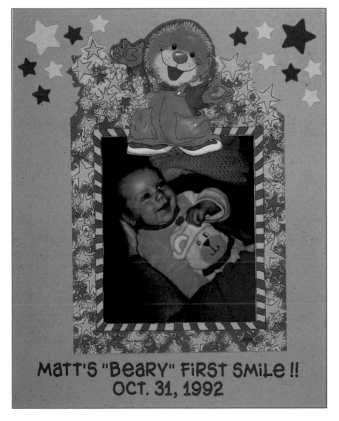

Cropping photos in circles works great with a button theme (above).

Journaling can be done with sticker letters (above) or by hand (below).

In these four examples, background papers were used and journaling was added by hand or printed on a computer.

Some photos won't need a mat (lower left) while others look great with a single (lower right) or double mat (above pages).

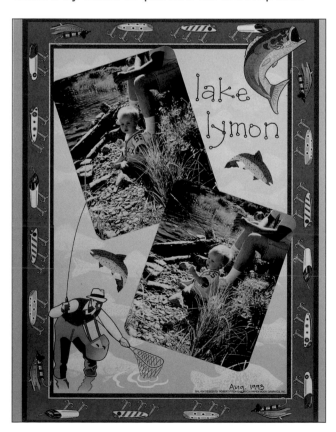

Punches and die-cuts are very versatile. In the page below, balloon die-cuts were used as an accent and the cupcake for journaling. In the lower-right page a leaf punch was used to punch out leaves from the background paper. Small squares of complementary colors were then glued to the background paper to fill in the "holes" with color. Other leaves were punched to embellish the photographs and the rest of the page. The letters were also cut from colored paper and added for the title. To finish off the page, decorative-edged scissors made a perfect edge for the photograph mats.

On the opposite page (upper right), the snowflake punches are placed over and under the photographs. This serves as a snowy mat for the photographs and gives the illusion of snow falling. Think of other creative ways to use punches.

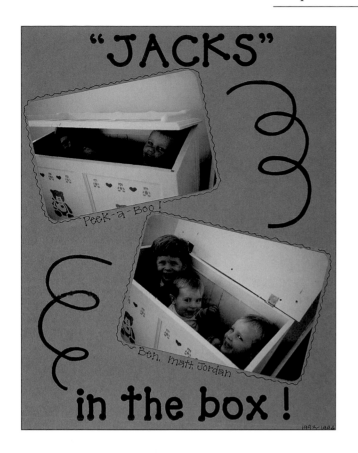

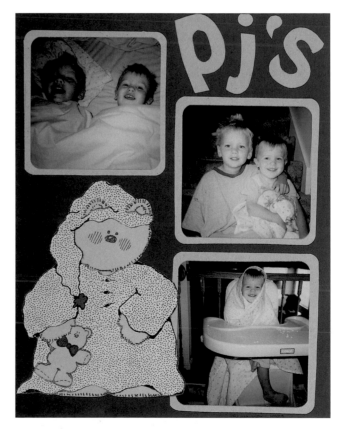

Print-out titles or graphics on a comptuer before adding photographs (above and below).

Try matting titles or letters on your pages. The letters (above) were hand-cut. The caption (below)was printed on the computer.

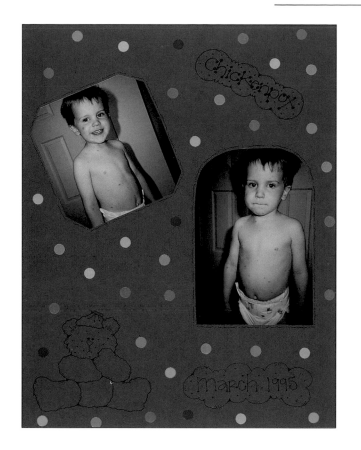

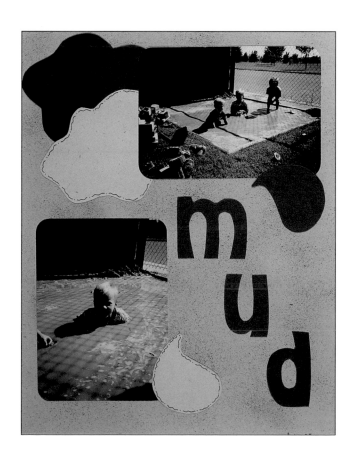

Where is Tom Sawyer when you need him?

Painting the Shed!

HOWDY

PARDNER.

West Yellowstone Grizzly Discovery Center, Aug. 1995

Golf... Golf... Golf... Golf... Golf... Golf... Golf... Golf...

"Nice chip shot"

"FORE!"

PGA here I come

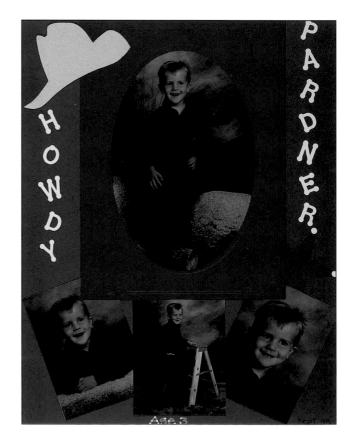

Age 3

Photographs can be adhered to your pages in a number of ways. The method you choose depends on the photograph and the subject.

On the opposite page, the upper-right page was put together with a prepackaged kit. The lower-right page used professional portraits and a precut mat. This page was enhanced by using several poses from the portraits taken, die-cuts, and sticker letters. The upper- and lower-left pages were mounted without mats and the corners were rounded.

The page to the left uses silhouetting to make the subject the focus of the page. This is a terrific technique that requires a small pair of craft scissors or craft knife to make detailed intricate cuts. Below, the photographs have been single-matted. Experiment with different ways to mount your photographs.

When you have several snapshots of a memorable event, make a collage (above).

Items other than photographs give a page sentimental value (below).

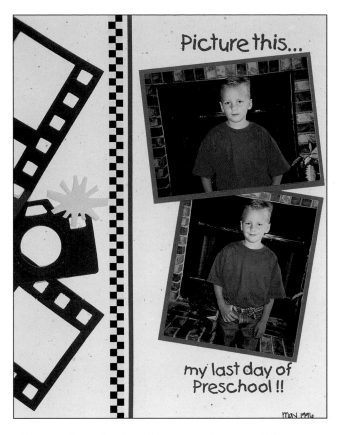

Some photographs include scenery that is important to the event (above), and don't require cropping.

Remember that colors can be used to accentuate a photograph or to complement an entire page.

Countless background papers are available that make putting a page together as easy as adding a title and photographs. They work well for single or double pages.

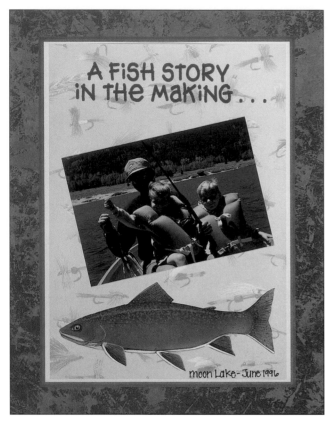

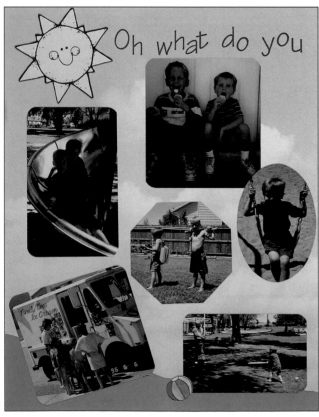

Enhance school pictures with computer printouts and stickers.

Not so great photographs can be an excellent way to preserve family memories.

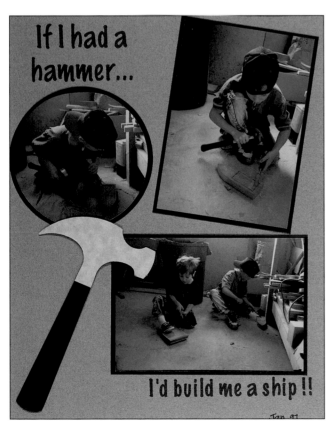

Children are God's way of telling us that tomorrow will be beautiful.

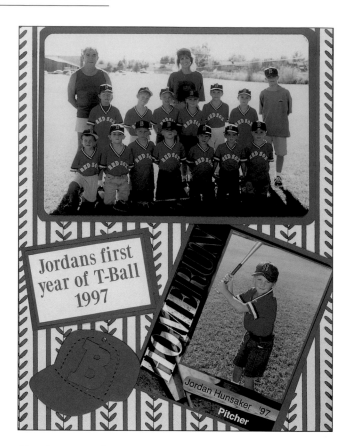

Jordans first year of T-Ball 1997

HOMERUN

Jordan Hunsaker '97
Pitcher

Journaling does not have to be facts or titles. A poem or quote can add sentimental value (above).

Background paper can be used as it comes packaged (above), or cut out and used to decorate a page (below).

It's a sleepover party !!

The gang all got together for a sleepover at the Halversons. We really didn't get much sleep but we sure did have a fun time !!

The Green Dragons

Region 239 AYSO 1997

Coaches: Larry Hunsaker, Darren Smith
Clayton Mabrey, Daniel Moyes, Jordan Hunsaker, Taylor Smith
Trevor Knowlton, Nick Romney, Anthony Bassett, Kyle Harvey
Missing: Kyle Ortega, JayDee Germer, Michael Collins

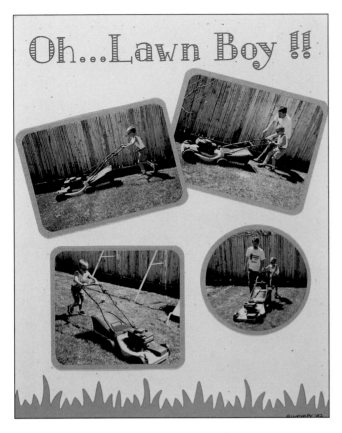

You can add simple lines to die-cuts to strengthen their look (below).

Coloring black-and-white clip art (above) enhances the look of the page.

Notice the variety of ways to create a page about water and swimming.

Print a graphic on several colors, cut them apart, then adhere in layers (below).

Double-page spreads don't have to end with double pages. They can extend onto other pages to include an entire vacation or family event. Use lettering and color to tie them all together.

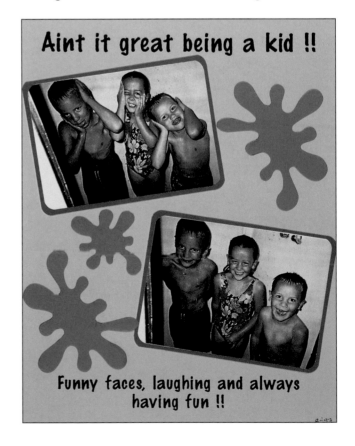

Don't be afraid to overlap graphics with your photographs, it will add interest to your page (above and below).

Computers offer not only access to graphics and artwork but also offer a wide variety of fonts (above and below).

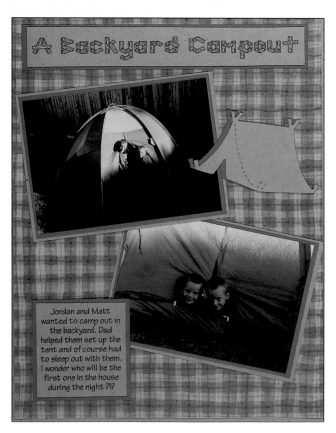

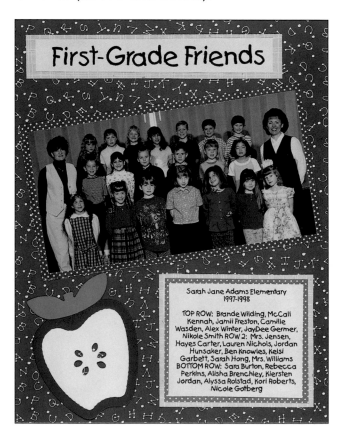

These pages use double and triple mats, punches, stickers, coordinating colors, computer-generated and handwritten lettering. Don't be afraid to mix techniques.

Try tilting or overlapping photographs. This will add interest and variety to your pages. Accents and borders can also overlap as shown in this double-page spread (above).

Torn white paper and a stationery cutout help this page look like the perfect tubing hill (above).

Remember that you can include items in your scrapbook that help others visualize the story (below).

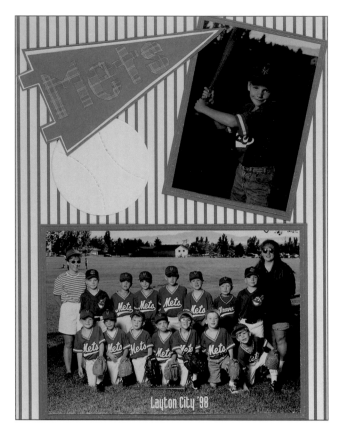

Use patterned papers to give added interest to double or triple mats on a photograph or a double-matted page (below).

Photographs of favorite hobbies as well as special events help to preserve a variety of special memories (above and below).

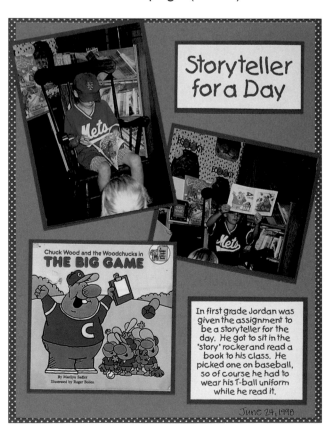

> I know that I am only an instrument in the hands of the Lord, but I'm a stradivarius!

Beary Best Friends
Jordan and Hunter

Add your own personal feelings about the subjects on your page. It will mean a lot to those who see your pages in the future.

Spontaneous shots of siblings become precious keepsakes (above), but don't forget the posed group shots (below).

> Great joy comes in seeing our family enter another generation.

Family Reunion

Using a complementary background with journaling creates a mood (above).

Whenever possible try to leave a date on your page for future reference (below).

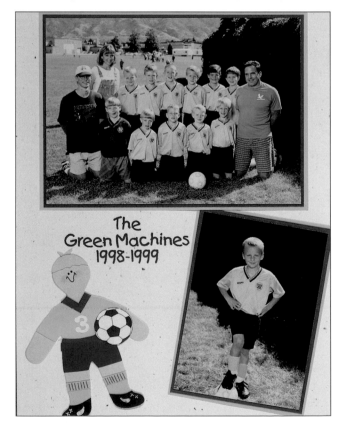

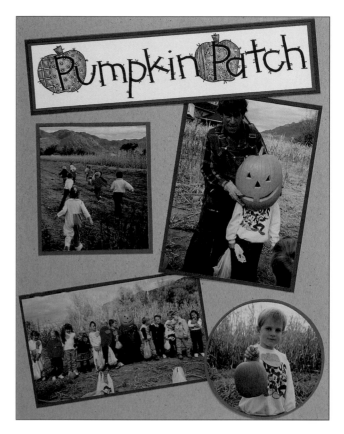

Stickers are available in any shape or form you can think of. Use them to accent or to create an entire page (below).

Die-cuts of different colors, cut apart, then pieced together make a bright multicolored graphic (below).

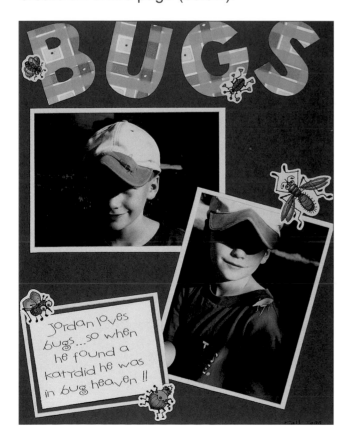

Your photographs and the memories behind them are precious. Journaling, or writing about them is vital to keeping the memories alive. Although the details and dates may seem very clear at the present time, they won't be in a few years. Be certain to include names, dates, and places wherever appropriate. These statistics are the easiest to forget. Try to recall feelings as well as facts so that others who see your pages in the future will have a better understanding of the events shared on your pages.

The page to the right needs only a brief explanation to summarize the hunting trip. On the opposite page (upper left) a slightly longer paragraph gives the details of the forgotten lunch box. The brief journaling on the upper-right and lower-left pages utilize fun fonts from a computer. The pages below use only a playful title.

The Forgotten Lunch Box...

Jordan was always forgetting one of his two lunch boxes at school. After forgetting both lunch boxes, mom was teasing him about it and he said, "I'm just a little boy with a little brain !! I have to remember to get up in the morning and get dressed, I have to go to school and remember everything to do there, I have to remember to come home and play and do all those other things and you want me to remember my lunchbox !! "
March 1999
Age 8

The Big Ones That Didn't Get Away !!

21" German Brown

19" German Brown

The Biggest Fish Yet...
22 in 4 lb Cutthroat
Strawberry Reservoir
Dec. 1998

First Day of Cub Scouts

Chapter 8: *Ideas from Shirley*

Shirley Pilkington (pictured with her granddaughter, Rose) attended Weber State University in Ogden, Utah, with an emphasis in Literature and English. Her poetry has been published on several occasions.

After only six months of scrapbooking, Shirley was hooked and opened up her own store, Daisy Dots & Doodles. She teaches scrapbooking classes several times a week and also designs scrapbook kits and papers. Shirley's own pages are full of texture and dimension and have been published in several scrapbook magazines.

Shirley lives in a beautiful rural town where she and her husband are active in their church and community. She is the mother of three children and the grandmother of six, which gives her a multitude of photo opportunities for her scrapbook pages.

Ralph J. Osmond Family
Donna, Lydia, Ralph, Dennis
Betty and Shirley

• Choose background paper carefully. Make certain that it will complement your photographs.

• Stickers can be used in a variety of ways. Cut them apart for even more possibilities. Foil stickers add shine to your pages.

• Run word strips around borders and make blocks to write journaling.

• Handmade tissue and paper add texture and dimension to pages. There are many different kinds available that are archival.

• When you are taking snapshots, move in close. Practice with a roll of film to see how close your camera will allow you to get for a great close-up picture.

Lydia Tullis

Lydia T. Osmond

The background papers in this double-page spread were softened by laying vellum over printed paper (below). Laser-cut photo corners give an antique look.

Ralph J Osmond

Ralph J Osmond

Mack with his Gram and his cream puffs.

Using different fonts from your computer makes titles more exciting and interesting to look at (above).

Sometimes a photograph taken from a different view, such as a back view (below), captures a great memory.

The background paper (above) was chosen specifically to complement the photograph.

Use circle and square cropped photographs on the same layout (below).

For candy corn, adhere three different sized and colored circles together. Cut the circle into eight pieces and mat each piece. Try to create other fun embellishments.

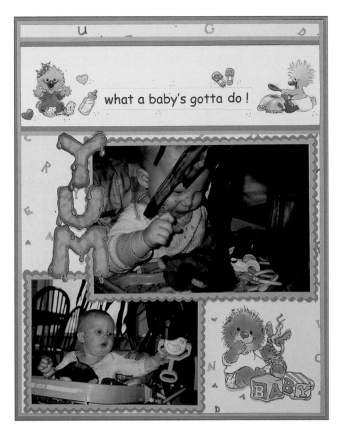

Brown glossy paper was used to cut out the chocolate bunny (below).

"A picture is worth a thousand words" holds true (above), so keep your camera ready.

Using a favorite nursery rhyme or song helps to capture a special memory (below).

The toy box (above) opens to display a photo or journaling.

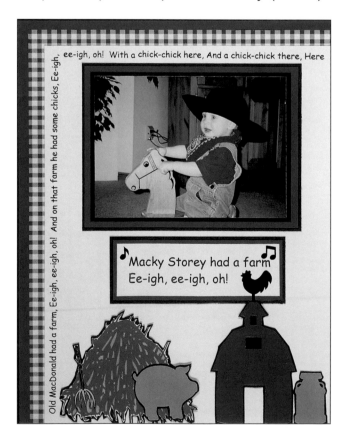

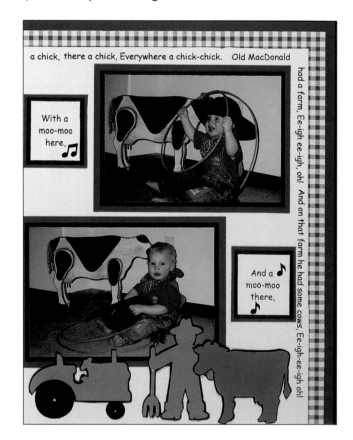

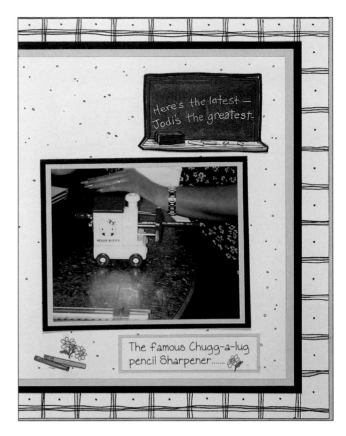

Matching mats on photographs and pages coordinates your layout (above).

Photographs of favorite places or things (below) will preserve cherished memories.

Letter stickers in different fonts and sizes make lettering easy and give your scrapbook pages a professional flair. Large letters lend themselves to this double-page spread.

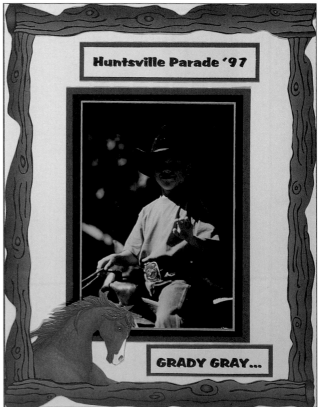

The fence in this double-page spread (below) is cut from textured brown paper to give it a "real" look. Twine was used for the rope. Be certain that any items used are archival.

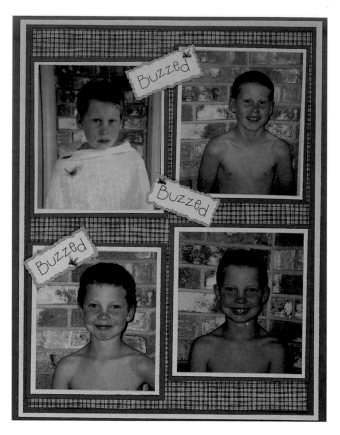

Punches and die-cuts were used to create the daisies (above).

Multiple mats (above) are pleasing to the eye and add interest to pages.

Acid-free adhesive spray was used to add a little splash of fine glitter. Die-cut lettering, confetti, and a basketball make these pages a celebration of fond memories.

A collection of stickers and paper cutouts make up this layout (above).

Try layering stickers. A cowboy hat was added to the bear sticker for fun (above).

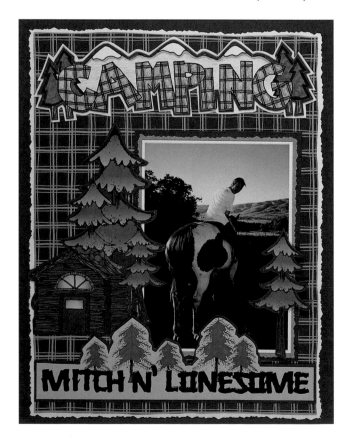

Mixing and matching coordinating prints are a fun way to highlight pages (below).

Bleeding embellishments off the page can create a different effect (below).

Make good use of a special card by cutting it out and using it to decorate scrapbook pages (below). Don't forget to use acid-free protection spray before you put it in your scrapbook.

Adhere stickers to colored paper. Leave a small border and trim. This will help to coordinate colors on a page or emphasize a favorite color.

Mat your photographs and pages with a lacy look. Choose decorative-edged scissors that complement your photographs and cut all layers of double mats (below).

This laser-cut frame (below) is oh-so-easy, but exceptionally effective.

The lace paper (below) was double mounted by trimming and staggering edges.

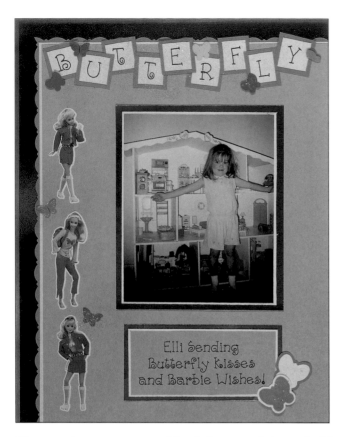

Try cutting your own block letters (above). Use a computer printout caption in your favorite font, stencils, or sticker letters. Cut into blocks and stagger them on your layout.

Self-adhesive foam will give dimension to accents (above).

Cutting stickers apart (below) gives you endless possibilities for accents.

Decorative-edged scissors come in large and small patterns. Use a small pattern to create the mats for these pages (below).

Patterned and colored paper scraps are great for cutting out shapes (below).

Stickers make great accents, but they also make great backgrounds (above).

Take a small notebook on vacations to write down thoughts (below). This will assist when compiling scrapbooks.

Save memorabilia from vacations (below). With acid-free protection spray you can preserve additional interesting information.

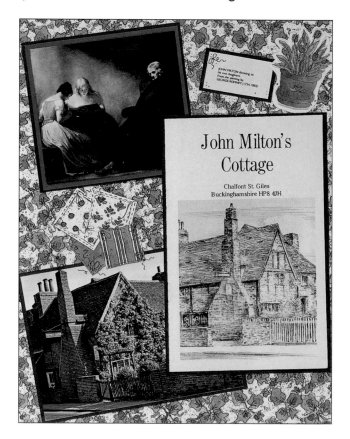

The floral arrangement (above) was made with punches from different colors of paper.

The close-up photo of the teacup (above) is one of a set purchased on this trip.

Holidays provide the perfect theme for a scrapbook page. Use bright colors, cut scraps of colored paper and create the perfect accent. Puffy stickers (above) are a unique way to give dimension to your holiday fun.

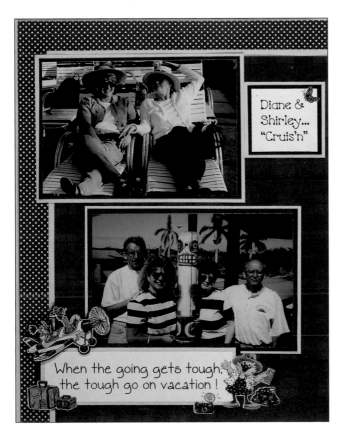

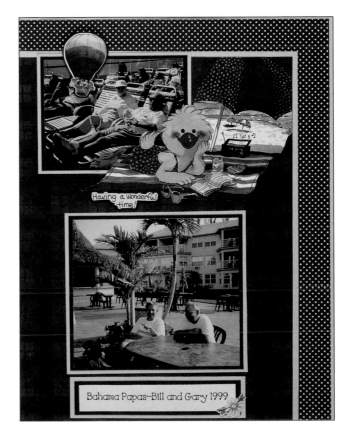

Notice the muted colors and simple design of these pages. The desire was to reflect the more serious, sober feelings that this trip evoked.

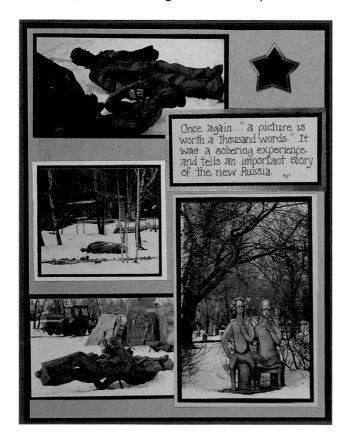

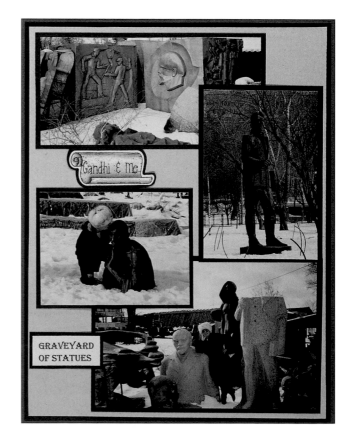

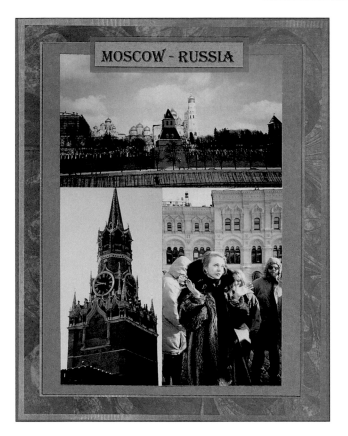

This double-page spread (below) uses computer clip art, die-cuts, sticky die-cuts, stencil lettering, and more. Notice the mats created with decorative-edged scissors to suggest alligator bites.

Tearing paper is an enjoyable technique that lets you create a unique shape. The background paper on this double-page spread (above) is a perfect complement for the winter photographs.

To highlight a special photograph, put it on a page all its own (above).

The textures of handmade paper leaves (below) are rich and give a look of fabric.

Chapter 9: *Cutout Patterns*

Solid lines indicate a cut line. Dotted lines may either indicate detail or a fold line. Do not cut patterns from book. Enlarge or reduce cutout patterns to desired dimensions with a copy machine.

0123456
789
ABCDEFG
HIJKLMNO
PQRSTUV
WXYZ?'(!)

0123456

789

ABCDEFGHI

JKLMNOPQ

RSTYVWXYZ

abcdefghi

jklmnopqrs

tuvwxyz??'(!)

Accordion Card

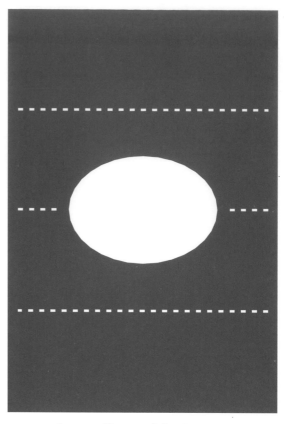

Accordion with Cutout

Angel #1

Apple

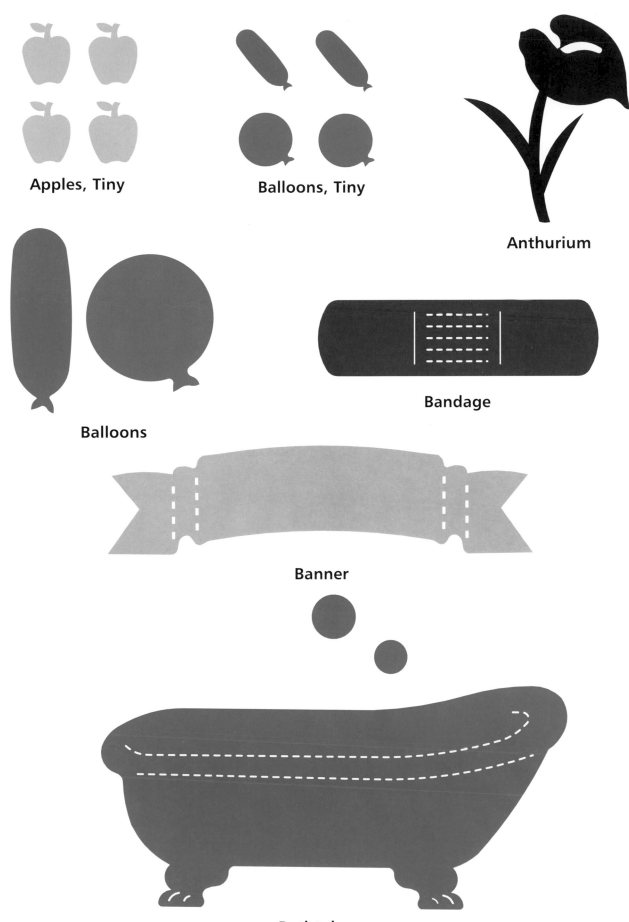

Apples, Tiny

Balloons, Tiny

Anthurium

Balloons

Bandage

Banner

Bathtub

425

Beach Ball

Bird #4

Bird #2A

Bird of Paradise

Bluebonnet

Bookmark, Heart

"Birthday"

426

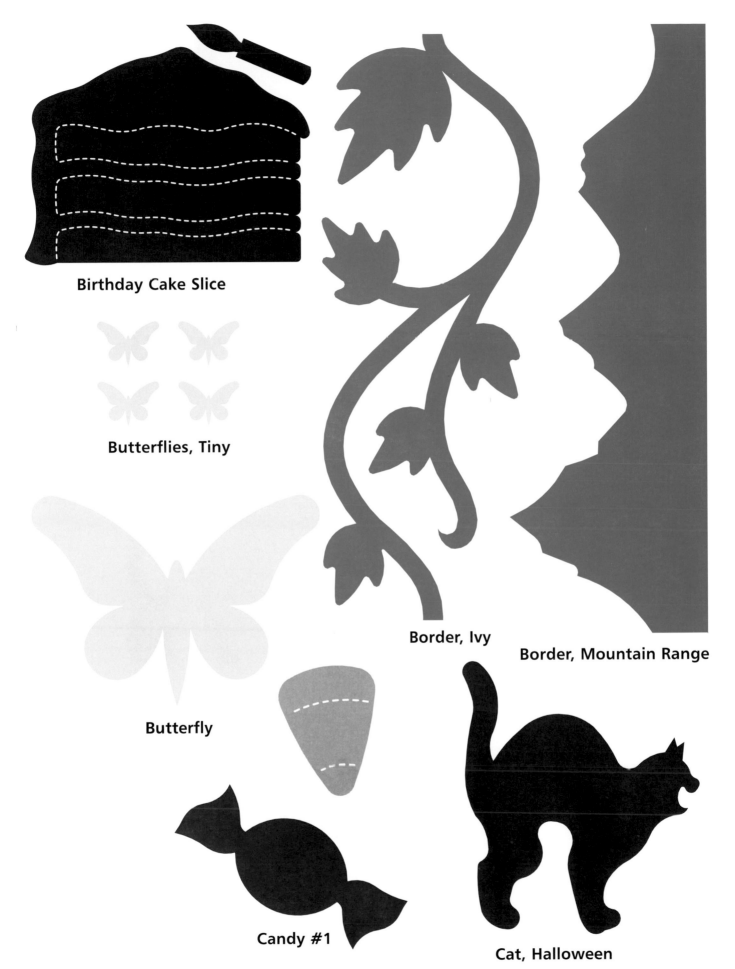

Birthday Cake Slice

Butterflies, Tiny

Butterfly

Border, Ivy

Border, Mountain Range

Candy #1

Cat, Halloween

427

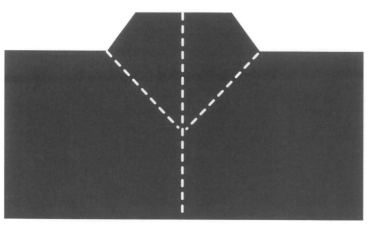

3-D Card, Plain

Christmas Tree #2

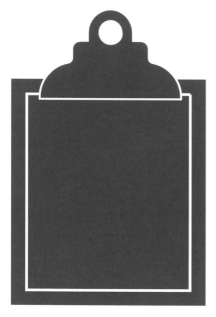

Clipboard

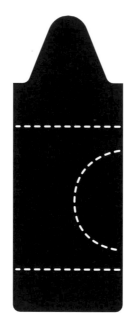

Crayon

Daisy

"Congrats"

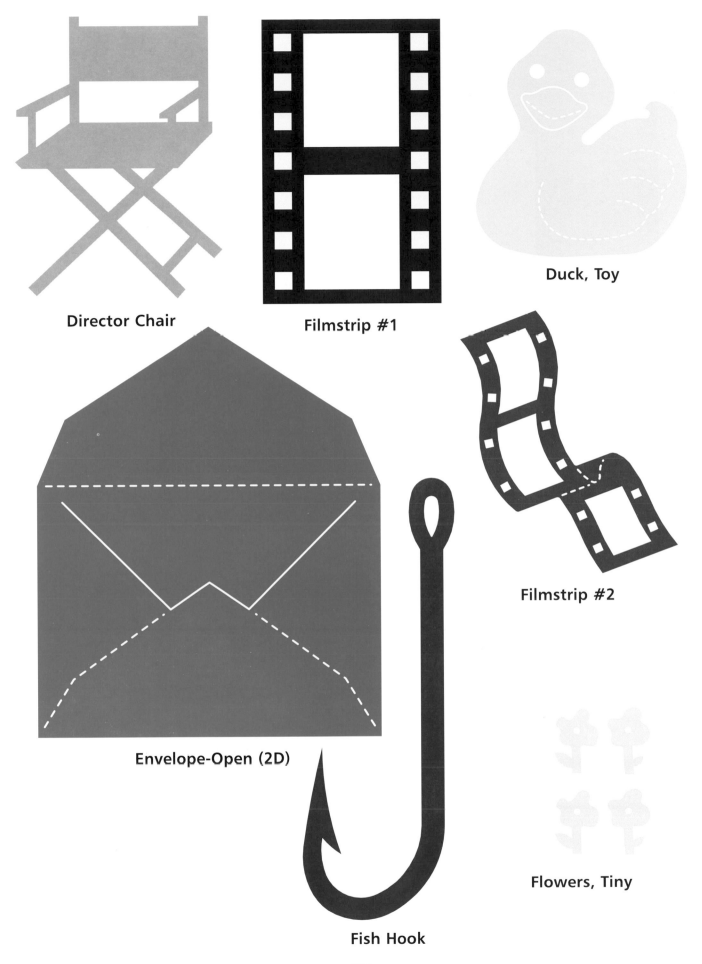

Director Chair

Filmstrip #1

Duck, Toy

Envelope-Open (2D)

Filmstrip #2

Fish Hook

Flowers, Tiny

429

Frame

Front/Umbrella (Diorama)

430

Ghost #2

Gift Card with Insert

Gift with Ribbon

Guitar

Hair Dryer

"Happy"

Hawaiian Lei

Heart, Primitive

Heart #1A

Heart #1B

Heart #2

Hearts, Tiny

Holly

Iris

Ladder

433

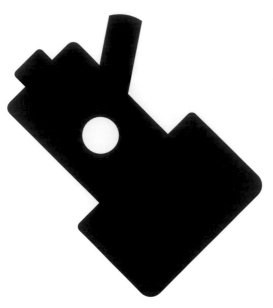

Light, Spot

Leaves, Tiny

Light Beam

Lips

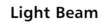

"Love"

Middle/Flowers (Diorama)

Middle/Waves (Diorama)

Mission

Mitten

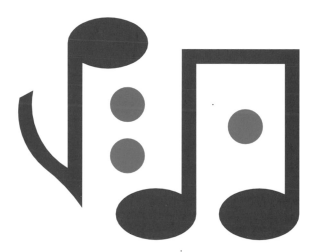

Musical Notes MX

Nose

Palm Tree #2

435

Party Noisemaker #2

Pencil

Pine Cone

Pitcher

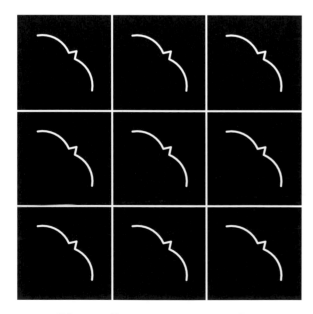

Photo Corners, Decorative

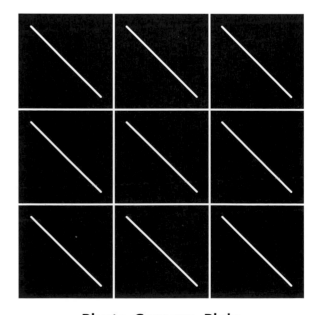

Photo Corners, Plain

Pop-Up, Double Page

Pop-Up #1B

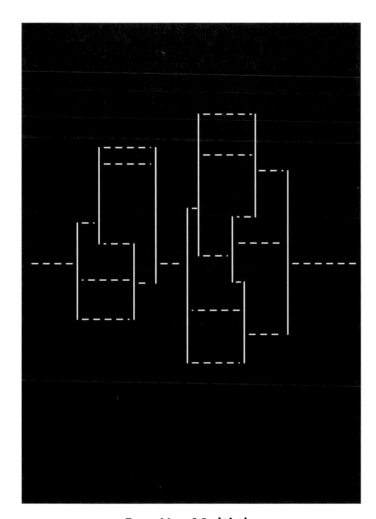

Pop-Up, Multiple

Pumpkin #1A

Pumpkin #1B

437

Row Boat

Road Sign, Country

Rose

Scissors

School Bus Back

Skier

Seed Packet

Square

Snorkel & Mask

Stars, Primitive (2 Up)

Stethoscope

439

(Flap)

Slider Card

(Slot)

Slider Card Cover

Sunglasses

Sunflower

"Thanks"

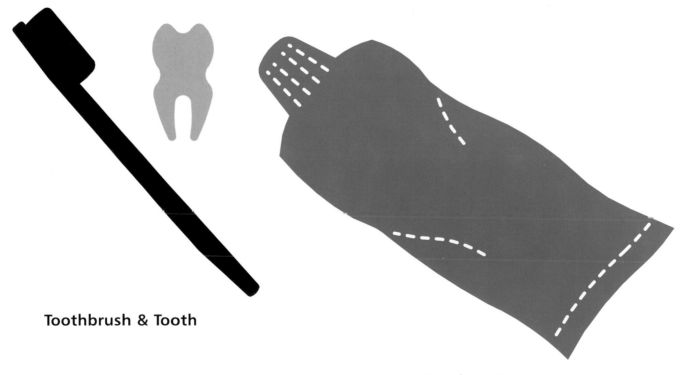

Toothbrush & Tooth

Toothpaste

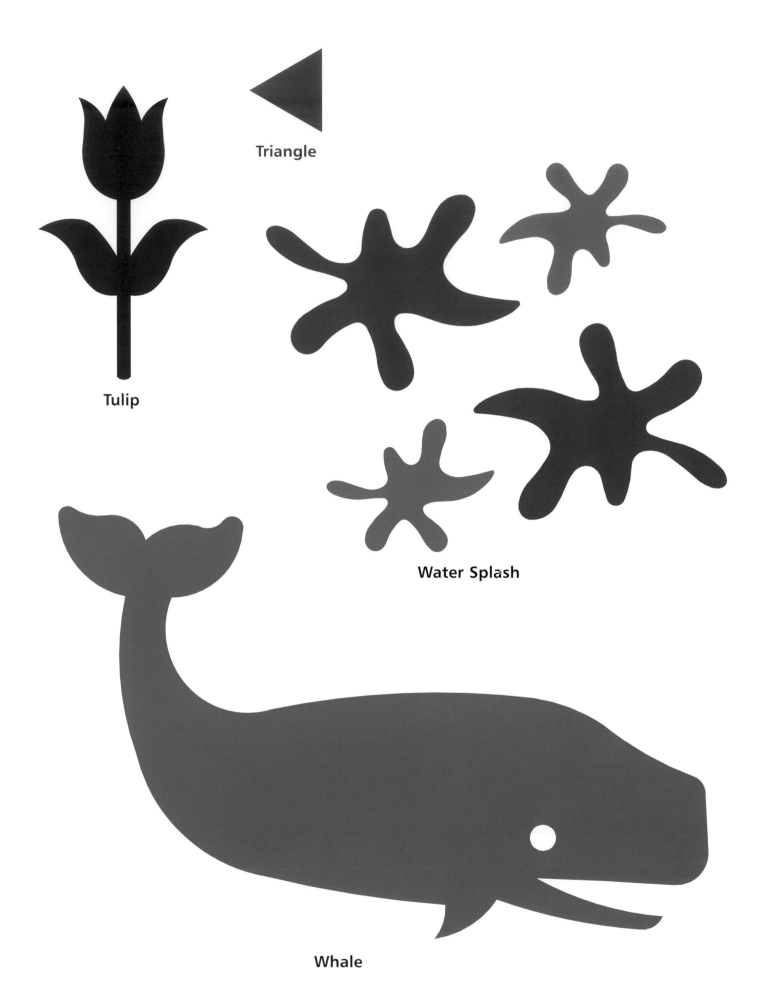

Triangle

Tulip

Water Splash

Whale

442

Bonus Cutout Patterns

Acorn

Airplane #2

Baby Booties

Bat

Beach Chair #2

Bear

Border, Bats

Border, Fence

Border, Filmstrip

Index

Metric Equivalency Chart

cm—Centimetres
Inches to Centimetres

inches	cm	inches	cm	inches	cm	inches	cm
⅛	0.3	5	12.7	21	53.3	38	96.5
¼	0.6	6	15.2	22	55.9	39	99.1
½	1.3	7	17.8	23	58.4	40	101.6
⅝	1.6	8	20.3	24	61.0	41	104.1
¾	1.9	9	22.9	25	63.5	42	106.7
⅞	2.2	10	25.4	26	66.0	43	109.2
1	2.5	11	27.9	27	68.6	44	111.8
1¼	3.2	12	30.5	28	71.1	45	114.3
1½	3.8	13	33.0	29	73.7	46	116.8
1¾	4.4	14	35.6	30	76.2	47	119.4
2	5.1	15	38.1	31	78.7	48	121.9
2½	6.4	16	40.6	33	83.8	49	124.5
3	7.6	17	43.2	34	86.4	50	127.0
3½	8.9	18	45.7	35	88.9		
4	10.2	19	48.3	36	91.4		
4½	11.4	20	50.8	37	94.0		